P9-CRN-609

FLYING
UNDER
FIRE

Canadian Fliers Recall the Second World War

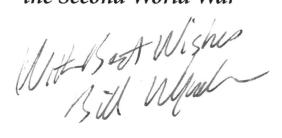

Selected and edited by
William J. Wheeler of the
Canadian Aviation Historical Society

FIFTH
HOUSE

Introduction © 2001 William J. Wheeler
Excerpts © The Authors

All rights reserved. No part of this publication may be reproduced, stored in a retrieval system, or transmitted, in any form or by any means, electronic, mechanical, recording, or otherwise, without the prior written permission of the publisher, except in the case of a reviewer, who may quote brief passages in a review to print in a magazine or newspaper, or broadcast on radio or television. In the case of photocopying or other reprographic copying, users must obtain a licence from the Canadian Copyright Licencing Agency.

Front cover painting of Typhoon © Les Waller. All rights reserved.
Cover and interior design by John Luckhurst / GDL

The publisher gratefully acknowledges the support of The Canada Council for the Arts and the Department of Canadian Heritage. We acknowledge the financial support of the Government of Canada through the Book Publishing Industry Development Program for our publishing activities.

Printed in Canada by Transcontinental Printers.

02 03 04 05/ 5 4 3 2

NATIONAL LIBRARY OF CANADA CATALOGUING IN PUBLICATION DATA

Main entry under title:

Flying under fire

   Stories originally published in: Journal of the Canadian Aviation Historical Society.
   ISBN 1-894004-79-5

   1. World War, 1939–1945—Aerial operations, Canadian. 2. World War, 1939–1945—Personal narratives, Canadian. I. Wheeler, William J., 1930– II. Journal of the Canadian Aviation Historical Society.
D792.C2F59 2001   940.54'4971'0922   C2001-911268-8

Editor's Note: Rather than interrupt the narratives in these stories, we have chosen to retain the language of the storytellers, which reflects the time in which they were written. Metric conversions have not been added.

Published in Canada by
Fifth House Ltd.
A Fitzhenry & Whiteside Company
1511-1800 4 Street SW
Calgary, AB
T2S 2S5

First published in the U.S. in 2001 by
Fitzhenry & Whiteside
121 Harvard Ave.
Suite 2
Allston, Massachusetts
02134

www.fitzhenry.ca

Contents

Acknowledgements

A s must be the case with an anthology such as this, many people, including the twelve whose stories I have used, have made important contributions to this book. I would like to express my most sincere gratitude to all of them: Russ Bannock DSO, DFC and Bar, for his Foreword; Mrs Angela Bell, wife of the late Don Bell DFC; Jack Brown; Michael Collins; Jim Coyne DFC; Charlene Dobmeier, now Publisher at Fifth House, for again demonstrating great patience; Doug Faulder; Bob Fowler OC, for not only providing a story but giving invaluable help with the Glossary; Dave Godfrey, for advice on many technical aspects of the Glossary; Bill Hagarty; John Luckhurst, the talented designer of this book; Krista McLusky and Richard Janzen, my editors; Larry Milberry of CANAV Books, for advice and encouragement; Geoffrey Norris for permitting me to excerpt a story on Jackie Rae which he wrote for a 1957 issue of *RAF Flying Review*; Catherine Radimer for her enthusiasm and promotional knowhow; Jackie Rae DFC; Ed Rice, CAHS National President; George Stewart; George Topple, for scanning pre-computer text to disc; St Solo Computer Graphics for scanning many of the images; Les Waller, for a striking cover painting; Vi Warren and her late husband, Arnold; my wife, Pat Wheeler, for once more suggesting much of the Glossary's content; Alan Williams, for unearthing CAHS *Journal* material and digital communication assistance; and Alan Wingate, for contributing both a story and Glossary assistance.

William J. (Bill) Wheeler
Markham, Ontario, July 2001

Foreword

In his previous book, *Skippers of the Sky*, Bill Wheeler gave us a selection of stories chosen from the *Journal* of the Canadian Aviation Historical Society that highlighted the role played by bush pilots in the development of Canadian aviation. In *Flying Under Fire*, Bill presents a further dozen outstanding tales told first-hand by pilots and ground crew who participated in a variety of operational and training roles during the Second World War. These men and women were young Canadians who enlisted or otherwise became involved at the first available opportunity. Alan Wingate's account typifies the contribution made by over two thousand civilian pilots who filled the important role of staff pilots at Air Observer Schools. Vi Warren's recollections of her experiences in the Air Transport Auxiliary remind me of Lois Butler, then a fifty-year-old grandmother, who delivered Mosquitoes to my squadron when we needed replacements. When I joined the de Havilland Company after the war, I was surprised to find that she was the wife of the company chairman.

All of those whose stories appear in this book went on to successful post-war careers in aviation, industry, or the arts. Bob Fowler, for instance, was a high-altitude photographer, then he joined de Havilland Canada, eventually becoming chief engineering test pilot and playing a prominent role in the development of the Dash 7 and Dash 8 series of regional transports. Jackie Rae has thrilled Canadians for decades with his Spitfire band.

I can identify with the contributors to *Flying Under Fire*, my own career being typical of many airforce pilots who joined at the outset of the Second World War. Having a commercial pilot's licence at nineteen, I was recruited to the RCAF as a Pilot Officer only three days after Canada declared war. Additional whirlwind training led up to my wings by March 1940. After an instructor's course, I spent three years teaching flying instructors at Trenton and Arnprior. For three months in the summer of 1942, I was loaned to Air Transport Command in Montreal to instruct American civilian pilots hired to ferry bombers across the Atlantic and Pacific. After reading only a *Pilot's Handbook* on the type, I found myself in the cockpits of Hudsons, Venturas,

Michells, Fortresses, and Bostons. Early in 1944, I was posted to the United Kingdom where I completed two tours on Mosquitoes. Most of my operational flying was similar to that described by George Stewart in his gripping account of a night intruder operation. During June and July of 1944, I participated in patrols over the English Channel, intercepting flying bombs. After the war I moved on to the aircraft industry, joining the de Havilland Aircraft Company of Canada where I filled various roles, starting as chief test pilot and retiring as president.

There have been many accounts written by and about airmen outlining their personal experiences from the day they signed up until their departure for "civvy street." Bill Wheeler's carefully chosen selection of widely varying stories provides the reader with an excellent broad-brush picture of how Canada's young airmen and ground crew made a major contribution to winning the Second World War.

Russell Bannock DSO, DFC and Bar
W/C RCAF (Ret)

Introduction

A Legacy of Courage and Determination

The thousands of young Canadians, many still in their teens, who volunteered for service in the RCAF, RAF, and other air services during the Second World War have left a proud legacy. Their gallantry and sacrifices must never be forgotten.

Much has been written about the exploits of Canada's airmen but because of the sheer magnitude of the war in the air their accomplishments can never be fully documented. There will always be other stories to tell and fresh insights to be discovered. Sadly, those who can provide them are aging and their numbers diminishing. The importance of recording their accomplishments while this is still possible is obvious. The Canadian Aviation Historical Society (CAHS) is one of several organizations striving to this end. The following accounts, all first-hand recollections, are from the pages of the CAHS *Journal*, a sampling of the many such stories preserved by the Society.

By 1939, scarcely two decades after the end of "The War to End All Wars" of 1914–18, Canada was again at war. In the earlier conflict, aviation had been in its infancy with the aeroplane tentatively pressed into service as a weapon—albeit an increasingly sophisticated and effective one. The demands of war had spurred unprecedented progress in aircraft development. During the 1920s and 1930s, in spite of the Great Depression, aircraft performance improved steadily. The aeroplane became a potent fighting machine. Air power would play an ever more critical role in the coming struggle, matching—and complementing—the contributions of land and sea forces.

Canadian airmen were involved from the earliest days of the "Phony War" with its propaganda leaflet raids, the disastrous Battle of France, the glorious Battle of Britain—when the tide of war began to turn—through the gradual

Hawker Hurricane

ascendancy of the Allied forces until the final Axis surrender. Their contributions were second to none. Stirring times begat stirring tales, typified by the following accounts, which reflect as well the changing aspects of the war. In the early years, with Nazi air power seemingly invincible, the fight was carried to the enemy only at great cost—exemplified by Mike Lewis's account of an RAF squadron's struggle flying an unreliable aircraft, under daunting circumstances. As the tide of war turned, Allied air forces gradually achieved air supremacy. Improved aircraft and more effective weapons enabled such daring missions as the *Tirpitz* raid, recalled by Don Bell, to be flown with reasonable hope of success.

Few aspects of the war did not involve flying. Airmen served on tactical and strategic bombers, flew fighters in defensive or offensive roles, carried out anti-submarine patrols, flew photo-reconnaissance (recce) sorties, attacked surface targets in close support of the army, transported troops and supplies, ferried aircraft, test flew aircraft, delivered VIPs—the list is almost endless. It would not be possible in a book of this size to offer a thorough coverage of Canadian wartime flying. With this in mind, the following stories have been chosen to provide a cross-section of Second World War aerial activities.

Along with accounts from fighter and bomber pilots, *Flying Under Fire* contains recollections of an intruder pilot, a pilot trainee, an Air Observer School (AOS) pilot, an army observation pilot, a flying ground crewman, a torpedo pilot, and an Air Transport Auxiliary (ATA) pilot. In view of today's vast expansion in the scope of women's activities the latter is of special interest. During the Second World War, although women did not fly operationally or serve in combat—except in the Red Army—they participated significantly. A good example is that of Vi (Milstead) Warren who flew with the paramilitary ATA in England ferrying first-line combat aircraft to squadrons, an assignment that in less pressing times would definitely have been "man's work."

Many of the following stories begin with the writer's experiences passing through the various levels of the British Commonwealth Air Training Plan (BCATP). In the case of a pilot, from enlistment successively to Manning Pool, Initial Training School (ITS), Elementary Flying Training School (EFTS), Service Flying Training School (SFTS), possibly an Advanced Flying Training School (AFTS, only in England), Operational Training Unit (OTU), and finally to a squadron was the usual progression. In the early stages it was back to classrooms very similar to those they had just left in high school, but with new motivation. The very real and ever-present fear of washing out often made achievers out of formerly marginal or disinterested students.

The majority of recruits hoped to become fighter pilots, but only a small percentage attained their goal. Luck, obviously, was important. Also aptitude, as measured by a trainee's performance in the Link trainer, was undoubtedly a key factor. Size was another consideration. A big man would be at a disadvantage in the cramped cockpits of most fighters; yet, if he flew well, he might pilot a bomber. Education was a further consideration. Mastering even basic navigation, for instance, required some academic ability. However, air force requirements were probably the most significant factor in aircrew streaming. If gunners or wireless operators were in short supply then current recruits would be directed to those "trades" until the need was met.

While former members of the RCAF tell most of the following stories, not all Canadian airmen served with Canadian squadrons. Sixty percent of RCAF personnel flew with RAF units. Other Canadians, like Mike Lewis, joined the prewar RAF when that service was recruiting pilots and the RCAF was not.

Handley Page Hampden

Unprepared at the start of hostilities, the RCAF had scarcely four thousand men in service. Fortunately recruits from all corners of the then British Empire were welcomed into Britain's air force. Later refugee aircrew from Axis-occupied countries joined them. After training they would be melded into one of the world's most powerful air forces. This very diversity of nationality and background often created a feeling of camaraderie and purposefulness in a unit. Many Canadian airmen did successive tours with both RCAF and RAF units. The contributors to this book are not all pilots: an especially gripping adventure is related by navigator Don Bell while ground crewman Mike Collins tells how he accumulated more flying time than many aircrew.

Other wartime pilots and navigators belonged neither to the RCAF nor RAF but flew as civilians—notably delivering aircraft across the Atlantic with Ferry Command. A large percentage of instructors in the BCATP were civilians, especially with the Elementary Flying Training Schools and Air Observer Schools (AOS). Their contribution to the war effort, maintaining the flow of trained aircrew for overseas service, was vital not only to the successful pursuance of the war in the air but also to the Allied effort as a whole. Because of the more than 130,000 airmen who obtained their wings through the BCATP, Canada was recognized by Franklin D. Roosevelt, president of the United States, as the "Aerodrome of Democracy." Lester B. Pearson— later to become prime minister of Canada—while stationed in Washington had actually coined this apt metaphor. He had unofficially drafted the speech at the request of a friend who happened to be one of Roosevelt's advisors.

Many airmen and airwomen who made significant contributions flew only occasionally. Dedicated ground crew—who substantially outnumbered aircrew—were essential to the success of any unit whether operational squadron or air training school. The safety of all aircrew rested largely in the hands of those who maintained their aircraft. Spitfire pilot Jackie Rae's warm tribute to his engine fitter typifies the appreciation of aircrew for the men and women who kept their aircraft flying and the bond that was forged between them.

In the 1950s a number of well-known airmen, both Allied and Axis, published autobiographies chronicling their wartime exploits, or had them recorded by others. Douglas Bader, Johnny Johnson, Pierre Closterman, Bob Johnson, Adolf Galland, René Mouchotte, and many others produced wartime memoirs. Their books were avidly read, particularly by the generation that had been too young to participate in the war. With the lifting of wartime secrecy, these recollections afforded fascinating insights not to be found in censored wartime reporting. By the end of the decade, the publication of such books had dried up. When the Canadian Aviation Historical Society was formed in 1962, veterans of the Second World War were loath to talk about their operational experiences. Their memories—still painfully vivid—were too personal to be shared with strangers, however understanding. Because of this reticence, speakers at Society gatherings were often men who had flown in the 1914–18 war. Yet this would change. The need remember and record their personal roles in the making of history triggered in many instances by the curiosity of grandchildren. Thi was not limited to family. Surveys of CAHS readers made in the revealed that Second World War flying stories were the most p items, nudging out bush flying and First World War accour

The stories in this book, as with those in *Skippers of t* Fifth House volume dealing with bush flying, are to them an immediacy that can be lost in retelling by are adapted from articles that appeared in th Aviation Historical Society, often based upon ter meetings or annual conventions. M? remain for publication, it is hoped, in f'

The aircraft flown by the contribu* stories and are as diverse as is the ' famous Supermarine Spitfire, d

Avro Lancaster

Bristol Beaufighter to the Avro Anson, Fairey Battle, Northrop Nomad—all training machines—and such less-well-known types as the Bristol Beaufort, Westland Whirlwind, Avro Manchester, and even the humble Taylorcraft Auster. Because their machines so often brought them through extremely trying situations, airmen and especially pilots developed affection for particular types. Jim Coyne writes with obvious fondness of the graceful Whirlwind, Jackie Rae of the elegant Spit, Alan Wingate of *Faithful Annie*, George Stewart of the versatile Mossie, Bill Hagarty of the Auster, and Jack Brown of the ruggedly appealing Tiffie. Representative examples of all of these aircraft, with the exception of the Whirlwind, can be found in aviation museums around the world. While the only extant Typhoon resides in the RAF Museum at Hendon in the United Kingdom, the others can be seen closer to home in the Canada Aviation Museum, Ottawa, and in other aircraft collections across Canada.

The exigencies of war provided an unprecedented stimulus, speeding up aircraft development. More advanced variants were being designed even as latest versions entered squadron service. Because of this continual improvement in performance, first-line aircraft, often after only a year or so of operational use, were relegated to secondary theatres of war or to the training role. Fighting aircraft, although generally capable of sustaining large amounts of battle damage, were built for short periods of hard use, not longevity. Clapped out and battle-weary, many still sporting bullet holes or flak damage from their fighting days, they found their way to this command. The Anson Is, piloted by AOS staffer Alan Wingate, had been on coastal patrol while the Battles from which Michael towed his drogues were used (disastrously) early in the Second World War as day-bombers.

As these demonstrate, there was a special brand of service humour, wryly grim, which sustained most fighting men and women, aircrew. It enriches narrative and description alike, and it is seen in the whimsical jargon and euphemisms used by the airmen. These stories abound with wry descriptions: Jim Coyne telling of crashing which he fell on his head, having released his harness hanging upside-down in his Whirlwind; Don Bell recalling his Lancaster churning through the tops of pine trees in a dive, struggled desperately for a few more feet of height; a Focke-Wulf-versus-Auster dogfight with a Very pistol as his

10

The RCAF, at its peak with some 230,000 serving, ranked as the fourth-largest Allied airforce. Of this number, 14,541 lost their lives. Bomber Command, with almost ten thousand killed, was hardest hit. This collection of stories, penned by surviving participants in a long and difficult war, is dedicated to the memory of those, often friends and squadron mates, who did not return.

Manchester Debacle

Unreliable Engines Doomed
the Lancaster's Infamous Predecessor

W. J. ("Mike") Lewis DFC, CD

The Avro Manchester was designed to a 1936 RAF specification for a heavy bomber. Promising in concept, it would prove a disappointing failure in service, largely because of the unproven Rolls-Royce Vulture engines that powered it. Rolls-Royce hoped that the Vulture, a radical mating of two R-R Peregrine V-12 engines to produce a 24-cylinder power plant of "X" configuration, would deliver twice the Peregrine's 885 hp. This seldom happened, and the Vulture suffered even more problems. Just over two hundred Manchesters were built and served with only a single RAF unit. Flying missions deep into occupied Europe against ever-more lethal air defences in an unreliable aircraft, 207 Squadron suffered daunting losses.

Mike Lewis was born in 1918 on a farm near Welcome, Ontario. Graduating from high school with top math marks he was studying as a mechanical engineer when he decided to join the RCAF in 1938. That service was not training pilots, but Mike, with several other young men, was sent overseas to train with the RAF on a Short Service Commission. Completing Flying Training School, he entered the RAF School of Air Navigation and graduated in July 1939. Of the thirty-eight students in his course only six would survive the war, indicative of the terrible attrition among bomber crews. Mike was posted to No 44 Squadron flying Handley Page Hampden medium bombers at RAF Waddington, England. After a tour of thirty-six missions, Mike earned a "rest" as Link Trainer Officer and was then posted to 207 Squadron where he begins his story.

Released from a German prison camp three years and eight months after being shot down on his final Manchester Op, Mike returned to England and transferred to the RCAF. He would serve with distinction, retiring in 1965 with the rank of Wing Commander. Initially he flew with 412 Squadron transporting VIPs and then tested new aircraft with the RCAF Central Experimental and Proving Establishment. Later he commanded the Flying Wing at Winnipeg and instructed at the RCAF Staff College in Toronto. In 1955–58, he was Staff Officer in the Chief of Staff's Branch at Supreme Headquarters Allied Powers Europe (SHAPE) Paris, France. He finished his RCAF service in Maritime Air Command, the last four years as CO of the Maritime Command Operational Unit.

The saga of the infamous Manchester ended positively. Fortunately, in parallel with the Vulture-powered machines, designer Roy Chadwick had planned the Manchester III with four less powerful (initially) but infinitely more reliable Rolls-Royce Merlin engines. The Manchester III became the immortal Lancaster, arguably the most efficient heavy bomber of the war. Mike Lewis's story appeared in the Summer 1994 *Journal* and was developed from a presentation he made to the Toronto Chapter of the CAHS in November 1990.

On 1 November 1940, 207 Squadron was re-formed under the command of W/C Hettie Hyde as the first of several intended Manchester squadrons. Originally 207 had been created as No 7 Squadron Royal Naval Air Service in 1915, becoming 207 Squadron RAF on 1 April 1918. It continued in service until shortly after the outbreak of the Second World War when it was disbanded to form an OTU at Upper Heyford. In addition to the CO, the original officer pilots were S/L Charles Kydd, Flight Commander (British); F/L Burton-Giles (British); F/L Derik French (Australian); F/O Johnny Seibert (Australian); F/O Frankie Eustace (New Zealander); and myself, F/O W. J. "Mike" Lewis (Canadian).

Other than Hettie Hyde and Charles Kydd, all of us were serving on Short Service Commissions in the RAF when war broke out. By 1 December 1940, all except W/C Hyde had completed one tour of operations in 5 Bomber Group flying Hampdens. W/C Hyde was about halfway through his first tour as a flight commander in 44 (Hampden) Squadron when he was diverted to command the newly formed 207 Squadron. Charles Kydd was a DSO, DFC while the remainder of the F/Ls and F/Os were DFCs.

On or about 1 December 1940, Manchesters L7279 and L7280 were delivered to 207 Squadron at Waddington, an RAF station in Lincolnshire, followed closely by L7278. For the first few days, since there were no pilot's notes or other briefing materials available, we just pored over the aircraft. One of the first things we noted was the absence of an overall heating

The nine Canadians aboard the RMS *Aleunia* who left Montreal on 15 July 1938 and arrived at Tilbury, England, on 24 July. All nine joined the RAF. Only three survived the war: Mike Lewis (centre, front row), Bob Barr (left, second row), and John Graham (left, third row). *W. J. Lewis*

system. Closer inspection revealed electrical outlets at each aircrew position, another first—electrically heated flying gear. Now I might as well begin our tales of woe right here.

When we were issued with electrically heated Irvin jackets, trousers, boots, and gloves, all worked okay. But how were we supposed to get the equipment on? It was all interconnected, one electrical line for each piece of equipment. We could get everything on and connected until we came to the last gauntlet (glove). Struggling into a bulky winter flying gauntlet and then attempting to plug in the electrical connector so that you would get some heat was unimaginable. On top of this, the heating elements in the equipment soon began to short out. It was no surprise to have a crew member suddenly get a hot foot, a hot hand, or a hot anywhere. Immediate modification: throw out the electrically heated flying clothing and introduce a heating system. This was done by reversing the oil-cooling system.

The oil-cooler radiator was set in the leading edge of the wing outboard of the engine. A duct in the leading edge supplied cold air that travelled horizontally through the oil-cooler and then exhausted over the top of the wing. For heating, Avro placed a small radiator in the wing leading edge between the engine and the fuselage and connected it to the engine cooling system, similar to the heating system in a car. Outside air was ducted through the leading edge of the wing, through the radiator and straight into the fuselage in front of the main spar. There was no control to regulate the flow of air nor, initially, anything to deflect the air around the fuselage interior. It blew full blast on the wireless operator, and we had to carry a piece of cardboard or plywood to set beside him to prevent his being scorched. Eventually, a deflector did this job, but since there was never any ducting the distribution of heat within the aircraft remained extremely poor.

It was only a few days until we had our first of many Vulture engine failures and with it another problem. Frankie Eustace was taking off when his port engine quit at low level. Against all flying principles, he swung left, making a 225-degree turn into the dead engine and was able to get the aircraft back safely on the ground. The Manchester was parked in front of our hangar. As this had been our only serviceable aircraft, flying terminated for the day.

Four of us sat down to a game of bridge. I happened to be seated where I could see the aircraft parked outside and I noticed that the prop on the failed engine was unfeathered. (The Manchester, incidentally, had the first fully-feathering propellers in the RAF.) The sixteen-foot props were hydraulic constant-speed de Havilland propellers. I remarked on the state of the prop to my bridge partners and asked whether they had seen anyone come over from Servicing to unfeather it. No one had, and we went on with the game. I looked out again—the prop was re-feathered. A fast call to the engineering officer brought maintenance on the run.

They discovered the feathering solenoid was stuck, and the prop was sitting there busily feathering and unfeathering. We quickly realized that this could happen in the air. If a pilot feathered the prop on a dead engine and headed for the nearest airfield, en route the solenoid could stick. The prop would unfeather and he would go down like a lead balloon!

This engine failure was the beginning of a series of problems, which, from the beginning until the time that I was shot down in September 1941, were never completely solved. I think the main problems could be summed up in three categories: oil channels that were too shallow, incorrectly torqued connecting rods, and no silver in the main bearings.

These weaknesses became evident over the same period of time; the difficulty was to identify the particular one causing each failure. They occurred regularly, sometimes with shocking results. In one instance a pilot was running up his engines in dispersal during his pre-flight when two pistons came right through the side of the engine and the engine cowling. Fortunately, most of the engine failures took place—with some exceptions—in flight and at altitude so that the results, in most cases, were not disastrous. At least, I speak of engine failures that happened on non-operational flights. When aircraft went missing, there were no clues as to whether the cause was enemy action or an engine failure.

Regretfully, we lost our first aircraft to the RAF Defence Force, a term I use advisedly. We had six aircraft going out to bomb the port and shipping at Boulogne, France. Our routing was down to Aldershot (southwest of London) and thence direct to Boulogne, returning by the same route. For some reason, the Observer Corps plotted one aircraft as an "enemy"—and not the other five. Our operation and route had been given to Fighter Command who had passed it on to 10 Group HQ. Evidently it arrived during the change of controllers. The new controller pushed the operation order under a pile of paper and forgot about it. When the report came in from the Observer Corps, he dispatched a Beaufighter from Wittering to intercept the aircraft.

The fighter pilot identified the "enemy" as a Manchester and so advised the controller. The controller would not accept his identification and ordered the pilot to shoot down the aircraft. The fighter pilot again closed with the Manchester and reported the aircraft as having roundels and gave its aircraft and squadron designator letters. Once more the controller refused to accept the identification, saying that the Luftwaffe had captured some bomber aircraft and were flying them over the United Kingdom. Again he ordered the pilot to shoot down the "enemy." This time, unfortunately, the fighter pilot complied.

Johnny Seibert was our first loss to enemy action. He held the Manchester long enough for his crew to bail out over Holland, but he did not get out and perished with his aircraft. The crew became POWs. Johnny went in March and the next to go was W/C Hyde, who was shot down over Kiel, Germany on 8 April.

Two nights earlier, I had had a somewhat terrifying—yet interesting—experience. As this incident was the result of a hydraulic failure, I should say something about the system. The Manchester had one of the first "high pressure" systems. While it would not be considered high today, four hundred pounds per square inch, in 1940, was high. When the system was actuated, for instance, to pull up the undercarriage, the pumps went into action and did their job. After the undercarriage had fully retracted, the pressure would continue to build until it reached six hundred pounds. Then a cut-out valve put the system into idle at four hundred pounds. A number of hydraulic failures on flights were the direct result of the whole system being built without "olives" in the joints or angles. But this night something new occurred.

We took off with Brest as our target. I remember the incident rather well. The night was as dark as you-know-what. I lifted off in pitch black (not unusual), retracted the undercarriage, and "went on to the clocks" (blind flying instruments). At about 50 feet the undercarriage came home, and suddenly the cockpit was filled with a fine oil spray. Pumped under high pressure, it covered everything including my flight instruments. I found myself trying to wipe them—flying at 100 feet! Fortunately I succeeded.

What had happened? On the engineer's panel, there was a rotary switch to move the radiator flaps from "open" to "trail" position. The washer on this control, we later learned, was made of compressed paper (a wartime economy measure). As the wheels came home—and before the pressure reached six hundred pounds and the cut-out valve operated—the washer blew. The pumps continued to operate, however, pumping the entire hydraulic supply into the cockpit.

This was bad enough, but we still had another hurdle to leap—getting the bomb bay doors open. The designers had thought of this one. Holes bored in the lower side of the bomb door hydraulic actuators were filled with plugs connected to a steel cable running to the front of the bomb bay, inside the nose section. Pulling this wire withdrew the plugs from the hydraulic jacks, and the oil drained by gravity. The bomb doors sagged enough for the slipstream to catch them and whip them fully open. We could drop our bombs, but we would have to fly from then on with the bomb doors open, a considerable drag. We pressed on.

Arriving at Brest, the navigator went down to the nose and pulled the cable. Nothing happened! I must have spent an hour flying around in the

F/O Burton-Giles DFC, one of 207's original pilots, in the left seat of a
Manchester's cockpit. *Unknown*

Brest area trying to shake those doors open by every G-force I could apply.

"To hell with it!" I finally said. "We're going home." Halfway across the English Channel, the bomb doors opened. I was faced with a dilemma: what do I do? Quick calculations showed that I did not have enough gas to go back to Brest, drop the bombs, and then return to Waddington—with the bomb doors open. So, there was no choice but to drag home with the open bay and the bomb load of fifteen 500-pounders still on board. When I arrived at Waddington, I told them that I was going to land with our bomb doors open and bombs still onboard. Later I found out that there wasn't a head above ground when I touched down.

I must describe one of the least glamorous Heath Robinson modifications that was ever carried out on an aircraft. Although the Manchester was built to a design specification allowing for a 4,000-pound bomb, no such bomb had been designed or built by the time the aircraft were completed. When the bombs were finally due to arrive, the bomb bay of the aircraft was modified by removing the central bombing point and installing what could best be described as an enormous hook. Woe to everyone when the bombs arrived.

When the first one was winched up into the Manchester's bomb bay, the bomb's diameter was such that the bomb doors would not close. Hence the Heath Robinson mod. A section was cut out of each bomb door sufficiently large so that when the doors were closed, the "cookie" could drop through without touching them. Two pieces of alclad (aluminum alloy), cut and hinged to the bomb doors, were held closed by large bungee cords; small fairings at the front and rear of the doors improved air streaming. To load the bomb, the bungee cords were detached and the bomb doors opened. After the cookie was winched up, the bomb doors were closed and fastened with nuts and screws. Then the modified sections of the doors were closed, and the bungee pulled tight to hold them in place.

When the time came to drop the cookie on the target, the crew merely selected master switch 'on' and pressed the release button at the proper time. The cookie was released from the hook and dropped on the metal slabs inserted into the bomb doors. The weight of the bomb stretched the bungee cords and the slabs opened, allowing it to fall free. Once the bomb was gone, the bungee cords pulled the slabs closed.

Simple? Sure! But imagine the process in operation. You released the cookie, which fell on the bomb doors with a loud crash. The slabs were thrust aside and the bomb fell free, but as soon as the doors came open, the slipstream got into the act and whipped them so far around that they clapped hands with the side of the fuselage. More frightening bangs. Then the bungee cords went into action yanking the slabs closed. Since the cords never functioned with equal force, one slab would close before its mate, making for a further pair of loud and disturbing reports.

Dropping a cookie could be disconcerting in a different way. One night, taking our act to Cologne, Germany, we found the audience definitely hostile. The footlights were exceptionally bright and applause (in the shape of lead) was considerable—and noisy. Just as the Nav shouted, "bombs away!" the aircraft gave its usual lurch upward. To avoid further interaction with the locals, I did my customary hard turn, putting the nose down to pick up as much speed as possible. When I pulled the aircraft out of the dive, it felt heavier on the controls than normal. Politely, I queried the Nav as to whether he had actually dropped the bomb. When his answer was in the affirmative, I requested that he check the bomb bay through the window in the bulkhead—to ensure that it really was gone.

I was not surprised when his inspection revealed that the cookie was still with us. He had not turned the master bomb switch on! Following a tense second bomb run to the continuing applause of the still appreciative audience below, we dropped the bomb and returned to base. Inspection of the aircraft after landing led me to believe that, during the first bomb run, just as the Nav shouted, "Bombs away!" we took a burst of heavy anti-aircraft fire under the aircraft. This had given us that deceiving lift—similar to that of a bomb being released. The flak had left its mark on the aircraft, but not, fortunately, on any of the aircrew.

Avro, in its usual efficient manner, came up with modified bomb doors in very short order. It accomplished this by bowing the doors in such a manner as to enclose the bomb. If you look at any museum Lancaster today, note the line of the bomb bay doors. You will see that very definite bowing.

I must give praise where praise is due. Avro was great in coming up with almost instant mods to the airframe when there were deficiencies. In addition, as the prototype Lancasters were already being built, all of these mods were immediately introduced into the new machine. From the squadron, we visited Woodsford every two weeks to back up our telexes and letters regarding problems. This resulted in the airframe bugs being cleared very rapidly with efficient, well-designed mods. By about May 1941, the airframe was in good shape and was never again modified—until the dorsal fin on the fuselage was removed and the wider horizontal stabilizer and elevators installed, along with larger vertical fins and rudders. These mods created the Manchester IA, and it was this fuselage and empennage that were retained in the Lancaster.

With this change came the large ammunition storage in the fuselage with tracks to carry the ammo back to the rear turret. The mid-upper turret on the Manchester never did function properly. When rotated, it set up a disconcerting vibration in the airframe. The Air Ministry finally circulated a letter permitting the squadrons and Avro to remove the turret if desired. I always had the mid-upper turret removed from my aircraft, giving me an extra 10 mph in speed and improving the single-engine performance immensely.

During May, we began having problems with high oil temperatures. At first we thought this was another engine problem, and to some extent it was. For me, there was an interesting sidelight. I was on my way to Frankfurt, Germany, one night (12 May, to be exact) when my starboard engine oil temperature started to creep up. We were routed that night on a course that headed us straight for Cologne, Germany. Just short of Cologne, we turned right, up the Rhine to Frankfurt. It was after passing Cologne that my oil problem made itself known, so we chose to bomb our alternate target, Coblenz, directly enroute. I returned to base with my starboard Vulture throttled back.

We arrived home to find that a Luftwaffe intruder had decided to terrorize Waddington that night. I declared an emergency and requested landing lights. Flying Control declined my request and told me to circle. In good, descriptive English, I explained that I was not in a position to remain cir-

Manchester IA, L7515 of 207 Squadron (code EM). For improved control, the central fin of the Mk IA was removed and the vertical tails enlarged. *A. V. Roe*

cling. Again I asked for landing lights and once more I was refused. I advised Control that I was landing anyway and joined the circuit. At this point one of our ground defence searchlights decided to join the fray—on the side of the enemy. He promptly illuminated me at about 500 feet above the ground. A colour-of-the-day got him out of the action, and I managed to land safely in darkness using only my landing light for the last fifty feet.

The intruder—who dropped four 250-lb bombs alongside my landing path, quickly put my accomplishment into perspective. Fortunately, he wasn't able to line up very accurately and his bombs fell far enough away that we were not damaged. He did tear three big holes in the airfield. The fourth bomb landed on an old First World War hangar at the south side of the airfield, one of several used by a Maintenance Unit (MU). All the intruder damaged were a few trucks, but he did add a little excitement where, really, none was needed.

On 20 May, Ops with the Manchester were stopped to investigate the previously mentioned overheating problems. We did a lot of test flying, especially at altitude, where most of the difficulties evidenced themselves. We did not go back on operations until 21 June, when, my logbook tells me, we went to Cologne.

In early June we became involved in another seat-snapping series of flights. At this time, the Brits adopted their first radar-predicted anti-aircraft guns. The first guns so fitted were the ack-ack at Nottingham. For some unknown reason, the "pongos" decided that the radar might not pick up an aircraft—such as a glider—with no engines running. Having the only aircraft in the RAF with fully feathering props (and thus able to glide efficiently), we were directed to carry out some flights over Nottingham with both engines fully feathered. If you don't think that this was an exercise to snap the buttons off your parachute, think again—remember that the sticking problem with the feathering solenoids had not yet been fully resolved.

In practice, the flight was carried out by climbing the Manchester to max height (with full gas but no bombs we could get to about 19,000 feet). We did this about twenty miles upwind of Nottingham. Then we feathered both props and glided down over Nottingham until we were about twenty miles downwind of the city. At about 2,000 feet we set about unfeathering the engines. Our lengthy "glide" had had its memorable moments.

The Manchester had no venturi tubes (to create air pressure) and all instruments were driven by vacuum pumps, one on each engine. So with both props feathered—look daddy, no flight instruments! As I once pointed out in discussing this little episode in a letter to the Editor of *Intercom* (the Aircrew Association newsletter), to have waited for a clear day in England to carry out these flights would have been tantamount to waiting for the Second Coming. It would have defeated the purpose of the exercise, as far as testing the ack-ack gunners was concerned. So, these descents were carried out in cloud. Anyone who thinks he can fly a Manchester in a straight line in cloud—by the seat of his pants—has another think coming. However, the radar tracks that came back from the pongos showed that we only wandered within reason.

I did two of these flights (23 May and 11 June) and each was successful. By "successful," I mean that I did the flight and got the props unfeathered without incident. Here my memory fails me, but I know that on another flight one of the pilots did not get his props unfeathered. He landed dead stick in a field after blowing his wheels down and did only very minor damage. The aircraft was quickly repaired, and Charles Kydd flew it out of the field.

In June, we lost Charles Kydd, a quiet but inspiring flight commander. He was flying ops and tests on equal frequency with the rest of the other pilots he had led "from the front." Taking off on a test flight, his port Vulture engine failed. He was barely off the ground and had no time to pick up single-engine speed. In fact, he had not cleared the hedge. Having no other option, he pulled off power on the starboard engine for a belly landing in one of our dispersal fields alongside the airfield. All might have gone well except for the eccentricities of the English countryside. The surrounding hedge grew to the level of the next field, three to four feet higher than the dispersal. When the aircraft slid through the hedge and hit the rise hidden just beyond, the whole front section was crushed. The entire crew except the wireless operator perished.

I mentioned earlier that we had gone back on Ops on 21 June, but the effort was short-lived. The engines continued to be more trouble than ever. It was becoming increasingly apparent that the main bearings, manufactured without silver, were just not standing up. My logbook shows that I did Ops on 21, 24, and 29 June. Grounded again from Ops, we set out to get 125 hours engine time on each of two aircraft. I note that I did flights on my aircraft (L7321) on 1, 2, and 3 July. At this point, the aircraft were completely grounded until replacement engines with new silvered bearings, new torques, and new oil channels could be fitted.

We were temporarily equipped with Hampdens and continued Ops with

F/O W. M. R. "Smitty" Smith DFC (L) with the author, F/L W. J. ("Mike") Lewis DFC in front of the officers' mess at RAF Waddington, July 1941. *W. J. Lewis*

these smaller but well-tried aircraft. To most of us, it was a relief to have an aircraft with reliable engines. We operated the Hampdens through 5 August. Early that month (my logbook says 4 August), the re-engined Manchesters were again available for test flights. On 5 August, I test flew L7373, did a night flying test on Hampden AE247, and an Op that night with the same Hampden to Karlsruhe. On 7 August my new aircraft, L7422, was available for testing and Ops. That night I flew it to Essen, Germany, in "Happy Valley."

I would like to digress briefly to recall a gratifying personal experience. On the morning of 9 August, the station commander (G/C John Boothman of Schneider Trophy fame) called to ask if I would take him down to Wittering for lunch that day. (John Boothman was the squadron commander of 44 Bomber Squadron when I reported to the squadron at the beginning of August 1939. He left us in December of that year but came back as station commander on 1 April 1941.) He wished to go to Wittering to have lunch with his old friend, G/C Basil Embry. My having lunch with these two famous men was interesting enough, but it became even better when W/C David Atcherley, commanding the Beaufighter squadron at Wittering, joined the luncheon. After lunch, Dave took me down to the flight line, gave me a short briefing on the Beaufighter, and then sent me off flying it. It was a very enjoyable half hour indeed!

Ops continued through August, and to my great regret, I lost my best friend, Mike ("Smitty") Smith, on a raid to Berlin on 12 August. After an Op to Mannheim on 25 August, I was informed that I was to have a week's leave, but before going on leave I would do one more test flight. In an attempt to improve the airflow through the air cooler a small metal spoiler had been placed on the leading edge of the wing, just forward of the oil-cooler exhaust port. This may have helped, but what it also did was disturb the airflow over the wing just enough to stall the wing at high load at altitude. This had occurred a couple of times previously, no one paid attention to the warning.

On the night of 25 August, "Kipper" Herring could not get his aircraft (L7316) above 11,000 feet so he dropped his cookie in the North Sea and came home. Fortunately, the squadron commander was flying with him as co-pilot that night. The next day, John Boothman insisted, over my protest, that I test-fly the aircraft in the same configuration as it was the night before. This I did—and I could not get it above 11,200 feet. At that altitude, I could feel a gentle, high-frequency vibration in the wing, and the aircraft refused to go any higher. Another curative mod had proven worse than the malady.

Manchester L7380, EM-W, the squadron "dog" in which Mike Lewis was shot down on his sixty-first mission, 8–9 September 1941. *RAF*

Then I was informed that I had completed my second tour of Ops and was sent on a week's leave. I returned on 7 September and a signal from Group informed me that I was posted back to 44 Squadron on 9 September. The squadron was to be the first equipped with the Lancaster, and I was to be in charge of its conversion to the Lancs.

That afternoon my old squadron commander approached me in the mess and asked if I would fly one more operation—a captain had gone sick. I should have stayed in bed! The Op was to Berlin (on L7380), and I was shot down by a night-fighter. I spent the rest of the war as a prisoner of war (POW).

I had never counted the number of operations that I had flown until I came back from POW camp, and on transferring to the RCAF, was asked for this information. I counted them up in my logbook and discovered that the one on which I was shot down was my 61st. The RCAF also totalled them up and awarded me the two-tour badge

Summing up the Manchester: the airframe that we flew during the summer of 1941 was excellent. The ailerons were very light with the possible bad characteristic that they became lighter the faster you flew the aircraft. In a dive at 250 mph you could roll her with only your little fingers on the yoke. Horizontally, it was too stable. In training, a pilot would become fatigued after three circuits and landings. This was resolved in the Mark IA.

Even if the engines had been reliable, the aircraft was badly under-powered. Two engines each occasionally giving their rated 1,750 hp are not enough to operate a forty-eight thousand pound aircraft. Single-engine operation with a top turret was almost impossible. An idea of flying a Manchester can be gained from a description of a takeoff on a summer evening with full bomb load and full gas. The longest run at Waddington was southwest-northeast, about forty-two hundred feet. This was the landing run for our Lorenz system (our blind-landing system). There was a low transmitter building similar to the instrument land system (ILS) shack at a modern airfield. Three miles away there was a small country church with the usual tower. I would tuck the tail against the hedge along the Sleaford Road at the northeast, hold her on brakes as long as I could at max power, and then let go. If I lifted off and my wing tip was above the Lorenz shack light as I crossed the upwind hedge, I felt that my takeoff had been up to par. I'd have the undercarriage on the way up. After it was up, I would start to bleed the flaps up. If I had wheels and flaps up and I crossed over the church at 100 feet, I felt that I was getting everything that the aircraft could give me on takeoff.

The basic design was good. With two powerful and reliable engines, it could have flown well. The Lancaster was proof of that, with its fuselage being unchanged from the Manchester 1A. Ten feet were added to the wing centre section, as well as new outer panels, designed to carry the outboard engines and additional gas. There you had the Lancaster. I would have given my butt end to have had the Lancaster II (Hercules-powered) to fly on Ops. The failure of the Manchester has to be blamed entirely on the Rolls-Royce Vulture engine—it was unreliable and did not have enough power. That the aircraft was used at all was the fault of the RAF. Rolls-Royce had already stopped development of the Vulture before we started using Manchesters on Ops in February 1941. That the RAF continued to fly this aircraft was, in my view, a mistake in judgement.

My strongest feelings from this period in my life are about my peers: the aircrew who flew these aircraft. Until about June 1941, the captains, navs, w/ops, and tail gunners were all men doing their second tour of Ops. Only when losses decimated their ranks to the point where the air force was incapable of supplying experienced personnel as replacements, first-tour personnel began to feed in.

These determined men went unrewarded for their magnificent efforts. Whether it was right or wrong, it was usual to recognize aircrew with decorations for outstanding performance. In 207 Squadron, the first Manchester unit, from the time that we started Ops on 24 February until I was shot down, (7–8 September 1941), the only decoration awarded to the squadron aircrew was a Bar to his DFC for Burton-Giles. During this time, we received no visible support from Bomber Command and little or no morale support from 5 Group. From the squadron's formation in November 1940 until I was shot down, the Air Officer Commanding (AOC) 5 Group visited the station only twice and did not talk to any squadron aircrew other than the squadron commander. That we were able to keep morale high was due solely to the quality of the men involved.

From the Deck to Thirty Thousand Feet

Beautiful and Lethal, the Spitfire Was a Joy to Fly

J. A. (Jackie) Rae dfc

Is there a more famous aeroplane than the Supermarine Spitfire? More than six decades after its first flight, the Spitfire's mystique remains as strong as ever. Restored examples—when available— are a bigger attraction at today's air shows than the latest military jets. Beautiful yet lethal, R. J. Mitchell's graceful little fighter was flown throughout the Second World War in ever-improved marks that more than matched opposing machines. Few pilots have not dreamed of flying the Spitfire. Jackie Rae, with most of his wartime flying on Spits, was one of the fortunate few who realized that dream. He flew 192 missions of all kinds with the RCAF's 416 (City of Oshawa) Squadron, a very successful fighter unit.

As the founder and leader of Canada's famed Spitfire Band, Jackie Rae's name will be familiar to many Canadians. His connection with show business actually extends much further back—he was a child performer at the age of three! As mentioned in his story, his musical skills occasionally proved useful overseas. Following the war he resumed his career in broadcasting with the CBC, producing the *Wayne & Shuster Show* and other comparable programs. As well he created spectacular CNE Grandstand Shows featuring major stars of the day. Around 1959, he returned to the United Kingdom to star as vocalist and band leader for three years in his own television show. Jackie Rae's entertainment accomplishments merit a book on their own. His Spitfire Band, conceived almost two decades ago to play big band classics from the 1940s, remains extremely popular.

Jackie Rae recalls his wartime flying experiences with insight, humour, and warmth. This account first appeared in the Winter 1996 CAHS *Journal*, adapted from a September 1994 talk to the Toronto Chapter.

I was eighteen when I went to a recruiting centre on Wellington Street in downtown Toronto. The recruiting officer, a jolly fellow, thought I was of the height, stature, and size to become an air gunner. "That's fine," I said. "I'd like to be in the air." Quite frankly, I didn't really know what an air gunner was but I became one, theoretically. In the recruiting centre, after the medical, I noticed two stacks of files, one with a large letter "E," the other with a "W." I asked the corporal sitting there what they meant, and I was told that those under the "E" would train in the west and those under the "W" in the east. While he dozed, I moved my file from the east to the west, which meant I trained in the east.

I recall very clearly the guard duty at Manning Pool, Toronto, with Ross rifles from World War I and no ammunition. I was trying to figure out just what I was guarding there—it seemed I was guarding the garbage. I recall one night in particular. Two young fellows, AC 2s—there was nothing lower than that—came along drunk, really paralyzed. I knew that I was supposed to present my rifle and say, "Halt! Who goes there?" These two fellows wobbled up to me "Halt! Who goes there?" They were singing and weaving back and forth. "Halt! Who goes there?" Then they were behind me, and I'm repeating, "Halt! For God's sake, stop!" but no one paid any attention to me.

I began by telling you that I joined the Air Force at the tender—and gullible—age of eighteen. At Manning Pool, our introduction to the RCAF, we noticed a lot of airmen with white flashes in their forage caps so we asked some of the more experienced fellows—who had been there two weeks— what the flashes meant. They indicated, we were told, that those fellows all had clap (venereal disease). Then we found out that, no, they were just air recruits, like the rest of us.

Then we were posted to Initial Training School (ITS). It involved strict discipline and many tests. I was to become an air gunner. Like everyone else, I flew the Link, and I seemed to have a certain affinity for flying. Somewhere along the line, I became a pilot trainee and was posted to an Elementary Flying Training School (EFTS) at Goderich, Ontario, on the Fleet Finch. I'd like to tell you briefly about my first solo there. My instructor was a fellow called Jack Teguenat, a civilian like all of the other instructors at that time— except the Chief Flying Instructor (CFI).

One morning, when I had six hours and fifty minutes of dual flying, he said, "Give me a good circuit today and I'll let you go solo." I gave him a really beautiful circuit, you couldn't ask for better. We taxied to the end of the field and he reminded me that the Finch would be lighter in the tail without his weight in the back, so I trimmed accordingly. He got out and I got a green light from the tower. I took off into the wind—it was a big grass field—for my solo. It was a wonderful takeoff, then great crosswind and downwind legs and back on final. I was sitting there beaming with joy. It was a wonderful sensation, flying the Fleet with nobody in the back seat. I levelled out at about eight or ten feet and I bounced! I bounced so heavily that I should have put the nose down, opened the throttle, and gone around again, but I didn't. I just let that Finch bounce and bounce until it finally stayed on the ground.

When I taxied back to Jack Teguenat, he hopped on the wing and said, "Congratulations."

"Thank you, Sir."

"Not because you soloed. Because you just escaped the jaws of death!"

He stepped into me with a barrage of invective and profanity that I will not repeat—I don't want to hurt your shell-like ears, but I can tell you, he ripped a strip from me. He later sent me on cross-countries, one of which was actually a trip to Kitchener to pick up his laundry from his mother. I finally accumulated eighty hours EFTS flying time and was posted to Camp Borden.

I was doing very well there, not getting into too much trouble, until night flying started to increase. We had to do a takeoff under the hood (flying blind) during the day if we were going to fly that night. One of the senior students realized very quickly that I could take off down the flare path with no problem, but under the hood I had difficulty. I thought I was going to get canned for sure. Then a guy from a class graduating three weeks before us, gave me some advice. "When you're under the hood," he said, "line yourself up on the runway, and uncage your gyro at zero. Then take your hands and feet off. Just keep your hand around the control column and your feet near the rudder pedals, but don't do anything. When he says 'Let's go,' just open the throttle slowly." The airplane took off beautifully, because this instructor was a very capable pilot (with his feet on the rudder pedals and his hand on the stick) and he didn't need any assistance from me. I got away with it!

Then my instructor asked me to wash his car. I think I was an LAC by then. I was really climbing up the ladder, and I didn't think it was the right thing to request of me or anyone else. "No, Sir," I said. Our association kind of soured from that time, but I still think of him fondly.

I had my wings' test with F/L George Phillips, who I understand was fifty-seven years old at that time. Taking me through the required exercises he asked, "Do you see that field of goldenrod?" Now, I was a city boy and I didn't know what goldenrod looked like, but I wasn't going to admit that to him. "Yes, Sir, I do," I answered. "Give me a forced landing," he ordered, and closed the throttle on me. I spotted a kind of yellowish looking field and began making the customary approach to do a precautionary landing. Hovering over this field with the flying speed getting so low, I wondered if he was going to open the throttle—or if I should. Finally, he whacked it open and we went around. "Take me home," he said, which I did. At Borden I landed and he hopped out of the aeroplane and stomped away. I thought I was finished. Some instructors (especially fifty-seven-year-old ones) liked to keep their students guessing.

I still got my wings and became a Sergeant Pilot. I had ten days leave and was then posted to the United Kingdom, to an operational training unit near Carlisle. I had two hours on a Miles Master and then about thirty hours in some very beat-up old Battle of Britain Hurricanes.

After that I was posted to 416 Squadron, a Canadian Spitfire unit just then forming in Peterhead, in the northeast corner of Scotland, some distance north of Aberdeen. Half the squadron, 'A' Flight, was in Aberdeen. I was with 'B' Flight at Peterhead. We were flying Spitfire IIs. In winter Peterhead was dull, and the weather was really foul; but we practised formation flying, battle climbs, and low-level attacks—almost always in really frightful weather.

I recall one instance when I and a Number Two were scrambled, the controller assuring us he had a wonderful hostile plot. He directed us farther and still farther out to sea, until we were almost out of his radio range. Finally, we came across a Lockheed Hudson. We made a few gentle passes at it so that they could see who we were. Then we shot some gun camera footage—delightful pictures. That crew never looked better! When we got back into the controller's radio range, we immediately contacted him.

"Congratulations, *Grass Seed*," (that was his code name). "You did a wonderful job! We got a Dornier 17. It was sensational! We got great pictures."

"Oh, that's great! Simply wonderful!"

Then we landed back at Peterhead and showed the film.

"My God, you shot down a Lockheed Hudson! This is dreadful!"

"You _ _ _ _!" I can't repeat what we called him, my colleague and I. "You send us out over the North Sea in terrible weather, so far that we can hardly hear you—and you tell us it's a hostile all the way, until we finally come across this old Hudson!"

We did let him off the hook, but for a while he was a very worried man.

I seem to be dwelling on the fact that Peterhead weather was so terrible. It was. On another occasion I was scrambled with another fellow who slipped off the runway on takeoff. I got away and when I came back there was a terrible blizzard at the airfield. I couldn't get down. I had the odd glimpse of the control tower and of the runways as I tried to make a pass and line myself up, but I couldn't figure things out. I couldn't get straight with the runway. I was off either one way or the other. I was really flying low, at maybe 300 feet, when one of the ground crew came up with the idea of firing a green flare from a Very pistol along the runway. He thought that maybe I could get a line on the flare. He kept firing the flares until I got the idea and managed to get kind of lined up. I made the best landing of my life because of the wonderful ingenuity of that ground crew fellow allowing us to beat the weather. It was doubly sweet.

With us we had a fellow called "Huck" Murray from Woodstock, Ontario, who became the commander of 'B' Flight, my flight. He was disturbed because we were all flying with the precision that we had learned in flying school. He was from 11 Group, between London and the south coast, and he

Jackie Rae in the cockpit of his Spitfire V with two squadron mates, N. F. Houghton (in front of the windscreen), and R. A. Buckham (on the wing). *DND 15091.*

had come to Peterhead to take his first command. "You've got to get rid of this style of flying," he told us. He was a tough little cookie, a Jimmy Cagney type. He said, "You've got to change your ways and get rough with the aeroplane," and he took each of us up. When my turn came, I formated on him, and we flew up to about 10,000 feet. Then we broke away and did head-on attacks with our camera guns. He got behind me very quickly. When we came down and looked at the film, I saw that he had me in the frame all the time. All he had done was turn tightly—while I did slow rolls, rolls off the top, and loops, all useless for getting away from somebody. He showed me, and when I saw the film, I learned for myself.

Then he decided to take us down to the deck. He was leading and I was flying formation very close to him when he did a turn to the left—which meant I had him above me and the sea below me—with no place to go except up or down. I didn't want to hit him, and I certainly didn't want to go into the water. "Don't get your wing wet," he advised me. Since he had asked for radio silence from us I persevered, trying to do as well as I could. "Don't say a word," I said to myself, but because I had been "educating" the throttle back and forth considerably, my gas gauge was going down very quickly. Finally I decided I had to say something.

"*White Ox Blue One: Blue Two* here—I'm running short of petrol!"

"What do you expect me to do," was the reply, "piss in your tank?" I told you he was a fellow of rough humour.

On one of the many scrambles we did from Peterhead, we went to Skabrae in the Orkney Islands to fly cover for an aircraft carrier, some cruisers, and destroyers. What was interesting to us was that we were told to maintain readiness to fly from dawn to dusk. At that time of year in the Orkney Islands, dawn to dusk was something like twenty hours, a long haul for us, but only for a short time. We were happy to say that this very massive flotilla got into Scapa Flow without any problem.

Then I was called to Inverness for an interview to decide whether or not I was suitable to become a commissioned officer. I flew a little Magister up there with another fellow. A/V/M Coltishall, a hero of the First World War, interviewed us, seated at his desk with a wing commander to one side and another one behind the candidate. For some reason I was called first. "What do you know about the Singer sewing machine?" he asked me. And I had boned up on the Spitfire! "What do you know about the Singer sewing machine?" he repeated. I was stumped. "We never had one in our family," I finally replied—and he seemed satisfied. "Now, what about the tides? What do you know about tides?" Then his phone rang and he took it. "Thank God," I thought. The tides? I knew they had some relationship with the phases of the moon. I was pretty scared of this fellow and the two hawkeyes and couldn't think of a damn thing more. Then he put down the phone and said, "That's all." I was dismissed.

I came out and the other fellow, B. B. Brooks, asked, "How did you do?" What could I say? Then he went in. Shortly thereafter our commissions came through. I really have no idea why such inane questions were posed. I suppose he just wanted to see whether we faked, told the truth, or said, "Take two aspirins and call me in the morning." However, we got the commissions. I probably got mine because they needed a piano player in the officers' mess.

While we were at Peterhead, somebody decided it would be a good idea to prepare for a mission somewhere in Scandinavia, and we were sent to practise takeoffs and landings from a dummy carrier deck. Fortunately, the sweep was cancelled and we were delighted—one of our happier moments.

Our Squadron Leader, Lloyd Chadburn—someone I remember with admiration, affection, and even love—was a sensational leader on the ground and in the air. On the ground he was a very relaxed fellow, but in the air he was something else. On 13 June 1944, one week after D-day, he died in an aerial collision, of all things, after a very long and successful career as a fighter pilot. It was just lousy luck.

But back to Peterhead. "You know," he remarked, "flying in all this rotten weather we may only scramble for the odd enemy aircraft, do convoy patrols, and so on." Then he asked, "How would you like to go to Malta?" "Great!" we answered. "Anywhere but this place would be super." So we had the shots and we had lectures on what to expect in Malta. The inoculations were effective, but the posting was cancelled.

Mark Vs replaced our Mark II Spitfires. The following month, 416 Squadron led the whole group in flying time. Our total was over nine hundred hours, surpassing the next squadron by 350 hours. That was because of Lloyd Chadburn and Huck Murray, who gave us such great training, keeping us in the air constantly. This paid off as things got a little busier. Night flying increased to the point where some of us were classed as night operational.

In June 1942, the squadron moved to Westhampnet in Sussex. There my tutor in operational flying, Huck Murray, and his Number Two were shot down off the Isle of Wight. It was a huge personal loss to me. Huck taught us much—how to bend the aeroplane and survive. When I was commis-

W/C Lloyd Chadburn DFC, leader of 416 Squadron, leans on one of the unit's Spitfires bearing the squadron's official insignia, a leaping puma superimposed on a maple leaf. *DND PL 15079.*

sioned, he gave me his old beat-up hat because I didn't want to look like a new officer. He has a very special place in my heart.

During this time, our CO, S/L Chadburn, flew to RCAF Headquarters with his cockpit filled with whiskey—to coerce the brass into keeping us in 11 Group. As I mentioned, that was the area between London and the south coast. He came back bleary-eyed and successful, so we went to Martlesham Heath. During our first month we did ninety operational sorties, which jumped to 336 the next month. The squadron did indeed log considerable operational time.

On 6 July 1942, foul weather caused the decision-makers to postpone the Dieppe raid, but 416 Squadron carried on with penetrations into France, Belgium, and Holland. We went to Hawkinge airfield near Folkstone and Dover, just before the Dieppe raid on 19 August. Looking in my logbook, I discovered that on 18 August I took up twenty-one air cadets for circuits in 416's Miles Magister, with no inkling of what would happen the next day.

Those who participated in the battle at Dieppe—navy, army, and air force—are just now (1994) being honoured with a decoration. We have just been notified. I wonder why it took fifty-two years to make this decision. I hope it comes before I'm too old. Wow, fifty-two years between man and boy!

Canadian ground losses at Dieppe were horrific, but because of our height, the smoke, and the fire we weren't aware of that. We were supposed to patrol at 3,000 feet, but our altitude varied because of what was happening. Along with our own kites there were many Messerschmitt BF 109s, Focke Wulf Fw 190s, and Junkers Ju 88s, all crowded into a very small air space. We did four sweeps over the beach, flying a total of seven hours and twenty minutes. Our squadron's score was eleven enemy aircraft with no loss to ourselves, a great credit to the leadership of Chadburn, Murray, and the others.

We were at a grass airfield (Hawkinge) which could take twelve aircraft abreast, landing or taking off. Lloyd Chadburn was always on our backs about taxiing too fast. We had become so cheeky that we taxied with the tail off the ground virtually all the time. Yet, he taxied faster than anybody. Being the CO made it a different story.

On one occasion we did a crossover turn coming back from an Op. I was leading one squadron and Chadburn was leading the other one—and the wing. We did our crossover turn, which put us on one side, and we landed first. One of the fellows in my front squadron experienced a hydraulic leak while in the circuit. Switched off, he managed a good wheels-down landing, letting the aeroplane roll until it finally stopped. He sat there for a moment and then got out, carrying his parachute, and started to walk off the field. Lloyd, who had been after us so much about fast taxiing, landed with his squadron right behind us and taxied up the tail of this stalled aeroplane, chewing it up rather badly.

Our practice with Chadburn was to behave with army formality when he first arrived in the morning—and that would be our military discipline for the day. This time we decided that when he came we would all snap to attention. When he walked in, we all popped up like soldiers. He strode over to the fellow whose aeroplane he had mangled rather nastily.

"How many stripes have you got on your arm?" he asked.

"One, Sir."

"How many do I have on my arm?"

"Three, Sir."

"Well, you've got a goddamn nerve backing into the Wing Commander's aeroplane!"

Can you imagine?

We had a box in which we used to put money whenever we did anything stupid, like taxiing a wing tip into a tree. Lloyd went over to the box, put in five pounds (a nice sum), and stomped out. Whenever we got enough money in the box, we'd have a party.

About a month later we were posted to Redhill, which was a little grass field, sort of nestled in between Kenley and Biggin Hill, still in 11 Group. We were asked to meet the station staff that evening at the officers' mess. I was now a P/O, I think, or an F/O—I don't remember. We met the G/C and his wife, who was dressed in a lace curtain, and then the adjutants, and so on. We finished passing down the line saying, "How do you do? How do you do?" and ended up with station staff at one end while we were at the other. We seemed unable to join together in friendly harmony.

Then Chadburn called some of us outside, as for a briefing. "In Redhill, there's a hotel," he said. "I want you, you, and you to take the truck to that hotel and go into the dance. Don't get yourself involved, just get a girl." This would be considered terribly sexist today, but it went over okay fifty years ago. "Bring her out to the truck. Then go in and dance with another one and put her in the truck too until you fill the truck with women. Then bring it back to the mess." We did as we were told, and the station staff were still there when we got back. We had a wonderful party—global in its concept, but frightening in its sheer simplicity. (I don't know what the hell that means, but it sounds good, doesn't it)?

The next day, the station commander called Chadburn in to tear a strip off him. "It wasn't my doing, Sir," he explained. "It was Brooks, Foster, and Rae. They caused the problem, but if you leave their punishment to me," he continued, "I'll look after it." We were not punished because he knew we were going to fly with him that afternoon. It had been a good night.

It's hard to reflect back. When I think about the war, really, I like to think about the funny things. For instance, there was a lady in London who played piano in a place called Ottilino's. She played piano and sang. She would have been, I think, in her forties—a very, very attractive and classy lady all around. I was about nineteen. I would sit beside her on the piano stool, and we would sing together. At the end of the evening she would give me a little kiss, and I would go home to wherever I was staying. One night she asked me, "How would you like to come home with me?" Well, at nineteen, you know, it was difficult to make those decisions. "Well, by George," I decided, "yes, I think I would like to." (Her name happened to be George—and if you believe that ...) So, we went. We drove to Cricklewood in a cab, and she didn't find it too difficult to kiss me and hold me with some degree of affection. I thought, "This is it! I'm home. This is beautiful. I've got it made!" We arrived at the door of her little house and her tiny, sweet little mother opened it. "Oh, come in, come in." Then, "Here's your room." I was taken to a bedroom, and I wondered to myself, "Hey, what am I doing in this room, by myself with a nice little old lady about to bring me a cup of tea? It's really unfair. It's unjust." Still, the lovely, piano-playing lady was adorable. She came to my door to tell me, "Now, there'll be tea here for you in the morning. You did say you have to get up and be back at the airfield by 06:00 hours. Isn't that six o'clock in the morning?" Then she left. "What should I do? Shall I get a cab from Cricklewood back to Piccadilly, or should I stay until the morning?" So, what is the moral of this story? *Never accept invitations from lady pianists!* Forgive me, ladies.

At Redhill, "rhubarbs" were plentiful, low-level attacks on trains, usually in sections of two. I found the erks who serviced our aeroplanes were very dependable—really unsung heroes. My engine fitter comes to visit me now and again. He has just turned eighty. When we were on the squadron together, he would say to me, "Hi, Jackson!" Then he would salute me. When I was about to take off on a mission, he'd hop up on the wing and say, "Now, listen, Jackson. Don't fool around and break my aeroplane." Then he would

A group largely composed of 416 Squadron pilots in November of 1943. Lloyd Chadburn is on the right. *DND PL 22193.*

39

jump down and salute again. He was one of countless ground crew who put their work far above themselves. I have great affection for them, and I'm not alone. Any pilot worth his salt held his ground crew in the highest esteem.

Here's to aircrew gone missing—bright, intelligent, aggressive young men who, had they lived, would have made worthwhile contributions to this world. So, bless them all, the long, the short, and the tall—and bless you. Thank you. Questions?

QUESTION: Having had so much fun flying the Spitfire during the war; did you go on doing any flying as a weekend pilot after the war?

MR. RAE: Yes, I did. I went back to England in 1960 to do television stuff, and there I started flying a Percival Prentice, a low-wing machine with turned-up wing tips. When I came back to Canada in 1976, I had the pleasure of flying a great deal with Gordon Schwartz in his Tri Pacer. He flew that little aeroplane with his knees right up in his face. I didn't have the same problem. And I've got a Harvard ride arranged, very shortly.

QUESTION: With regard to your tight turns with the Spitfire, what were the effects of "G?"

MR. RAE: If we did a hard recovery from a dive or a tight climbing turn, your cheeks would sag down around your shoulders. That was a daily experience. However, I had a feeling at that time that if I kept in shape it would take me longer to black out than perhaps it would otherwise.

QUESTION: The Hurricane was rugged and could stand up to a great amount of rough use. But the Spit—so aerodynamically clean—what happened when you hung things on it? How did it handle? Or did you want to keep the aircraft clean?

MR. RAE: The Hurricane was certainly a strong gun platform and very sturdy. However, my flying time on it was only thirty hours, not really a great deal of experience. Aerodynamically, I think the Spitfire, with all its cleanliness and manoeuverability, was the aeroplane, and one stayed with it if one had a choice.

QUESTION: Can you say a bit about briefings and your response to wartime tensions.

MR. RAE: Briefings lasted only about thirty or forty minutes. There was seldom a great deal to tell since our sweeps would only take an hour and forty,

A Spitfire IXB of 416 Squadron in France during June 1944. The white and black invasion stripes around the fuselage and on the wings identified Allied aircraft operating in Europe. *DND.*

an hour and fifteen, or an hour and ten minutes, that sort of duration. We emptied our pockets—most of us had nothing in them anyway. Then we did the sweep. It was a period where our various personalities came to the fore. Some people became withdrawn. In my case, I never even thought about it. My way, I suppose, was to be a cheerful, happy kind of guy, regardless of the fear I might be feeling. Then there were others who were very quiet and maybe wrote home—that sounds kind of corny, but it's true—mainly writing to mothers, not wives, not girlfriends. That was very obvious. It was a short time by yourself before getting strapped in the cockpit, a few very quiet moments. A lot of things were happening although not in terms of today's technology. We would be checking our oxygen bottle, our microphone, and the other elementary things there were, waiting for the CO to wave his hand. Most of us would say a kind of a prayer. We used to talk about it after. Then "whoof," off we would go, in four or twelve across, or whatever the takeoff formation may have been.

QUESTION: Was 'B' Flight really the origin of the Spitfire Band?

ANSWER: No, the Spitfire Band started when I was working at Standard Broadcasting, which controlled CFRB and other stations. I was running the record side of that organization when someone asked me what I was going to do next. I answered that I thought it was time for a resurgence of big band music. There was agreement, and we decided to do just that.

"What are you going to call the band?" I was asked.

"I have no idea."

"Well, if you're going to start playing 1940's music, you should include aeroplanes."

That seemed like kind of a nice marriage. Hence the Spitfire Band. That's how it all began.

The following is excerpted from a brief article entitled "I'm No Hero Says Jackie Rae" by Geoffrey Norris that appeared in the April 1959 issue of the now defunct *RAF Flying Review*. It affords insights into the flying career of Jackie Rae DFC, which complement the foregoing rather modest account. As author Norris points out, Jackie Rae, the extrovert entertainer, had acquired the British penchant for understatement and self-deprecation. The first incident described occurred on 14 May 1943.

Alone over Mardike, in Holland, a Canadian Spitfire pilot anxiously scans the skies for the rest of his squadron. There has been a mix-up with some Focke Wulf 190s and now that it is over, this pilot finds himself in an unenviable solitary position.

But he is not quite alone. He stiffens as he peers through the side of the canopy and sees, some way away, three squat shapes flying on a course parallel to his own. He does not have to be a recognition expert to identify the aircraft as Focke Wulf 190s.

The Spitfire pilot feels uneasy, to say the least. By all the rules three 190s should be able to make mincemeat of his single Spitfire. But the Canadian does not hesitate for long. Smoothly he pushes his stick over and turns into the attack ...

If you ask Jackie Rae about that scrape he'll tell you that turning into the attack was the safest course to take. That is a matter of opinion. He'll also stress that he "properly got the twitch" when he saw the three 190s.

Nevertheless, he turned and bore down on the Germans. For a second it seemed that they had not seen him coming—until suddenly the two outside aircraft half-rolled away and down to safety, leaving the centre one to face the Spitfire.

Rae wasted no time. As he came into range and the Fw 190 flashed in his sights, he fired. It was good shooting, and no repeat performance was called for. The 190 fell out of control toward the ground.

It was Rae's sign to turn for home. "I pushed the throttle right through the 'gate,'" he recalls, "and kept it there all the way home. I roared off at top speed and ended up zooming around the circuit like a bomb. Those 190s had given me the creeps."

I asked him how he had come by his DFC.

"Well, you know," he said, "they gave a lot of those away. Sort of good conduct medals in a way."

Good conduct!

Press him further and he'll say that it had something to do with shipping strikes—and then adroitly change the subject.

Just for the record, let's quote the London Gazette for August 27, 1943, on the subject of J/15493, Flight Lieut John Arthur Rae, RCAF.

This officer has completed sixty sorties and throughout has displayed skill and determination of a high order. He has taken part in many telling attacks on shipping, and while in combat he has destroyed at least two enemy aircraft. His fighting qualities and excellent leadership have contributed materially to the high standards and efficiency of his Flight.

That is the citation that accompanied the award of an immediate DFC.

Rae will tell you that he was just another fighter pilot ... But it is not every pilot who is awarded the DFC. And it is quite an achievement to spend the greater part of the war in the thickest of the air fighting in England and Europe—and end up with a bag of eight aircraft as Rae did.

"I was flying Number 2 to Lloyd Chadburn (during the Dieppe sweeps), who was leading our squadron. On one sortie he picked up a squadron of Ju 88s, which was about to bomb some shipping. He led us straight into the attack. I saw a Ju 88 right in front of me, lined up and fired. It flew away with smoke pouring from it."

With the advent of winter, the pressure eased off a little, and it was not until the spring of 1943 that Rae found himself in the thick of things.

'Johnnie' Johnson was again leading the Canadians when the Wing ran into a flock of Focke Wulf 190s over the Belgian coast. Rae saw a 190 flying straight across his front. He lined up, allowed for deflection, and fired. Shells ripped through the enemy, which did not crash. Official credit was given to Rae for one more damaged.

It was around this time that Rae found himself flying Number 2 to Johnson himself. G/C Johnson now Station Commander of Cottesmore "V" Bomber

Station (in 1959), has no hesitation in referring to Rae as "a first class fighter pilot. He stuck well and was aggressive."

Rae was to have plenty of opportunity to show his prowess as a fighter pilot and his aggressiveness a little later in 1943. Squadron 416 began to specialize in providing fighter cover for Beaufighters out for shipping attacks in the Channel and the North Sea. July 18 was one such occasion.

Beaufighters were out in force to attack a convoy, and Rae was in one of the escorting Spitfires. They found the convoy sheltering under an umbrella of escorting 109s. As the Beaufighters swept in low to release their torpedoes, the Spitfires closed around the German fighters. The 109s "bounced" from one squadron of Spitfires to another in their attempts to escape.

Flying close behind Lloyd Chadburn, Rae followed him into the attack. The two Spitfires chased one 109, which crashed into the sea before they could fire. They found another, and Chadburn opened up at short range. Rae followed in closely and poured cannon and machine gun fire into the German fighter. He watched his shells striking home around the engine and then, without warning, the Me fell like a stone into the sea.

Again, a few days later, the Spitfires were flying at 1,000 feet when they saw two Me 109s coming around the end of a German convoy.

One of the Mes made a half-hearted attack on the Spitfires and fell an easy victim to S/L Geof Northcott, who was leading the Canadians. Rae spotted another Me and immediately gave chase as it streaked toward shore. Steadily he closed into range and then fired. As the 109 reached the shore, it crashed into the beach.

This was Jackie Rae the fighter pilot. He remained with 416 throughout the war, operated from the Continent, and followed closely behind the Allied armies as they advanced across Europe ... Although Rae the fighter pilot is now a thing of the past, he still gets in as much flying as he can. One of the first things he did when he came over to England last July was to join the Surrey Flying Club. His one criticism of England is that our Air Traffic Control Rules are a bit puzzling for a stranger. But we must remember that the last time he flew in England, Rae had the virtual freedom of the skies. Freedom which he himself had helped to win.

Flying the Whirlwind

Interception and Ground Attack with an Unsung Yet Remarkable Aeroplane

J. P. (Jim) Coyne DFC

Circumstances occasionally foil the development of promising aircraft to their full potential. Such was the case with the RAF's innovative Westland Whirlwind, a fine aeroplane ahead of its time. The German Luftwaffe's Messerschmitt Me 262 was another such example. Jim Coyne flew with the only squadron to operate Whirlwinds substantially, from their introduction almost to their retirement. His extensive Whirlwind experience may be unmatched. The same can be said of his enthusiasm. The following account, a much-expanded version of a 1991 CAHS Convention presentation, appeared in the Winter 1999 CAHS *Journal*.

Jim Coyne was raised in The Pas, Manitoba, where bush pilots were an important part of the scene. Their exploits captured his imagination. Jim's chance to fly came with the outbreak of war, and he enlisted in the RCAF on 10 October 1940. From Manning Pool in Toronto he went to Trenton, where he did guard duty—but managed a flight in a Fairey Battle. From there he was posted back to Toronto for pilot training. At this point he picks up the story.

His Whirlwind tour capped with the award of a DFC, Jim was appointed president of the RCAF Aircrew Re-Selection Board, a six-month desk assignment. After leave in Canada, he returned to the United Kingdom, where he converted to the de Havilland Mosquito, joining the RCAF's famed 418 Squadron as a Flight Commander. He flew with 418 as part of the British Air Forces of Occupation (BAFO) until 418 was disbanded in August 1945. Remaining in the postwar RCAF, Jim flew photo-survey Lancasters out of Rockcliffe, on the outskirts of Ottawa, and in his spare time acquired

45

a degree in geology. He retired from the RCAF in 1965 to teach school, ultimately becoming audiovisual co-ordinator for the Bruce County (Ontario) Board of Education. He continued to fly until 1997 when he gave up his licence and sold his Cessna 150.

I see my wartime career as being pretty much average for a fellow joining the air force in the early days. I was fortunate to be selected during Initial Training at the Hunt Club in Toronto for pilot training while a lot of fellows were arbitrarily streamed to become air gunners, navigators, and other trades people.

My solo on a Finch at No 1 Elementary Flying Training School (EFTS), Malton, was disappointing. I was expecting something magical to happen when I went up alone that first time—and it really didn't. That magic came later. From the Finch I went onto the "metric" Yales (taken over from French orders) and then Harvards at No 2 Service Flying Training School (SFTS), Uplands (Ottawa). The only thing notable was that our senior course was the one that was filmed for the well-known Cagney movie *Captains of the Clouds*. I was an extra in the film—and thus became famous! Another memorable aspect was meeting John Gillespie ("Maggy") Magee who later wrote the immortal sonnet "High Flight." I was on guard duty with him not only at Trenton but at the Hunt Club ITS and SFTS at Uplands. Maggy was one place ahead of me on Wings Parade held on 10 June 1941 when A/M Wilf Curtis made the presentations.

I soon made sergeant pilot and was sent overseas. After a little cruise on an armed merchant cruiser, HMS *Ascania,* we stopped at Iceland for a few weeks at a transit camp, where we slept on the floor, sixty to a hut, and washed in a glacier-fed stream behind the hut. I had my first introduction to the RAF. To put it mildly, the commanding officer there was a little eccentric—others had different ways of describing him. I can't remember his name, but he was a First World War pilot who rode around the narrow dirt roads on a high bicycle, stopping any airmen that he met and delivering lectures on how our experiences with poor food and poor accommodation would do us good. The food *was* poor. Sparse and monotonous, it came from England rather than Canada. The daily main meal was mutton stew and brussel sprouts, sometimes with potatoes or rice, and sometimes not. The normal dessert was rhubarb—without sugar.

And, believe it or not, I got joed into working in the kitchen, opening cans of hard tack which, instead of bread, we had for tea, with a dab of margarine just like axle grease. These cans were big square metal containers with a ring soldered on the top. Stamped on that, with a broad arrow, was the year 1917! I kid you not.

Next came a very unpleasant journey on a troop ship, SS *Leopoldville*, overloaded with British army troops who had been on garrison duty in the north of Iceland. It was very crowded: on our mess deck we had three layers. One layer slept on the floor, one on the mess tables, and the other in hammocks. It added up to five days of very uncomfortable living. We arrived at Greenock on 15 August and had only one week at Bournemouth, a seaside resort town used as a reception centre for Canadian aircrews. Some people spent three or even six months there before posting to a unit.

Sent to 55 OTU, Usworth, we flew Miles Masters and Hurricane Is. I flew my first Master, N8002, on 26 August and my first Hurricane, P3589, the next day. That magic I didn't experience soloing in the Finch happened at OTU. On 3 September I was told to sign out a beat-up Battle of Britain Hurricane (7400)—with patched bullet holes still evident—to fly for one hour at 20,000 feet. It was a beautiful fall day over the Lake District with towering cumulus clouds spotted here and there. Bright autumn sun shone on the cloud tops, the valleys, and through the spaces between them. It was a most wonderful feeling to swoop and soar and dive and stall-turn or spin in that wonderland of cotton wool. That feeling was enhanced on 24 September when I flew Hurricane 3413 with another aircraft, the pilot's name forgotten, to dogfight at 25,000 feet in similar conditions, this time for an hour and twenty minutes. In contrast, that flight was followed immediately by deck-level flying in a formation of four aircraft.

We thought we were on our way to becoming Canadian fighter pilots on Spitfires or at least Hurricanes; but at the end of the course when our squadron listings were posted, ten RCAF sergeant pilots were to be sent to 263 Squadron. "What was 263 Squadron?" we asked. "Where was it, and what did it fly?"

Somebody thought that 263 flew Whirlwinds. "What are Whirlwinds?" we wanted to know. No one at the OTU, including the instructors seemed to know anything about the Whirlwind because it was on the "Secret List." All kinds of rumours began circulating, strange stories about this odd machine, heard second- or third-hand. Fairy tales would have been a better description. Other than it having two engines, the originators had no real knowledge of this fine aeroplane. One claim was that it could not fly on one engine. Later I would fly one back to base on one engine. Twice! Another story had it that, on a nose over, the four cannons, which were mounted virtually in your lap, would break loose and separate the top half of your body from the bottom half. Not so! I would seriously bend Whirlwind P7108 by running it off the runway into boggy ground, flipping the aircraft on its back. I was unhurt except for one toe. No sooner had the aircraft come to rest than a whole gang of airmen appeared and mightily lifted up the tail. I pulled the pin on my Sutton harness and landed square on my head. Crawling out from under, I vented my anger by giving the aircraft a mighty kick—breaking my toe. This kept me off flying for a couple of days. Of course, expecting Spits or Hurricanes, we knew that we wouldn't like the Whirlwind at all.

The night before we were to have a formal interview with the CO, we ten new RCAF pilots decided *en masse* to tell him we did not wish to fly twins and to demand a posting to a Canadian single-engine fighter unit. The next morning, needless to say, Pugh, the CO, tore off great strips from our hides and threatened us with dire penalties—court martial and other unpleasantness. We would all fly the Whirlwind, he firmly stated. He guaranteed that we would grow to love it. As we waited for transport to take us back to the field, wondering what our fate was to be, Pugh's Whirlwind appeared. Diving down on us, he pulled up into a series of upward rolls and treated us to a fantastic series of low-level aerobatics—the likes of which I would never see again. Maybe, we thought, it won't be too bad having to fly this strange aeroplane.

All of us did fly the Whirlwind. Bob Brennan and John McClure would be transferred to 137 Squadron when it was formed from a nucleus of experienced 263 pilots. Ed Brearly, Don Gill, Hap Kennedy, Bill Lovell, Jack Michener, Mick Muirhead, Dick Reed, and myself would remain with 263. Bob Brennan became the first casualty from our group, and John McClure returned to 263 when 137 was re-equipped, becoming 'B' Flight Commander—I commanded 'A' Flight. On 7 November 1942, Don Gill would be killed on a rhubarb with me to the Cherbourg Peninsula. On another trip to Cherbourg Peninsula, on 16 April 1943, Ed Brearley would go missing on a "night intruder," (We sometimes referred to single aircraft "night rhubarbs" as "intruders"). His body was washed ashore just south of our airfield. Sadly, I commanded the Honour Guard when we buried him in the village churchyard at Warmwell.

Hap Kennedy did eventually convince the CO to arrange his transfer to a Canadian Spitfire squadron and finished the war as a highly successful and well-decorated fighter pilot. Bill Lovell would transfer to a USAAF P-38

Lightning squadron and lose his life during the North African invasion. Jack Michener would enter hospital a few months after joining 263, and on recovery, somehow manage a posting to a Canadian Spitfire squadron and serve with great distinction. Mick Muirhead was posted to a non-op unit for a short period and then to 401 Squadron RCAF flying Spits and was killed in a mid-air collision 12 February 1943. Dick Reed, the other American national in our group, would also transfer to the USAAF. I have no knowledge of his subsequent activities.

Returning to my story, on 7 October I arrived at Charmy Down near Bath and reported to 263 Squadron along with nine other RCAF sergeant pilots, two of whom were American citizens. That was just the beginning. We were the first "colonials" to arrive at this RAF squadron; with ten of us, some unusual activities took place. You can imagine the feelings of ten keen, and brash, young pilots arriving at an RAF squadron that had had no experience of such "outlanders." We found many of the customs and sayings strange. There was some misunderstanding at first but flying this unusual aircraft—which some of us got to like—brought us together.

The Whirlwind was designed in 1936 for Westland Aircraft by W. E. W. Petter—later of English Electric Canberra and Lightning fame—to the oper-

Six of the ten Canadian Sergeant Pilots posted to 263 Squadron. (L-R): Bill Lovell, Ed Brearley, John McClure, Jack Mitchener, Bob Brennan, and Hap Kennedy. *J. Coyne*

ational requirement specification F.37/35, almost the same, I think, as the Spitfire and Hurricane (F.37/34), except that it called for two engines.

It was clean, sleek, and relatively small for a twin-engined aircraft, with a forty-five-foot wingspan and a length of thirty-one feet, six inches. The fuselage was mainly of magnesium, which made it a little different from contemporary aircraft. A low-wing monoplane, it had very smooth surfaces and was built in three major sections. The engines were mounted on the wing centre section. Leading edged slats were installed initially, but these were permanently locked as a result of a fatal accident. One of the slats broke loose during a high-speed stall, causing the aircraft to crash.

The engines were Rolls-Royce V-12 Peregrines rated at 885 hp at 3,000 rpm, driving ten-foot diameter variable-speed propellers, which could not be feathered. There was a 67-gallon fuel tank in each wing feeding the adjacent engine, but there was no crossover from one tank to the other. The lack of feathering and crossover feed were two very unsatisfactory features. The throttle, pitch, fuel, and mixture controls were hydraulically operated by the "exactor" system. Armament was four 20-mm Hispano cannon mounted in the nose, immediately in front of the cockpit—right in your lap—with sixty rounds per drum-fed gun. The Whirlwind was the first Allied monoplane fighter to be designed around cannon armament.

The cockpit was roomy and well organized for its time. The seat was amply protected by armour plate, and the windshield was bulletproof. There was a substantial crash pylon right behind the pilot's head in case of a bit of unexpected (but extreme) nose-down, tail-up attitude. Access to the cockpit was by a three-foot retractable ladder, stowed in the fuselage during flight. The first prototype flew initially on 11 October 1938—unintentionally—as a result of a too-fast taxiing trial.

Number 75 Squadron flew one of the prototypes and two of the production aircraft during June 1940 but turned them over to 263 Squadron, which was reforming and re-equipping after a disastrous campaign on Gloster Gladiators in Norway. By the time I joined 263 Squadron, some twenty-one Whirlwinds had been lost or written off and there were only ninety-three left. Westland built only 114 out of an order for 440. I flew thirty-three of the ninety-three Whirlwinds, probably more than anybody except Harald Penrose, Westland's chief test pilot.

What was it like to fly the Whirlwind? I can say that it was scary for those first few flights. There was no two-seat version for dual instruction, no way of learning how to manage an aircraft with two engines, how to taxi it, or

An unusual rear view of the Whirlwind emphasizes the distinctive high horizontal tailplane. *J. Coyne.*

become familiar with any odd characteristics. Much later we did get an Oxford, but only for twin-engined ground handling. Even the Whirlwind's landing speed—in excess of 25 mph beyond that of the Hurrie or Spit—was daunting. We didn't even have a manual for the aeroplane. Visibility from the cockpit was excellent and in my view, even better than the Mk VI Mossie that I later flew. The bubble canopy, which wound back on a single crank system for normal opening, was great. I don't think that there was an emergency canopy jettisoning system, because of the high fin and raised tailplane. The *Pilot's Notes* I picked up several years ago in the United Kingdom at the Shuttleworth Collection's bookshop make no mention of one.

We were allocated one of the experienced sergeant pilots on the squadron who became our tutor with a "show and tell" approach. From him we were expected to learn how to fly the Whirlwind. We also learned other useful things by going over to the maintenance hangar and inspecting the emergency systems, armament, and such things.

On 12 October, three days after beginning this course, the flight commander asked my tutor if I was ready to fly the aeroplane. Assured that I was, he told me to get my parachute and sign out Whirlwind P7003. I sat in the cockpit for what seemed like an hour—actually about ten minutes—being vigorously grilled by the flight commander. Suddenly he slapped me on the shoulder and told me to get it into the air. Since this was the first time I had even sat in the aeroplane, luck had to be the rule.

As I sat in that cockpit on 12 October, I knew very little about this curiously unconventional aeroplane. All I could think of was how in hell do I get the damn thing up, and more important, how do I get it down again? My mind was filled with all the half-believed rumours about it being a hard aeroplane to fly, a killer that couldn't fly on one engine. It was also said that if that you lost an engine on takeoff, the plane would proceed to roll upside down, or, on the other hand, it might climb out of sight. There was no shortage of *pukka gen*. (RAF slang for accurate information, a term originating years earlier in the Far East.)

My tutor had primed me with all of the procedures necessary to get out of scrapes, but I only half-believed him when he said it was a great machine to fly. My immediate concern had to do with the Whirlwind's fast acceleration. Unlike the Spit and the Hurricane, which had monstrous cooling radiators hanging down below the wings or fuselage, the Whirlwind had its rads set right into the leading edges of the wings, inboard of the engines. While it was very clean-looking, this feature made the engines prone to overheating on the ground, so a quick takeoff—as soon as you started the engines—was essential, and I had a long way to taxi. There were two engines to deal with, and I wasn't completely familiar with the RAF's new system of hand brakes. I had to taxi this two-engined, marginally cooled thing with a scant supply of air pressure. It was a daunting picture.

But this was it. What to do? Don't forget to prime the exactors (hydraulic lines rather than the rods and pinions that normally went to the throttle), pitch, fuel, and mixture controls of the engine. Remember the speed numbers. Use full plus-nine boost on takeoff and full fine pitch. Don't let the rads boil. Remember, it will fly on one engine at 140 mph—no, better make it 150! I was just a little worried, but I told myself that I'd already coped with 194 hours of flying so I should be able to put in at least one more.

When I looked around to see if everything was clear, my two ground crew—bless their souls—who obviously knew that this was my first flight in the Whirlwind, gave me great big grins and vigorous thumbs-up signals. I started the engines. Quickly now, hydraulic pressure okay, check flaps down

Jim Coyne as a Flight Commander in the cockpit of his Whirlwind. The device painted below the cockpit denotes that this aircraft was purchased with funds subscribed by the Bellows Fellowship. *C. E. Brown via J. Coyne*

and up, pressures building, set max cooling flap, cooling and oil tempera-tures okay, plus-two boost, check prop, pitch change okay, open up to plus-five boost, check them on four mags, taxi out. Prime the exactors again, run the engines up to plus-nine boost at 3,000 rpm, complete minor cockpit check. Then quickly taxi out onto the runway.

My takeoff was remarkably quick. Little, if any, differential throttle (to control swing) was needed. The tail came up very quickly, and the large rud-der kept the aircraft straight down the runway. Three hundred feet up, I rolled the coupe top closed. The Whirlwind was the first fighter to have a retractable tail wheel as well as a single-piece canopy that wound back and forth on rack-and-pinion rails. These were nice features.

So, now we're in the air, boost back, revs back, and climbing away at 180 mph. I level off and cruise at 240. Temperature is okay, so I close the cooling flaps, try a few gentle turns, risk a slightly steeper one, and then some dives and climbs. Wow! This thing climbs like a bat out of hell. I throttle back one engine, add a little boost to the other and with a touch of rudder trim it flies hands off. I sit back relax, and enjoy. Pretty soon realization comes that maybe, just maybe, I'll be able to cope with this machine, and possibly con-vince the CO to post me to a Spitfire squadron.

Okay, now it's time to land. Join the circuit downwind, throttle back to 150 mph, prime the exactors, lower undercarriage, set the cooling flaps, turn in, props fully fine, slow down a little, flaps down a little more, set at 125 mph, come over the fence at no less than 110, and drop onto the runway. (While there was a runway at that particular time, we usually operated from grass fields.) Whoops! I didn't get the final speed down quite enough. So I float for a bit. Never mind, there's plenty of room on this one thousand-yard runway. Those great big Fowler flaps really slow you down.

Wow! One year and two days after being sworn in, I had finally flown a real fighter on a real fighter squadron. Comment in my diary was very brief: "These things come in really fast. Mail: 300 cigarettes from the 25-Cents-a-Month Club—and I don't even smoke."

For half the time when I was with 263, we were a normal day-fighter unit. The other half, we operated in the fighter-bomber role. My logbook for the month of June 1942 shows a fairly typical month of normal fighter readiness. In this list I have noted that there were thirty days of readiness, twenty-four flying days and that I made fifty-four flights of which twenty-two were con-voy patrols or as they say in the Gulf, combat air patrols. There were eight scrambles, two average basic sea patrols, one ramrod offensive sortie, one defensive operation, and six miscellaneous—all on Whirlwinds—and seven miscellaneous on Miles Magisters and one air test. I loved flying any aeroplane at every opportunity.

Normal readiness meant that one flight must be on "immediate" standby and the other flight on thirty-minute stand-by—at all times. If an alert occurred, then the thirty-minute flight would be up-rated to "immediate." Being on the thirty-minute flight meant that you could do some practice flying and could at least go down to the mess to have your meals and sleep in your bed at night. Immediate readiness meant that you had to be available to be in the air within two minutes. This required that each pilot who had been allocated an aeroplane had to ensure that his parachute, oxygen mask, gloves, and maps, and all his other odds and ends were in the aircraft, and that he was in suitable flying gear, wearing his Mae West. It was essential that he never stray more than a few hundred feet from his aircraft. In other words you were tied to your aeroplane with a two-minute umbilical cord.

This went on from dawn to dusk. Every pilot was on readiness from noon to dusk one day and then from dawn to noon the next day. Then he joined the thirty-minute proposition. Of course, when the hooter went it was for

Westland Whirlwinds of 263 Squadron, RAF, are seen in loose "finger-four" formation above the clouds. *J. Coyne.*

the two-minute readiness flight. As the old saying went, "If you hear the bell, then run like hell!" and get into the air. Flights changed duties at noon, and the flight that went on immediate readiness was then charged with first ops or any scrambles or convoy patrols.

The evening meal—brought down to the immediate readiness flight— was most unappetizing. It was delivered in a "hay box" and I wondered where they got the term. I watched them bringing these tin boxes and I assumed it was a term coined in the early days of the RAF when straw was packed around the food in the boxes to keep it hot.

During the long summer days, there were very few hours of darkness, and as a result, having to be on duty from one half-hour before dawn until one half-hour after dusk added up to a long stretch. At least three of the sec-tions—six aircrew—had to sleep in the dispersal hut whereas the thirty-minute aircrew could sleep in their own beds. Again, the latter was more pleasant.

As far as convoy patrol went, at the crack of dawn, "operations" would come through and give the location and details of any convoys we would have to cover that day or at that particular time. If we were to be over the convoy at first light, Grey Section would have to scramble and get into posi-tion. The patrol time over the convoy was normally one hour, and the tran-sit time varied depending on the convoy's location. At the time we were based in south Wales from where we covered the Bristol Channel, up into the Irish Sea, and then down as far as Lundy Island, a small rocky island off the coast of Cornwall. As soon as your hour was over the second section would be on its way. When you saw them off in the distance, and once they were in range, you hurried back to base, refueled, and resumed readiness as quickly as possible. Sometimes we might have two or even three convoys to patrol.

One of the more interesting convoy patrols would occur almost every afternoon or early evening near Milford Haven. A couple of beautiful naval ships would come out of the Haven and head southwest. They were the high-speed minelayers, HMS *Manxman* and HMS *Welshman* and they really moved! I'm sure they must have been capable of thirty or forty knots and were as fast as an MTB (motor torpedo boat). They were up and down the Bay of Biscay laying mines at night or in the approach to Brest, France, where the convoys go in all kinds of weather.

Normally a scramble was caused by an unidentified bogey stooging around somewhere. The Luftwaffe maintained daily weather and shipping recces from their bases in Brittany, up past Land's End into the western approaches, and into the Irish Sea. Quite often we were scrambled to intercept these Junkers Ju 88s and just as frequently we were mistakenly sent up after Wellingtons or Whitleys from our own Operational Training Units. We didn't see many Ju 88s except from a distance because as soon as they saw us they would nip off into clouds that always seemed to be conveniently located for them. Occasionally we saw them and gave chase but never got close. Sometimes, happily, we chased them into the arms of the radar-equipped Beaufighters of 125 (Newfoundland) Squadron, our sister unit.

Another type of assignment was the Irish Sea patrol, which was along similar lines. Occasionally Intelligence would tell us that one of these enemy recces was expected into the area at such a location and at such and such a time. To put a stop to this sort of cheeky invasion of our turf, we developed a joint strategy with the Beaufighters. On these operations, the eight or twelve Whirlwinds involved would spread out in a long line abreast and sweep across the Irish Sea until we sighted Ireland. Then we would swing around 180 degrees and return—back and forth. Usually two or more Beaufighters would be higher, also on the lookout, ready to intercept any Junkers we flushed out, when they made a run for the cloud. We had varied luck with that tactic, but the Beaus were a little more successful. On the mixed flight of 27 June, my logbook states that "The Beaufighters got another one today."

As for offensive operations, I list only one for this period, and it was a low-level attack on a ground target, in squadron or higher strength. We planned to attack the twin airfields at Morlaix and Lannion on the Brest Peninsula. We were to shoot up Lannion and 'B' Flight would head for Morlaix. We made a satisfactory landfall and had a good attack. I shot up a line of three Ju 88s and then another one in a small maintenance hangar, setting it on fire. This was also my first experience of anti-aircraft guns seen close up.

I was almost certain that the three Ju 88s had been dummies and so that was what I told the intelligence people, but they said there was no way they could be dummies because dummies had never been used in that particular area. They might have been real, but I don't really know. Anyway, it had been pretty hot and exciting. However, on the long haul back—with a fair amount of water just twenty feet below my heels—between Brest, France, and Predannack (an airfield near Land's End on the southernmost tip of England), it sure felt good to have those two engines. Never again did I hanker after a Spitfire. I did fly one once, but that's another story.

On 10 February 1942, the squadron moved to a new airfield in the south of Wales, Fairwood Common, near Swansea. This field was built on a bog with runways that not only rolled up and down but also twisted in a corkscrew pattern. On the 13th I returned from a convoy patrol at dusk and landed in a bit of a crosswind. I couldn't hold the swing and came to rest off the runway, and as previously described, upside down with the top of my head a few inches from the ground. Two days later I was told to report to the Group Commander for an interview. I thought I was headed for a target-towing job, but A/V/M Orlebar—of Schneider Trophy fame—a fine old gentleman, smoothed my ruffled feathers and set me at ease regarding my mishap. He said that he was interviewing me for a commission, and a couple of weeks later, it came through.

About eleven months after I joined the squadron, our aircraft were fitted with bomb racks, and after about a week of stand-down to fit out and get a little practice, we carried out our first fighter bomber operations by sinking two coastal ships near Alderney, one of the Channel Islands. We took over all fighter bomber duties for Ten Group replacing 174 and 175 Squadrons. Fortunately our normal state of readiness went from immediate to thirty minutes, which was a much more agreeable lifestyle.

Code names had been invented to distinguish the various forms of offensive operations involving our fighter aircraft. I will try to explain them.

Rhubarb: an offensive operation for a section of two aircraft. The essential (hoped for) requirement for this operation was solid low-level cloud cover over the target area to give the section somewhere to hide on the flight home if the opposition became too intense. Targets were usually the enemy's transportation system: lock gates, trains, railway yards, barges, small ships, dock installations, and other targets of opportunity, always with the proviso that the well-being of the French populace would be kept in mind. It was, in short, a dash across the Channel for a shoot-em-up and then a dash home—hoping to avoid any fighters that had been stirred up by nipping into the cloud.

Ramrod: usually a squadron-strength, low-level operation with additional fighters along for cover and to add to the sound and fury of an attack on a larger target such as an airfield or port installation.

Ranger: similar to a Rhubarb, but usually at night in flight or squadron strength—with aircraft operating singly to cover a wide area.

Roadstead: similar to a Ramrod but with a shipping convoy as target.

Dive-bombing (no code name): a full squadron operation usually against airfields. In the early days of the war, as our strength grew, there was a concerted attempt to draw the Luftwaffe into the air and establish a high rate of attrition.

Squadron activities increased until June 1943 when I was off on leave. In April and May, my logbooks indicate that I made fifty-two flights in thirty-one flying days and of those I made twenty-two offensive ops, ten were day-armed shipping recces, and five were night-armed shipping recces. We only flew on moonlit nights, not in full darkness. We operated more or less the same at night as we did in the day. However, we flew individually at night whereas during the day we flew more formation flights with other aircraft. We did three dive-bombing operations, two night shipping attacks, one day shipping attack, and one night ranger.

By way of explanation, the armed shipping recces and strikes, both day and to some extent night, resulted from reports from our other recce groups. At that time the army co-op people in Mustangs were getting practice going across the sea. Unfortunately their reports were not quite as reliable as those from some of the experienced squadrons. I don't know how many times they identified a nice row of reefs near Alderney as a convoy. We would go out after the convoy and find nothing there but that little old reef. However, Alderney got lots of target practice with their coastal guns just as those on Jersey and Guernsey did.

Sometimes as few as two aircraft, if the information wasn't considered very reliable, went out on a rhubarb—providing it was rhubarb weather, meaning, as I've explained, that there was local cloud cover that you could nip into. Otherwise, four or more Whirlwinds, usually escorted by a squadron of Spits, would be sent. On a lot of these shipping recces, when we got to the designated area, the ships that had been reported were not there and so we turned around and came back. We returned to base and landed, still with our bombs, in order to save them. The night armed shipping recces, as I said, were done individually and again in the same area. If you found anything, you attacked it.

Dive-bombing was rather interesting. Our dive-bombing missions to France included the bombing of power stations at Caen, large ships in Cherbourg Harbour, and airfields near Guipavas near Brest and Maupertus near Cherbourg. The procedure was that we acted as decoys—the cheese in a mousetrap consisting of Spits and Tiffies. At the end of 1942 and early 1943 we were trying to gain air superiority by drawing their fighters into the air and shooting them down. There were lots of circuses whenever there was squadron or wing availability. Eventually the Germans got wise and wouldn't come up if radar showed that the attackers were all fighters. As a result, our slightly bigger Whirlwinds with their twin engines would be sent in first and we would do a little damage with our two 500-pounders. Then, when the opposition came up, a massive Spitfire formation would arrive to take care of them.

I recall one beautiful early morning takeoff from Warmwell, down near Portland Bill. It was a squadron effort to dive bomb Cherbourg airfield. Our squadron took off and circled Warmwell in a wide sweep around to the right. As we came over our own airfield on the way south, the Exeter wing, three squadrons right on the deck, joined up on our starboard side and the Ibsley wing, coming from a little east of us, arrived at exactly the same time, from the west. There we were, thirty-six Spitfires here, another thirty-six there, and our twelve Whirlwinds—all right on the deck. It was a beautiful sight.

The procedure for dive bombing airfields was to fly out down on the deck below radar until we were within fifteen minutes of the target, where we climbed in weak mixture at a rate of 1,000 feet per minute until we reached 15,000 feet. We heard the Spit pilots screaming that we were climbing too fast and that they couldn't keep up, particularly in weak mixtures so we had to slow down and waft through the air with our cooling flaps open. At 15,000 feet we came in just past the target, usually slightly to the right, did a ninety-degree turn to the left behind it, and then, as we reached it, peeled off, again in another ninety-degree turn. We dove straight down onto the targeted airfield—at a screaming great rate of knot, I assure you.

Again, the Spits couldn't keep up. We were heavier and a little faster diving. We would release our bombs at about 6,000 feet, pulling up gently but keeping the nose down. We would be doing about 400 to 440 mph. Hell, we were back home in about ten or fifteen minutes which was pretty nice. The Spitfires were left to deal with the hornets' nest that we had stirred up.

Now, here is a little about a night shipping attack. Arthur Lee White, one of the very few Whirly fighter pilots in Canada, was on that particular shipping attack. (There were four of us left in 1991.) This attack took place forty-eight years ago (as of 1991) on 21 May. Our group of pilots was working very hard and we were tired. We needed a rest and our CO arranged with Group

The "old sweats" of 263 Squadron, RAF Warmwell, in the spring of 1943. (L-R): Ken Ridley DFM; Joe Holmes DFC; "Simmy" Simpson DFM; "Blackie" Blackshaw DFC; Jeff Warnes DSO, DFC; Jim Coyne DFC; and Don Tebbitt. *J. Coyne*

that, since we had finished our day's operations and it was toward the end of the moon period, we should have a stand-down at dusk.

We had a friend near Bath who owned a butcher shop—steaks and other nice cuts of meat were scarce in those days—and we sent the Miles Magister up and loaded the back seat and luggage compartment with steaks, chops, and kidneys, and God knows what. The Maggie returned and everybody forgot about readiness and looked forward to having a nice dinner. It was about an hour after normal mess time and we were just getting in a few good "noggins" (mugs of beer) when there was a hell of a scream on the Op's line.

"How many aeroplanes can you get into the air?" There was a convoy bound toward Cherbourg from the Channel Islands, and they wanted us to get out there. We had five serviceable aircraft and we looked around to see who would be the five pilots most capable of flying those aeroplanes. One happened to be Jeff Warnes, the Squadron commander who was, to the best of my knowledge, the only fighter pilot in World War II who wore contact lenses. The others were 'B' Flight commander, Joe Holmes; myself; an

Australian named Max Cotton; and my good friend Arthur. The CO got off first and we followed at two-minute intervals, heading for Cherbourg.

We found the convoy—five ships—and came up behind them. The CO attacked the lead ship and then pulled off, circled, and did a running commentary like a Pathfinder. Joe Holmes, the flight commander came in next. Jeff wasn't even shot at. The convoy was just about to enter the mole of the harbour at Cherbourg and obviously the gunners were stood down—probably looking forward to a night ashore.

By the time Joe got there, things started happening. When I went in, I ended up getting a stray shell in my aircraft. Max Cotton was behind me and he got fairly well beaten up. Lee, coming in last, got very badly beaten up— with an engine on fire. By the time I got back, he was halfway across the channel where Jeff reached him on the radio and told him to get over land and bail out. "I don't think so," replied Lee. He landed the Whirlwind, and as soon as he slowed down, the engine flared up and he had to cope with a little fireworks. That was quite a night! Of the five ships, we sank two and severely damaged one other.

Those two months were very busy and we flew many more missions than I've discussed here. From 2 to 15 April alone, my logbook shows that I carried out operations from Warmwell, Tangmere, Harrowbeer, Exeter, and Predannack. We were moving about quite a bit, depending upon where our targets were. During that time, I lost four of my closest pilot friends, including our flight commander and his deputy. This resulted in my taking over command of 'A' Flight.

These casualties occurred in June, and by April of 1943 all of the highly experienced pilots on the squadron were posted or became time-expired, including the CO and the other flight commander. Group decided that since I had only recently been promoted, I was going to stay behind and earn my stripes and help to train all of the new arrivals in 263 procedures.

The crop of new pilots was posted in and the Squadron moved to a new grass field at Zeals to work up. This airfield was used as a training ground for "airfield commandos," ground crew who would accompany the squadron when it moved to Europe after D-day. They would be trained to defend the airfield from attack as well as to fuel and service all types of aircraft. The Commando Unit CO happened to mention to me that his people needed real practice at rapid rearming, repairing, and refueling. Since they had no pilots on strength, he suggested that I might be interested in flying some of his aircraft. Always game, I did a few flights in their Mk IV Hurricane and then had a go at their Mk IX Spitfire, again without benefit of a handbook or even good advice. I took the Spit down to the Gunnery Range in the Channel and fired away. I was startled when the Spit suddenly went into a great skid. Immediately I stopped firing and pulled out of my dive—realizing that I had had a cannon stoppage. No doubt it had been "fixed" to give the ground crews the previously mentioned practice at rearming and fueling.

The Squadron returned to ops on 12 July, and after a few trips on similar types of operations, they expired me in the middle of August. (Tour-expired meant the completion of a sufficient number of successful missions to warrant change to a non-operational job for six months prior to returning to Ops.) I had been on the squadron just a few days under two years. My association with my favourite aircraft, the Whirlwind, came to an end.

There was no question that the Whirlwind was an aeroplane ahead of its time. Along with its limitations, it embodied some very interesting innovations. Compared to the Mk I Spit or the Mk I Hurricane, the Whirlwind was far in advance in speed and rate of climb to 15,000 feet. We had tremendous capability low down, but once we got to 15,000 feet performance dropped off disastrously. It was, however, a very successful fighter-bomber and one might wonder why its potential was never developed.

There were many reasons and I think everyone concerned shared the responsibility—Rolls-Royce in particular for not living up to their promises for the Peregrine. Selected for the Whirlwind, it was being developed at the same time as the Merlin. However, it soon became apparent that the Merlin was going to be easier to develop; therefore Rolls-Royce abandoned the Peregrine. The Whirlwind was the only aircraft ever powered by the Peregrine.

In the Air Ministry of 1935, decisions were being made by people who, in many instances, had never flown an aeroplane, and they wouldn't believe that a fighter could have two engines; that would dictate a monoplane configuration. Therefore, there were a lot of errors, delays, and procrastinations in its development. Nor did Westland pursue construction and development to the extent that they might have. Of course, Petter's rather arrogant attitude didn't go down too well with the Air Ministry. Thus the aeroplane was never developed beyond the Mk I.

But, in spite of it all, the Whirlwind was the best machine that I have ever flown in my fifty years in the air. It was just great, no question about it. It was easy to fly and the only tricky thing was that tremendous jump in speed with

The Whirlwind's cockpit afforded the pilot excellent visibility. Jim Coyne in his 263 Squadron (code HE) machine, RAF P7094. *C.E. Brown via J. Coyne*

---

which we were faced for landings and takeoffs. Once we got that down, we could land the thing without an airspeed indicator, relying only on the sound. It was indeed a very fine aeroplane.

Since I later flew the Mossie I've been asked to compare it with the Whirlwind. Basically, there can be no comparison: they were built for different purposes and in different time frames—each had its own genesis. I loved to fly both aircraft. I believe the Whirlwind had a quicker response on the controls and was fully capable of aerobatics. Compared to the Spit, it had a heavy punch of four 20-mm cannon concentrated in the nose; but the fuel tankage and the ammo supply were limited. The Mosquito VI was also a great aeroplane to fly, although not quite as aerobatic but with an even heavier punch. I liked the greater endurance of the Mossie, and the fact that it didn't rattle quite as much in a high-speed dive.

The Westland Whirlwind was a wonderful but neglected aeroplane. To remember all the positive experiences I had with it so many years ago, I am forced me to go back and do a little digging in my logbook and a few other long-neglected places. Rediscovering the interesting things that I have forgotten about the Whirlwind was an adventure in itself.

Typhoon Pilot

Hawker's Mighty "Tank Buster" Could Be a Handful

JOHN G. (JACK) BROWN

By any standards, the Hawker Typhoon was a formidable fighting machine. With its massive front and wide stance, it looked the part. Designed as a successor to the obsolescent Hurricane, the Typhoon was almost overbuilt, sacrificing speed for strength with an even thicker wing than its predecessor. Its Napier Sabre engine of well over 2,000 hp offered more than twice the output of the Hurricane I's Merlin. Loaded, the Tiffie weighed an additional three tons. Intended for the interceptor role in which the Spitfire excelled, it was deemed a failure. More Typhoons, unfortunately, had been lost through flying accidents than by enemy action. However, as Jack Brown will explain, one far-sighted pilot almost single-handedly gained the Tiffie the opportunity to prove itself. Close aerial support for ground forces was a role still being defined, yet this pilot foresaw the Tiffie filling the much-needed niche. Tanks and gun positions, attacked with cannon and rockets or bombs, were favoured Typhoon targets. Happily, the big fighter excelled to the extent that Tiffie pilots became a soldier's best friend and they were toasted and treated to free beer should they meet in bar or mess. Later, American machines such as the Republic P-47 Thunderbolt and Vought F4U Corsair, both of comparable size and power, performed similar duties.

But this new assignment brought fresh hazards. While relatively few Tiffies fell to the guns of enemy fighters, low-altitude operation made them especially vulnerable to light flak and even machine gun and rifle fire from ground positions. Pilots were grateful for the armour protecting them and vital parts of the engine; but attrition was high.

Toronto-born Jack Brown was twenty-one when he enlisted in the RCAF, leaving his job with Loblaws grocery store chain. After the war, Jack returned to civilian life and a job in the personnel department of Loblaws' head office. While he occasionally flew in light aircraft, Jack rarely took the controls. When he retired in 1981, he was the firm's safety manager. He spoke to the Toronto Chapter of the CAHS in December 1983 and his talk was adapted for the Summer 1984 *Journal*.

After graduating from the RCAF Initial Training School (ITS) at Victoriaville, Quebec, I began flying training on 30 October 1941 at No 21 Elementary Flying Training School (EFTS) at Chatham, New Brunswick, where I put in sixty hours on the Fleet Finch. During the first five months of 1942, I flew 135 hours on the North American Harvard at No 9 Service Flying Training School (SFTS) at Summerside, Prince Edward Island, where I was awarded my wings.

Of those graduating, two of us were posted to RAF Ferry Command at Dorval, near Montreal, to train as ferry pilots, although neither of us had flown anything but single-engined aircraft. We spent a month in ground school learning about fuel systems and automatic pilots in Hudsons, Venturas, Mitchells, and Marauders. For the flying training, we lined up in a room where the instructors selected four of us at a time. I changed places with another chap so I could stay with my classmate from Summerside. It was lucky for me that I did! Half an hour later, the Hudson, in which the instructor and four others were flying, lost a wing and crashed. All aboard were killed.

Russ Bannock, of Mosquito night-intruder fame, was our instructor. On our second trip, we were awaiting takeoff clearance at the end of the runway when an aircraft on the final turn of its approach suddenly spun in. Russ immediately took over the controls, took off, and flying at about 50 feet, directed the ground rescue squad to the scene. I can still see the tip of a church steeple off the end of the wing as we circled near Point Claire.

When it became evident that we could not learn to cope with twin-engined machines in the allotted time, we were posted to the RAF depot at Moncton, New Brunswick, and from there to the RCAF Holding Unit in Bournemouth, England. We arrived on the day of the Dieppe raid. From Bournemouth, I went to No 7 Advanced Flying Unit (AFU) at Peterborough, north of London, where we received twenty-seven hours of instruction on Miles Masters to acquaint us with British-type aircraft and with navigation in different geographic and atmospheric conditions than those to which we had been accustomed.

The maintenance at Sibson, the satellite airfield where we did our night flying, was very lax. One aircraft crashed when the glide path indicator at the end of the runway was set at the wrong angle. The instructor was killed and the student pilot badly burned. And it was here that I had one of my most frightening flights. Shortly after takeoff into a black, overcast night sky, I found that the control column would not move sideways. I was too low to bail out and I hoped and prayed the machine would not start to roll. When I reached 1,500 feet, the stick came free. I had no idea what had caused it to jam or whether it would do so again. I gently eased the aircraft into a turn and carried out an elongated circuit. Fortunately, I had not strayed off course since I had no radio aboard to get a homing signal and the runway lights were shielded so they could only be seen from one direction. As I rolled down the runway after landing, the column seized again. Later I learned that the rubber mouthpiece from the rear cockpit speaking tube had come off at some previous time, fallen to the bottom of the fuselage, and lodged in the control wires.

From October to December 1942, I completed sixty hours training on Hurricanes at No 56 Operational Training Unit (OTU) at Tealing, near Dundee, Scotland. On 29 December 1942, thirteen members of our OTU course, plus four from another OTU, arrived at Harrowbeer, near Plymouth, Devon, to form 193 Fighter Squadron which was equipped with Typhoons. The only "operational types" on the squadron were the CO and the two flight commanders. No one had flown Typhoons, there were none of them on the station, and it was several weeks before we even got to see one. We spent our time in a Hurricane familiarizing ourselves with the area. We learned as much as we could about the Typhoon from the *Pilot's Notes* and from watching and talking to the pilots of 257 Squadron, based at nearby Exeter who were already flying Typhoons.

The Hawker Typhoon was a low-wing, single-seater fighter powered by an amazing piece of machinery—a twenty-four-cylinder, liquid-cooled Napier Sabre 'H' type, sleeve-valve engine which, in its later versions, developed up to 2,260 hp. The Typhoon's wing spanned forty-one feet seven inches, the length was almost thirty-two feet and the height an impressive fifteen feet four inches. Four internal wing tanks carried 154 gallons of fuel and another 90 gallons could be carried in two drop tanks. She weighed 8,840 pounds empty, 11,850 pounds loaded, and with two 1,000-pound bombs aboard, reached a maximum of 13,980 pounds or nearly seven tons— double that of the contemporary Spitfire VB. It was a massive aeroplane

As typified by this factory-fresh example—MN624, not yet assigned to a squadron—the Typhoon was a ruggedly attractive aircraft. *Air Ministry*

indeed. Only the American Corsairs and Thunderbolts were comparable to the Typhoon.

Maximum speeds at usual operating levels were 413 miles per hour at 11,500 feet and 412 mph at sea level. The aircraft could climb to 1,500 feet in six minutes and had a range of 510 miles with two 500-pound bombs or 910 miles with drop tanks. We generally cruised at around 240 mph. Our armament consisted of four 20-mm Hispano cannon fed by belt from magazines carrying 155 rounds. The four cannon fired 760 rounds per minute, operated by a thumb button on the spade-grip control column. A camera mounted in the nose of the aircraft took a picture of the target whenever the cannon were fired. An illuminated reflector sight created a ring-and-bead image on a slanted piece of glass near the windscreen. The Typhoon could also carry eight 60-pound high-explosive (HE) rocket projectiles, two 500-pound bombs, or two 1,000-pound bombs.

For low-level bombing, delayed action fuses were used and identifying ribbons were put on the arming wires. One low-level "do" I was on was scrubbed, fortunately, at the last minute because of the weather. Climbing down from his machine, one of the pilots happened to notice that all of our bombs had been armed with instantaneous fuses. Our own bombs could easily have blown us up!

Diving on our targets, we used the reflector gunsight to aim the bombs.

We released them by pushing a button in the throttle just as the target appeared in the lower segment of the gunsight during pullout from the dive.

Designed by Sidney Camm, the Typhoon was one of a long line of notable aircraft produced by Hawker that included the Hart, the Fury, and the Hurricane. An accepted maxim for successful aircraft development is that future requirements should always be the principal concern of the design team, and so Camm was working on a replacement for the Hurricane in 1937 before the first production version had flown. Two prototypes were produced, the Tornado with a Rolls-Royce 24-cylinder 'X' type Vulture engine and the Typhoon with the 'H' type Napier Sabre. First flights occurred respectively on 6 October 1939 and 24 February 1940.

After the Typhoon had been selected as the aircraft to be produced, a litany of problems caused delays and almost resulted in program cancellation. Initially, the need for more Hurricanes and Spitfires, created by the approaching Battle of Britain, resulted in curtailed Typhoon production. Then the sleeve valves and pistons in the new and very complicated Sabre engines occasionally seized up. Flutter in the elevators weakened the rear fuselage so tail sections could fall off without warning. Carbon monoxide leaking into the cockpit could asphyxiate the pilot. (This happened a number of times before the cause of several mysterious crashes was determined.) Starting up the Sabre engine was often difficult. Performance at high altitude, where the aircraft had been designed to operate, was disappointing. The cockpit enclosure design afforded poor pilot visibility. (Our original aircraft had doors like those on automobiles, with roll up windows. The first production models had no visibility to the rear whatsoever as the designers apparently assumed that nothing could catch the Typhoon.)

Most of the aforementioned problems were the result of hurrying the machine into service without adequate testing. At a high-level meeting held to determine if the aircraft should be scrapped, Roland Beamont, CO of 609 Typhoon Squadron, made a strong presentation. He had seen how effective the Tiffie was in attacking ground targets and in catching and destroying low-flying Focke Wulf Fw 190s. Eloquently, he envisaged a future role for the Typhoon as a close support aircraft. Beamont's foresight and persuasiveness saved the Typhoon.

The Typhoon would more than prove its value in the ground attack role—and each of its problems was eventually solved. But at the start, the tails of two of our aircraft did come off. One fell off while the pilot was cruising over the moors. He crashed and was killed. The other came off in a high-speed dive and the pilot just managed to bail out in time. To counter this problem, adjustments were made to the elevators and the rear fuselage was reinforced. Engine failures occurred periodically as late as the summer of 1944. The carbon monoxide hazard was reduced by changing the exhaust stubs and by making it a rule that oxygen cockpit control valves be set for operation at 15,000 feet—no matter the altitude—as long as the engine was running. Starting remained unpredictable but experience soon enabled us to cope. The *Pilot's Manual* devotes two and a half pages to the procedure. Inadequate high-altitude performance ceased to be a problem when the Typhoon specialized as a medium- and low-level weapon.

Other than the occasional starting problem, the only difficulty I ever experienced occurred as we were thrashing around the sky in a squadron formation practice and the oil system packed up. Fortunately, I was near base and managed to return—a single pint of oil was left in the engine.

I found the Typhoon an excellent machine, responsive to the controls, steady in a dive, and as a gun platform. It was ideally suited to its role as a fighter/bomber. A big, strong aircraft, it could stand up to tremendous punishment whether from air combat, enemy flak, or forced landings.

I approached my first flight in a Tiffie with some trepidation. Obviously, we didn't know then what we would later learn about all the problems and their solutions. We were understandably in awe of the Tiffie's size and power. We had been warned of the violent effect of torque created by the huge propeller which caused a swing to the right on takeoff—of how different this was from the Hurricanes we had been flying.

On takeoff, I locked my left leg rigidly on the rudder bar and actually ended up going slightly to the left. I got off safely and flew around for a considerable time to accustom myself to the machine's handling. At times I felt as if the machine was flying me! When I lowered the undercarriage for my landing, the machine wallowed in a corkscrew fashion. To make sure I didn't stall it, I came in with a little too much speed. The runways at Harrowbeer were not exceptionally long and I could see a pile of bricks at the end coming up fast. Luckily, the brakes held and the machine stopped in time.

Our work-up training as a squadron consisted of practising formation flying, dogfighting, cloud flying, and strict air discipline. We visited the Group Operations Room to see how aircraft positions were plotted and controlled from the ground and to meet those who would be directing us. We visited an Air Sea Rescue Station and were taken out on a rescue launch. We

Resting on his 193 Squadron (code DP) Hawker Typhoon at Needs
Oar Point, England, in May 1944, Jack Brown poses for the photographer
(who, unfortunately, decapitated Jack's fitter in this picture). *J. G. Brown*

practised inflating a dinghy in the swimming pool of a local hotel. To
improve our deflection shooting, we had regular sessions of skeet shooting.
On poor weather days we practised in the Link Trainer. All of this was
invaluable training for situations in which we could find ourselves on future
operations.

As well, we had lectures from pilots who had either evaded capture or had
escaped from prisoner-of-war (POW) camps. We studied maps of the areas
in France over which we normally flew to plan what we might do if shot
down. On one exercise we were transported several miles from the aerodrome and dropped off with instructions to return to base without being
detected or captured. As for air fighting, we were supplied with recent combat reports from other fighter units to help us when we became involved in
similar situations. One of our axioms became "Beware of the Hun in the
sun." (In the First World War, patrolling fighter aircraft on either side tried
to climb as high as possible, positioned up-sun from where an enemy was
likely to appear.) We built up a rapport with the ground crew. When we
learned that the smoothness of an aircraft's skin improved its speed, we even
assisted in the cleaning of our machines.

When the squadron became operational, we began patrolling the coast in our area to counter "tip-and-run" attacks by Focke Wulf Fw 190s. These patrols were carried out by pairs of aircraft; one right down on the water, the other about a hundred feet up. Several fellows bent the ends of their props when they flew too low and actually touched the sea. We did standby duty, waiting at the end of the runway, ready to take off as soon as a Very pistol was fired from the control tower. We envied the pilots of 609 Squadron, based at Manston on the east coast, close to France, where they had lots of action.

Our first offensive operation involved escorting a Typhoon bomber unit assigned to attack shipping in the harbour at Brest, some two hundred miles over water from our base. We had no long-range tanks at that time and the thought of what might happen if we got into a scrap and used up the fuel that was to get us back over all that water left us a bit apprehensive, to say the least. We had been briefed nearly six hours before the "do" and so had a lot of time to think about it. I wandered around the crew room in nervous antic- ipation, looking for a suitable pair of escape boots, much to the amusement of those who were not going on the op. They tagged me with the nickname "Boots," which stayed with me throughout my service career. Just after we took off, the operation was cancelled and we were recalled. Over the next few months we carried out a number of shipping "recces" along the Brittany coast and managed to "prang" a few small enemy ships.

In January 1944, Fighter Command was disbanded to be replaced by the Air Defence of Great Britain and the Second Tactical Air Force. We became part of 84 Group, a division of Second TAF, which was later to provide close support for the First Canadian Army in the Northwest Europe Campaign. We began a series of moves from Harrowbeer to various airfields along the south coast, including Fairlop, Thorney Island, and Gravesend. In the event that we had to operate in France before our ground crew arrived, we were given instruction on refuelling and rearming our aircraft, and on driving a three-ton lorry. Fortunately, we didn't have to put any of this training to use. One of our fellows ran into the side of a London bus while learning to drive!

Throughout that spring our targets varied from flying bomb sites along the Channel Coast to marshalling yards at Mons, Arras, Bethune, Cambrai, and Rouen, to bridges along the Seine, to radar stations at Caen, Cherbourg, Gris Nez, and Le Treport.

On a typical fighter/bomber operation, Group Headquarters would give the squadron commander the target. Pilots were then assigned to their sec- tions and aircraft. Briefing took place about an hour before takeoff when the

The pilots of 193 Squadron pose with one of their aircraft and a 500-pound bomb at St-Croix-sur-Mer, Normandy, on 1 July 1944. *J. G. Brown*

target was described, with map references and photographs. The Intelligence Section provided maps, weather information, flak locations, and the anticipated enemy reaction. We were each issued a pouch of French currency and an escape kit containing a water bottle, chocolate, a needle and thread, a fish hook, a compass, pills to keep us awake, and a list of French, German, and Spanish words. Then we returned to the crew room, emptied our pockets of any identifying material, and donned life jackets and escape boots. These boots could be converted to street shoes by cutting off the uppers in the event that we had to wear civilian clothing to evade capture. In one boot we carried a dagger to deflate our seat-pack dinghy should it accidentally inflate in the air. We put on gloves and a flying helmet containing goggles, a microphone, earphones, and an oxygen mask. Then we signed the flight authorization book and the aircraft logbook, and climbed into the cockpit to sit on the combination parachute and dinghy. Seated in our machines, we fastened the seat belt and hooked up to radio and oxygen.

When the leader fired up, we all did. In the event of any aircraft not starting, a spare pilot and machine took that person's place. We lined up at the end of the runway in pairs, opening the throttle as soon as the previous pair became airborne. After one circuit, we were in formation and on course. The formation usually consisted of two "finger-four" sections—an arrangement loosely based on the relationship of the fingertips in a hand held out flat.

Each pair covered the other two in the section.

Clearing the English coast we maintained radio silence, dropping down to 50 feet above the sea to sneak under enemy radar. We remained at that height until within sight of the French coast where we climbed to 8,000 feet to avoid coastal flak-batteries. We continually scanned the sky above, behind us, and into the sun to avoid being "bounced" by the enemy. Approaching the target, we set our bomb selector switches and turned on the reflector sight and gun buttons. We slid into echelon starboard behind the leader. In turn, we peeled off, firing our cannon in the dive to discourage the flak gunners. At about 4,000 feet we released our bombs—just before pulling our aircraft out of the dive.

Heading home, we kept a sharp eye out for enemy aircraft. As we neared base, we went into a tight formation and sometimes maintaining these formations was as trying as the op itself. We swept in low over the runway in line astern, breaking off individually into steep climbing turns to spread ourselves out for landing. The distance between aircraft was not great and you often dipped a wing—involuntarily—in the slipstream of the fellow ahead. Once down, you might hear a frantic, "Keep rolling!" on the R/T (radio). Someone had slowed down too abruptly before turning off the runway. We taxied back to dispersal, shut off our engines, and climbed down to report to the Intelligence Officer who debriefed us.

Typical squadron accommodation: two of Jack Brown's squadron mates, Ned Statters and Jock Inglis, with their tent at Needs Oar Point, England. *J. G. Brown*

With other Tiffie Squadrons, we spent a week at an armament practice camp in Wales where we sharpened up on our bombing and rocket-firing techniques.

In April 1944, we arrived at Needs Oar Point, a newly constructed airfield on the south coast immediately opposite the Isle of Wight. Here we joined four other Typhoon Squadrons to form 146 Wing. The airfield, formerly a farm, had runways made of Summerfeld Track, a type of wire mesh. We went under canvas and were issued a camp cot, bedroll, and all that went with living in the outdoors. Just before D-day, Intelligence learned that a German suicide paratroop group was to attack airfields along the south coast and we were issued side arms. One night I awakened to see a shadowy figure entering the tent. Grabbing the pistol from under my pillow, I was prepared to use it when I realized that it was one of my tent mates who had been up to "answer nature's call!"

During the month of May, there was a tremendous buildup of ships in the Solent, the body of water between our base and the Isle of Wight. We could sense that something big was in the offing. We continued our attacks on enemy radar stations right up to 5 June 1944. That night our 'Winco' (Wing Commander), Reg Baker, briefed us on the invasion, outlining in detail the role each service would play in the huge operation. We heard the first of the many aircraft that were to take part flying overhead on their way to Normandy as we left the briefing.

We were up early the next morning—D-day—for which we had waited so long. Everyone wanted to be in on the first show of the day. But for our squadron, nothing occurred until early afternoon. Led by the Winco, six of us were detailed to carry out a recce behind the beachhead.

Taking off, we flew out across the Channel where a solid line of ships— four abreast—stretched from the Isle of Wight to Normandy. Nearing the invasion beaches we saw a row of the Allies' largest battlewagons firing salvo after salvo inland. Southwest of Caen, we spotted two enemy tanks at the side of a road. We dive bombed them then went in from all sides straffing. Later, viewing cine films of the attack, I watched my machine fly right through another aircraft's target area!

After the first few days, when the Germans brought up reinforcements, flak in the area west of Caen became deadly. I lost one of my best buddies six days later when we were attacking vehicles. The day after that, we lost Reg Baker, our Winco, the same way. His death caused a terrific letdown on the wing. "Lochinvar" had been his code name and we had all come to rely on his calmly reassuring "Lochinvar heah," over the R/T. He was a born leader, extremely well liked, and the pilots would have flown anywhere with him.

Flak was the scourge of Typhoon pilots. During the period of most intense activity, losses were estimated to be three to five aircraft per unit per month. Undoubtedly, this was due to the low height at which we flew most operations. Fire from lighter automatic weapons was a constant hazard and the versatile 88-mm German anti-tank gun could quickly be elevated to fire at aircraft. As a rule, the opening round was far enough away for us to take evasive action.

One evening I was leading our flight on a recce of the battle area, flying at about 7,000 feet, when I saw and heard a bursting shell between my Number Three and myself. His oil line was hit. With oil spewing up into the cockpit, he couldn't see. He headed for our lines, radioing that he was bailing out. Unfortunately his 'chute didn't open. It had probably become doughy (matted) from sitting around in a damp tent. He and I had been close friends since the squadron formed and we had just returned from leave together.

I have another vivid memory of flak from when we were attacking destroyers in a port in Brittany. Starting into our dives we could see the red blobs of tracer fire slowly rise toward us—or so it seemed—and then zip past our wing tips. Amazingly no one was hit. A sequence in the documentary film *The Fighting Lady* had dramatic footage of Japanese anti-aircraft fire illustrating exactly what I saw.

After D-day, we bombed enemy strong points and bridges in the Caen area. On 25 June 1944, three squadrons of the Wing carried out a low-level bombing attack on a bridge near Beaumont le Roger on the Seine. On these low-level attacks we spread ourselves out as we neared the target to avoid being blown up in the explosion of the delayed-action-fused bombs dropped by the aircraft in front. The idea was to keep the man ahead of you in view at all times. Flying Number Three to the Winco who was leading our squadron, I kept his Number Two in sight during and after the attack. But the Number Two had lost sight of the Winco. After the bombing, we maintained continuous circuits of the target area. Later, we learned that the Winco's R/T had packed up; with no way of communicating with us, he had headed back to England on his own.

The three squadrons having completed their attacks, I set course for base and found I was leading the wing! On the way back we received disturbing reports of bad weather along the English coast. The other two squadrons and our other flight broke off and headed for other airfields. As we approached the south side of the Isle of Wight I could see that the cloud base was below the level of the chalk cliffs. Rather than risk running into them, I turned out to sea and called for another course to base. Again we approached and made landfall—between the western end of the Isle of Wight and the Needles, a series of high-pointed rock formations. Short of fuel, my Number Two landed at the first base to which we came. I continued on for several miles to our own base setting down in driving rain. The three squadrons' aircraft were spread out on airfields over the whole of the south of England. That was one of many times I was thankful for the Link (blind flying) training which taught us to put full trust in our instruments.

As a fighter/bomber pilot I saw very few enemy aircraft. But, on 29 June 1944, I saw more than I ever wanted to—at one time. Our Wing Leader, Johnnie Baldwin, who had replaced Reg Baker, had downed more enemy aircraft than any other Typhoon pilot. He was leading ten of us on a recce near Rouen when we ran into twenty or thirty Bf 109s. I dropped my long-range tank and pulled into a turn toward them, firing as I did so. To avoid colliding with the 109s, I tightened the turn. They climbed and I followed. Looking back, I saw three others coming after me. I pulled my aircraft into a steep climbing turn trying to reach the cloud cover above. Over my shoulder, I could see the flame coming out of their gun muzzles—just as you would in a movie! Suddenly there was a bright flash above the engine and a thump on the cowling. As I tightened the turn, the aircraft went into a spin. I remember thinking, "This is it!" In a Typhoon, you were not supposed to be able to recover from a spin at that altitude. Fortunately, corrective action got me out of the spin and I found myself in a vertical dive to the north. I levelled out almost at deck level and headed for the coast. Looking back, I saw one of my pursuers go straight into the ground as he tried to pull out of his dive. The others gave up the chase as I reached the coast just east of Le Havre.

When I throttled back, the engine began to vibrate. I prepared to bail out near the ships that formed the bridge from England to Normandy, but the engine kept going and so I landed on one of the airstrips near the beach. The ground crew advised me that the magnetoes had been damaged—and there were three-inch holes in two opposite blades of my four-bladed prop that explained the flashes above the cowling.

I returned to England in a Transport Command Anson. Back at base I learned that we had shot down seven enemy aircraft and damaged two others. Two of us with damaged aircraft had force-landed in France. All of our pilots were safely back at base that night, and needless to say, we had a party.

On 17 July, our flight moved to St-Croix-sur-Mer in Normandy. Our other flight, which had preceded us by several days, was out on a recce when they spotted an important looking staff car accompanied by other vehicles on a road southeast of Caen. They attacked and saw the vehicle turn over. In October, when news of Rommel's death was announced, our squadron was headlined in the British press as the "Rommel Killers." Credit was later given to a Spitfire unit that was operating in the same general area. Rommel had been seriously injured in the attack but had recovered. His subsequent death was by his own hand. He had been implicated in the plot to kill Hitler.

Aside from a brief visit to the nearby Canadian "Tiffie" Wing, we never travelled too far from our base in Normandy. The water at our base was unfit to drink without being boiled. We received one bottle of beer a week. Usually buried in the ground to keep it cool, it was savoured on a hot evening when we were really thirsty.

One of the Tiffie wings sent a pilot back to England for a beer supply. He took a pair of carefully scrubbed long-range tanks to a nearby pub, and had them filled with beer. He also purchased a large quantity of bread and tomatoes that he packed into the gun bays in the wings. With the beer-filled long-range tanks installed, he began his takeoff down the runway. Unfortunately, one of the tanks fell off and he nearly pranged before he brought the aircraft to a stop. By the time he got the tank refilled and back onto the aircraft, the weather closed in. He was grounded for about three days during which time the tomatoes became soft, the bread got stale, and I'm sure, out of sheer frustration, he drank the beer!

Around this time the Germans launched a tank attack against the Americans at Mortain. The Americans called in the Typhoon squadrons who successfully thwarted the attack. The Americans openly expressed their gratitude and our CO was awarded an American DFC for his part in this operation.

The Germans had a long-range gun mounted on a railway car that they wheeled out of a tunnel at night to shell the beachhead. Intelligence learned where they kept it and six of us went over with two 1,000-pound bombs each. We skip-bombed each end of the tunnel, effectively sealing it.

Several of our pilots who had been shot down returned with exciting tales of their escapades. Bill Switzer from Edson, Alberta, who later became an MPP, badly twisted his knee as he bailed out after his aircraft was hit. Unable to walk, he crawled among the Normandy orchards for a week gaining sustenance from any fallen apples and quenching his thirst by sucking the dew from his battledress cuffs. At night he would often hear German troops talking on the other side of a hedgerow. An American army patrol finally spotted him at the side of the road and, because he was wearing a grey-blue uniform, took him to be a German. A few well-chosen obscenities convinced them otherwise.

Art Ross, son of the well-known coach and manager of the Boston Bruins hockey team, was one of our flight commanders. Art was shot down while attacking an enemy ammunition convoy. He bailed out in a wooded area and a nearby SS regiment searched for him. Hiding under a pile of leaves he narrowly escaped being killed when his pursuers fired into similar piles. With the aid of the French escape organization, he made his way to a village east of Caen that he hoped would soon be overrun by Allied troops. When it was not, he went to Paris where he took part in the liberation, sniping at the retreating Germans from the rooftops.

A fellow named Kilpatrick—who had safely bailed out when the tail came off his Typhoon at Harrowbeer—was later shot down and taken prisoner in Normandy. This was shortly before the German retreat. "Killy" and an American pilot convinced their captors to surrender and the pair turned over fifty prisoners to a nearby British unit. Killy received a DSO for his efforts.

The pilot of this 193 Squadron Typhoon, DP-K, is obviously pleased after landing safely, wheels-up, in a farmer's garden. His engine had failed as he approached his base. *J. G. Brown*

A pilot from another squadron in our wing evaded capture and lived in the attic of a French farmhouse, posing as a farm hand. Although he spoke neither French nor German he played cards with the occupying German soldiers. By the time the Allies overran the area and he returned to his unit, he was a nervous wreck.

Another of our lads, Ned Statters, had the most miraculous series of escapes. When his engine cut on a mission in Normandy he tried to force-land in the narrow fields. He went right through a house ending up upside-down in a ditch without sustaining a scratch. One of his elevators was later shot away in a dogfight, yet he got back safely. On another occasion, he had a tire blow on takeoff and managed to keep the aircraft clear of nearby machines. A similar accident, the day before, had resulted in the death of a pilot. When Boulogne was the only port in the Pas de Calais area still being held by the Germans, Ned mistook it for Dover and was shot down, landing wheels-up in no man's land where he was rescued by Canadian troops.

Capping it all, we had a visit from Winston Churchill who arrived in 83 Group Commander's captured Fiesler Storch, a German light communications aircraft. "Give it to those buggers!" he told us when we gathered around him.

In August, we went on recces looking for enemy transport, bombed tanks, tunnels, and troop concentrations. We flew fighter cover for a Wing "do" in which a radio beacon near Beauvais was destroyed. As the enemy was compressed in the Falaise Gap, we attacked vehicles near Trun at the eastern end of the Gap.

About a week after the Battle of Falaise, a number of us toured the area in a truck to determine what had happened to some of our missing pilots. We drove down the Caen-Falaise Road and then on to Argentan. Between Falaise and Argentan the sides of the road were strewn with a continuous line of smashed and burned out vehicles. Many of the dead had not yet been buried. Infantrymen and tank crews were sprawled, in grotesque positions, around their vehicles. It was a scene of total destruction, one which we, as pilots, had never seen before, and would never forget.

We returned to our base by another route and came through a village almost levelled by the advancing armies in their effort to drive out the enemy. The black humour of the day had it that the inhabitants had been "obliberated." An old Frenchman came out of what was left of a house and offered us a tiny glass of Calvados, a type of apple brandy for which the area is noted. This bottle must have been pure alcohol. Immediately after

I drank it I felt as if someone had hit the inside of my skull with a hammer.

The fleeing enemy raced toward the Seine and under cover of darkness crossed the river on barges. We dropped leaflets into the area to encourage them to surrender. We also carried out armed recces as far away as Arras. But, as the enemy moved only at night, we couldn't find much to shoot at. Our airfield moved to Lille. While this was taking place, we operated from Manston on the east coast of England and carried out recces of the Dutch coast. After a week at Lille we moved on to Antwerp, Belgium.

From there I was posted back to a Tactical Exercise Unit at Aston Down in the west of England—the last of the original 193 members to leave the squadron. As an instructor at Aston Down, I taught pilots, who had converted from Spitfires to Tiffies and other pilots fresh out of OTU, the tactics we used on fighter/bomber operations.

But the greatest hazard at Aston Down was the pilots in the bar. Once, a redheaded Scot, who went wild after a few pints, dove straight at me from the top of the bar. We ended up on the floor with my head inches from the sharp corner of a brick fireplace. I did manage to survive the war unscathed and arrived back in Canada on 1 August 1945.

I enjoyed flying the Typhoon. And I also enjoyed the camaraderie that existed on a squadron. It was something that I had not experienced before, nor have I known it since those days when our lives were on the line and we lived a day at a time.

Ned Statters points to the sort of damage the rugged Typhoon could sustain— a missing port elevator shot away in an encounter with a Messerschmitt Bf 109. *J. G. Brown*

Mediterranean Torpedo Pilot

Low-Level Shipping Strikes Were Difficult and Dangerous

MURRAY C. HYSLOP DFC,

WITH DOUGLAS J. FAULDER

Airborne torpedo attacks on shipping were among the most hazardous of wartime assignments. Allowing for the speed of the targeted vessel, the pilot of the attacking aircraft had to approach from abeam along a track calculated to achieve a strike. For the torpedo to function properly the pilot had to release it at a set minimal height and at a relatively low speed, close enough so as not to be avoided by the target. Unable to take any form of evasive action, the pilot was extremely vulnerable to defensive fire. Once the torpedo was released, flying very near the target vessel was unavoidable. Most pilots chose to veer toward the bows and pass to the forward where the flak might not be as intense. Added to this risky procedure was the frustration of torpedoes occasionally malfunctioning by not exploding or by diving harmlessly beneath the target.

A native of Edmonton, twenty-year-old Murray Hyslop spent the summer of 1940 working on Mackenzie River barges. At fall freeze-up, he returned home to take a course in aircraft engine maintenance. Early in 1941, his studies completed, he applied to join both the RCMP and the RCAF. On 5 March the RCAF accepted him. The RCMP also accepted him—but a week too late. From Manning Pool in Brandon, Manitoba, the RCAF sent him to No 2 Bombing and Gunnery School (B&GS) at Paulson, also in Manitoba, for guard duty. His next posting was to No 4 Initial Training School (ITS) at Edmonton where an aptitude for the Link Trainer earned him a posting to No 16 Elementary Flying Training School, where he picks up his story.

Following his discharge, Murray Hyslop obtained a degree in mining engineering, but instead of entering that industry he returned to the RCAF where the pay was better, working as a construction engineer. He resumed flying in 1952 and became current on a wide selection of RCAF machines. He retired in 1977. His story appeared in the Spring 1997 CAHS *Journal*.

I was in the air on 28 July 1941 for the first time as an RCAF trainee, in Tiger Moth 4134 with Mr. Cheety as my instructor. This was the first time that I had ever been in an aircraft, and I loved it! On 11 August I soloed in Tiger Moth 4189 after ten hours and forty-five minutes of dual instruction. While I was at No 16 EFTS the Duke of Kent visited us, and I have a photograph of myself in a very baggy flying suit shaking his hand. I finished in Edmonton on 12 September with twenty-nine hours dual and twenty-eight hours solo flying time.

Then I was posted to No 10 Service Flying Training School (SFTS) at Dauphin, Manitoba, where we flew Cessna Cranes from 30 September to 13 December 1941. Most often my instructor was P/O Beat, a nice fellow, but more interested in hunting than instructing. On one flight we saw some deer in the bush below, and he had me put down in a nearby field. He told me to go solo, while he went after the deer. I got my wings at Dauphin, and then I had six weeks leave over Christmas, after which I reported to Halifax.

I went overseas by boat to Liverpool, then to the Personnel Reception Centre at Bournemouth. Like so many others, I drilled, went to classes, dances, and on special trips, generally wasting time until someone higher-up figured out where to send me. I did get a chance to go to Glasgow to see my grandfather. Finally, in April 1942, orders came to report to No 2 Advanced Flying Unit (AFU) at Brize Norton, Oxfordshire. From mid-April to mid-June 1942 it was intense training in Oxfords—up to six flights a day. We practised map reading, navigation, night flying, and formation flying. I spent a week at Wattisham doing Beam Approach training, and when I finished on Oxfords, I went for a six-week General Reconnaissance course.

My training moved me inexorably closer to wartime action, and in August 1942, I was ordered to No 5 (Coastal) Operational Training Unit of Coastal Command at Turnberry in Ayrshire, Scotland. We flew Beaufort Mk Is and Mk IIs. To me they were not much different from flying an Oxford, but they seemed war weary, almost junk. From August 1941 to November 1943, eighty Beauforts were lost at No 5 (C)OTU. The Taurus engine that powered the Mk I must take some of the responsibility as it was unreliable and had a short life; but most of the losses were due to inexperienced, hurriedly trained pilots. On 1 September 1942, while waiting at the end of the runway to take off on my sixth flying day at Turnberry, I saw a Hampden (P1199) and a Beaufort (L9932) making landing approaches together but unseen by each other. The inevitable collision and crash followed. At the time it seemed to me that there was a crash every day at Turnberry, but actually only five or six Beauforts were lost while I was there.

At No 5 (C)OTU we fired on towed drogue targets as well as bombing fixed and moving targets. While my first month there went well, in October 1942 I had a few problems. My first incident occurred while I was wearing goggles to simulate night flying. Taxiing, I cut a corner too sharply and hit a runway light with my tail wheel. It was not too serious, but a portent of things to come. Shortly after that, I lost an engine that caught fire while I was landing. The rest of my crew jumped out once the aircraft had slowed to about 30 mph. I got out of the burning machine at about 5 mph.

On 28 October, the most serious incident occurred in a Beaufort Mk IIA while flying at low level for air-to-sea firing. We had been higher to give my navigator some practice, and when we came down to low level, I neglected to tighten the straps of my harness—with uncomfortable consequences. Suddenly, barely above the water, both engines quit. The Beaufort bounced off the water. With my straps loose, my head broke the windshield, shredding my helmet and cutting my scalp. On the next impact the aircraft stayed on

The Bristol Beaufort enjoyed modest success in its designed role as a torpedo bomber. This machine is a Mk I (Taurus-powered) of 217 Squadron. *Crown Photograph*

the water, sinking rapidly but thankfully not before the entire crew was able to get out safely. Later I was told that this was the first ditching without a fatality at No 5 (C)OTU. It was also lucky for us that we were only about a mile off shore, near Girvan just south of Turnberry. Our ditching had been witnessed and we were soon rescued.

An investigation found that we had run out of fuel; but the gauges were faulty, so I was cleared. In front of the board, I was asked how I could have hit my head if my belts were on? "It was a confused time," was all I could stammer. That was, coincidentally, my last flight with No 5 (C)OTU.

From the OTU, some of us went directly to operational squadrons, but it was decided that I would become a torpedo bomber pilot and I was sent for specialized training to the Torpedo Training Unit at Abbotsinch, Scotland. We studied the theory of torpedo-dropping in ground school, then practised with Beauforts against fixed and moving targets. HMS *Canterbury* and the *Isle of Guernsey* were our usual targets. They would steam at various set speeds such as eight, sixteen, twenty-four, or thirty-two knots while we would simulate attacks with various deflections. I finished on 10 December 1942, and I was assessed as an "Average Plus Torpedo Bomber pilot with a sound knowledge of Torpedo Bomber Theory."

I was off to war, assigned to 39 (Torpedo) Squadron on the island of Malta. During the last week of January 1943, I flew a bit at the Ferry Training Unit in Lyneham. On 6 February I left Lyneham with a Beaufort IA bound for Landing Ground 224, near Cairo. My three English crew members were P/O Bob Elliot, Navigator; and Sgt Harry Milner and Sgt Stan Hornsby, Wireless Air Gunners. We called Bob Elliot an old man because he was twenty-eight years old! We would stay together as a crew on 39 Squadron. On 16 February we arrived in Cairo, Egypt via Gibraltar and North Africa.

On 28 February 1943 we caught a ride in a Hudson from LG (landing ground) 224 to Malta, where 39 Squadron was based at Luqa, flying Beaufort IIs and IIAs. Their Pratt & Whitney Twin Wasps were much more reliable in a hot climate than the Taurus. By this time, the Axis forces in North Africa were reeling and were being driven to their final stand in Tunisia. They were desperately trying to supply their garrison there and it was up to the anti-shipping squadrons in Malta to stop them—the primary strike force being 39 Squadron. I did some familiarization flying from 6 March to 12 March; and then I did my first operation on 18 March, looking for shipping west of Sicily, especially a convoy that the squadron had attacked the day before off the toe of Italy. We did more shipping strike searches on 21 and 24 March with air tests between. The squadron enjoyed some success on 23 March. Just before midnight, P/O Ralph Dodd, a fellow Canadian, sank the tug *Tenace* that was towing a damaged merchant vessel to Trapani harbour on Sicily.

In April, with the loss of Tunisia imminent, the Axis were forced to curtail their convoys and our flying became mostly practice. I did a gardening (mine-laying) operation with five other aircraft on 4 April, putting our mines into Trapani harbour. Mines, being big round things, unlike torpedoes, could be carried only partly in the bomb bay. They barely cleared the ground. This was a night operation and I remember the hills around the harbour lighting up with twinkling AA guns. With the islands and harbours clearly visible in the moonlight, we did not have too many problems flying at night. Landing and taking off on a pitch black night was another story. We used flare pots along the runway, the small lights accurately indicating the level of the strip.

I did a shipping search on 13 April, again in follow-up to a successful attack carried out by other members of my squadron the day before, but I could not find the convoy. With the last Axis holdouts in Africa being cleaned up by the Allied forces, May 1943 was relatively quiet for 39 Squadron. I put another mine in Trapani harbour on 7 May, when ten aircraft went on another gardening operation. It must have been a rather dark night. I found myself too far into the harbour, once the guns started firing at us, so I went around, and on my second try I was able to put the mine in the harbour entrance.

On 9 May, four of us went out with our Beauforts, each carrying four 250-pound bombs, to look for targets around Marsala on the western tip of Sicily. On 13 May, I dropped a torpedo against a train ferry off Point Alice without results. We did two more fruitless shipping searches on 16 and 18 May, and then on 29 May the squadron was taken off operations and ordered to move to Protville, near Tunis in Tunisia, for a changeover to Beaufighters.

Before leaving Malta, I should mention a few other recollections. Our food was rationed, and we ate a lot of cabbage and potatoes. This made me slimmer than ever and I acquired the nickname "Bones." The higher-flying fighter pilots had a different mess with marginally better food. The cabbage gave them too much gas at their higher altitudes, or so I was told! We had one beer a week, and I was once lucky enough to buy an egg from a woman with a chicken.

On 1 June we flew to Protville, where our arrival was a complete fiasco. No one was expecting us! Without accommodation or food, we were obliged to scrounge and sleep under our Beauforts for two nights. Our plight was eased when we moved, temporarily, to Cairo. We flew on 3 and 4 May via Castel Benito and El Adem. After a few days rest, all aircrew were ordered back to Protville. With no available transport, we were told to use our Beauforts to get there! Arriving on 9 May, we found a primitive camp that our ground crew had set up. After a further six days' rest, orders came to deliver the Beauforts back to Maintenance Units near Cairo, so we retraced our route of twelve days earlier. On 20 May, I was able to get a ride in a DC-3 as far as Castel Benito and then on a Wellington to Protville, two days later. Our conversion to Beaufighters finally began in earnest.

The Beaufighter TF Mk X was a big step up from the Beaufort. Its two Bristol Hercules could speed it along at 300 mph, and unlike a Beaufort, it could fly on one engine. That they were not supercharged did not matter, since all of our flying was low level, usually cruising at 250 mph. With the Beaufighter we could carry a one-ton Mk XIV torpedo fifteen hundred miles. The four 20-mm cannon in the nose effectively suppressed anti-aircraft fire.

While there were three Beaufighter torpedo squadrons in North Africa

The Bristol Beaufighter has been aptly described as "two huge engines hotly pursued by a fuselage." This early example does not have the dihedral that was applied to the horizontal tail of later aircraft. *Air Ministry*

(Nos 39, 144, and 47) we rarely, if ever, operated together. My first Beaufighter flight was 23 June 1943, a familiarization flight with P/O Garland from 144 Squadron. The chaps in 144 Squadron had brought their Beaufighters from England a week earlier, and thus they had experience flying them. The Beaufighter had only one seat in the cockpit, obliging Garland to stand behind me on the checkout flight. Since the Beaufighter required only a crew of two, pilot and navigator, Bob Elliot and I bade goodbye to our gunners, Milner and Hornsby, who both transferred to a Wellington squadron also based at Protville. Harry Milner was killed on his second or third operation with his new squadron. For me, it was two weeks of almost daily practice flights.

Then on 10 July, the Allies invaded Sicily. All three Beaufighter squadrons were put on daily standby in case the Italian capital ships left their base at La Spezia to attack the invasion convoys. They never did, but we were busy enough. On 11 July 'B' Flight leader, S/L Stanley Muller-Rowland, led six of us against a convoy south of Naples. Four Beaufighters were carrying torpedoes and two, including my aircraft, were assigned to flak suppression. In the late afternoon we found the convoy (one merchant vessel, two destroyers, and a flak ship), and attacked. I had cannon strikes on the destroyer and saw torpedo hits on the merchant vessel and one of the destroyers. As it turned out, we sank the German merchant ship, *Tell,* and damaged an Italian warship. I also saw an Italian Cant floatplane in the area. On the return home we were attacked by single-engine fighters and F/L Ian McIntyre, another Canadian, was shot down and killed. His navigator, Sgt Fletcher, survived to become a prisoner of war (POW). Muller-Rowland's aircraft was damaged so badly that he was forced to crash-land it back at Protville.

How did we carry out our attacks? Flak suppression, it had been found, was vital to achieving good torpedo drops, so we usually tried to have six torpedo-armed Beaufighters teamed with at least three others for anti-flak work with their 20-mm cannons. Without the one-ton torpedo they were much more maneuverable and could maintain good airspeed. The torpedo-armed aircraft would fly in loose formation—line abreast—about a block and a half apart to try and bracket the target with their torpedoes. We would go in at top speed about five feet off the water, until we got to dropping range, when we would climb up to about 60 to 80 feet and slow down to 140 knots—which made us much more vulnerable to flak. Whenever we had enough aircraft for an operation to carry torpedoes in six of them, and still have four or five for flak suppression, we would have three aircraft attacking with torpedoes from each side. On takeoff we were told, "You are on port, you are on starboard."

Our squadron was busy for the first few days of the invasion of Sicily, but then things quieted down and I saw no action on my patrols until 21 July. On this day S/L Muller-Rowland again led six of us against a convoy off the east coast of Corsica, ten miles south of Bastia. This convoy had two merchant vessels well protected with four warships and four flak ships. The wall of flak prevented us from making accurate drops; and we lost one aircraft, although the crew, P/O Hunter and Sgt Booth, were able to ditch, becoming POWs. I flew about every other day until the end of July, and then not again until 8 August. On 10 August we were in the thick of it again, attacking two merchant vessels escorted by three warships. We had eight aircraft, four with torpedoes and four for flak suppression. Again we were off the east coast of Corsica near Bastia, this time led by F/L Stan Balkwill. We managed a torpedo hit on the larger merchant vessel, my torpedo I believe, and I saw my cannon fire pour into the bridge. Luckily we had no losses.

On my next operation, 16 August, we again found targets, this time about ten miles north of Naples. Muller-Rowland led us against two merchant vessels escorted by three warships. I was flying a torpedo-armed aircraft and was able to get a good drop away. We saw a hit on each merchant vessel with-

Personnel of 39 Squadron under the nose of one of their Beaufighters at Protville, Tunisia. *M. C. Hyslop*

out losing an aircraft. My usual aircraft at this time was Beaufighter LX907, carrying the designator letter 'W.'

I flew a few practice flights for the next three weeks, and then on 7 September I was involved in an attack that I would sooner forget. Our squadron leader, W/C Nelson B. Harvey, led ten aircraft on an armed rover around Corsica. West of Corsica, we found an unescorted merchant vessel which in itself was odd. I became really suspicious when no tracer fire poured up at us, as it usually did, following our every move. Getting closer I saw "SWITZERLAND" in letters ten feet high on the side of the hull, and I wondered if it was a neutral ship. I called "Don't drop! Don't drop!" over the radio, but two aircraft dropped torpedoes and another raked it from stem to stern with 20-mm shells—despite being warned long before they attacked. The ship was sunk. The whole thing was hushed up, no court martial or anything. That night on the Axis propaganda radio, it was reported that the Allies had sunk a Red Cross hospital ship. Later we were told that it was a neutral ship smuggling ammunition. We did not know who to believe. There were some trigger-happy fellows in our squadron. I recall one pilot who would shoot up the little Italian fishing boats that we occasionally saw although the rest of us objected. We knew we might have to be rescued by those fisherman if we were shot down.

I was pretty gung-ho myself. On one armed rover between Corsica and Italy, I came upon a little Italian float plane that didn't even shoot back. He was all over the sky trying to evade me, but I was so pumped up that I stayed right on his tail. I pulled the little handle on the control yoke to fire the 20-mm cannon, which would have blown him to smithereens, but nothing happened! It turned out that my navigator had not armed the cannon, their breeches being behind me in his compartment. When we got back, that handle was bent so badly from my pulling on it that it had to be replaced. I was mad as hell at him, but now I wonder what difference it could have made.

On 8 September 1943, the Italians announced their surrender. The next day, the Germans in Italy made the landings at Salerno tough going for the Allies. Surrendering Italian warships from La Spezia tried to escape from the Germans at this time. Near Sardinia they were caught by Dornier 217s and attacked with radio-controlled glider bombs, sinking the battleship *Roma*. Other Italian warships from Taranto sailed to Malta without a problem. While all this was happening, 39 Squadron took a back seat.

Then on 15 September, I was back in the action again. S/L Muller-Rowland led eleven aircraft, six with torpedoes and five with anti-flak, against a convoy made up of a tanker with four escorting warships. We were between the islands of Elba and Capraia when we found them and attacked. Six torpedoes were dropped, one of them by myself, but no hits were observed. The flak was intense and one shell exploded right under my air-craft, putting holes in the port engine nacelle and wing. Luckily my torpedo was already away. It might have exploded and I would not be here describ-ing it. Two of our aircraft were lost immediately, and on our way home to Tunisia another was forced to ditch southeast of Sardinia. We lost three air-craft, without one torpedo hit. Truthfully, we weren't even close. Were we ever chewed out over that one! The positive side of this operation was that all six crew men in the three lost aircraft survived. In one aircraft were F/O Howard and Sgt Goldie who were captured to become POWs. S/L Muller-Rowland went out the next day and located a dinghy containing F/O Ambrose and F/O Higgin from the Beau that ditched near Sardinia. Then he homed a high-speed rescue boat onto them, his last operational flight with 39 Squadron. The other aircraft shot down during the attack was crewed by F/O York and F/O Mathias, and I was relieved to see them already safely in their dinghy as the rest of us high-tailed out of there.

I could not believe it when York and Mathias walked back into our base at Protville two months later! They had been rescued by Italian sailors and were taken to the island of Capraia. The group of them sailed down to an

A Beaufighter is guided from the dispersal area at Luqa Airfield, Malta. *RAF*

Allied-held island off Naples and were then taken by Allied ships to Capri, then Malta, and then to Tunisia. In a cruel twist of wartime fate, they were both killed in March 1944 during a 39 Squadron operation near Marseilles.

I have to say more about our flight leader, S/L Stanley Muller-Rowland. He was a natural leader and one of the best torpedo pilots of the war. If we would have all been like him, the war would have ended a lot sooner. He was very serious and fought the enemy like he had to win the war himself. On one operation, his torpedo failed to release during his attack run. He went around, shaking his aircraft a bit to ensure the torpedo would come away, and then he made another run in by himself, without any flak suppression. He was a very brave young man, only twenty-one years old at the time. In Cairo or Protville, while the rest of us were partying the night away, he would be poring over books and action reports, developing new tactics. Like so many other fine men, S/L Stanley R. Muller-Rowland, DFC and Bar, did not survive the war. He lost his life on 3 October 1944 off the Dutch coast while flying a Beaufighter with 236 Squadron.

We did a lot of partying. It was our way of coping with the stress of operations. With only a 17 percent chance of surviving one tour, Torpedo bomber crews suffered one of the highest loss rates in the war. At Protville we found a lot of stuff left behind by the Germans, including motorcycles, cars, and cases of machine guns and ammunition. Just for fun, we would race the motorcycles and fire the machine guns into the air.

My next operational flight was on 23 September 1943. The Germans had withdrawn from Sardinia to Corsica in mid-September, and were now attempting to withdraw from Corsica to Italy. Our reconnaissance aircraft had seen large numbers of transport aircraft shuttling back and forth between Corsica and Italy, so we went after them as a fighter patrol not slowed down by torpedoes. I was in my usual mount, Beaufighter LX907/W, with my navigator, Bob Elliott, now promoted to F/L from F/O. For our 20-mm cannons, we used a mix of tracer, explosive, armour piercing, and incendiary rounds. Our flight of four aircraft found three Savoia-Marchetti S.M. 82 three-engined transports just northeast of Corsica and shot them all down. Later, on the 23rd, another 39 Squadron Beaufighter went out with two from 47 Squadron and shot down another S.M. 82 and a Junkers Ju 52, another tri-motored transport.

Still later in the afternoon two more from 39 Squadron went out only to learn that shooting down transports was not as easy as one might think. They brought down two Ju 52s of a formation of five; but both Beaufighters were lost to return fire, one crashing during the attack, the other being forced to ditch near Sardinia on the way home to Protville. The next day was more of the same. Four aircraft went out in the early morning, but one had to turn back with engine trouble. The other three found three Ju 52s and shot one down into the sea, but not before S/L Petch and P/O Williams had to ditch. Later in the morning, four aircraft, including myself in one and Wing Commander Harvey in another, found three Ju 52s and shot them all down with no loss to ourselves. A third sweep that morning got two Ju 52s but lost three Beaufighters, two aircraft into the Mediterranean, and another crash landing ten miles from Protville. One of the crews that ditched was killed—P/O Twiname and Sgt McCleod—but the other four men survived. Twiname had been my tent mate. We all lost friends and tent mates, but we carried on. The next day, two Beaufighters went out looking for the ditched airmen, with parachute containers to drop to them, but they ran into two Messerschmitt Bf 109s, and one was shot down. I did an air-sea rescue search on 30 September.

Then 39 Squadron was off operations for the month of October 1943. Rain turned Protville into a mud hole, so it was well that we were sent to No 5 Middle East Training School in Shallufa, Egypt, for more torpedo training and a bit of a break. For the flight to Shallufa, ten aircrew went in six aircraft, and with some ground crew that came along, we managed two or three extra personnel in each machine—quite a crowd for a two-place Beaufighter. From 10 to 18 October we flew one or two times daily, carrying out simulated torpedo attacks against Royal Navy vessels, principally HMS *Sagitta* and HMS *Niki*. On 19 October, I went out on a search for a crashed aircraft and the next day, with four passengers, made the eight-hour flight from Shallufa back to Sidi Amor, near Tunis, the capital of Tunisia. Along the way, we stopped at Marble Arch to refuel.

Our squadron had moved to Sidi Amor from Protville while we were gone. A detachment from 39 Squadron, including myself, F/L Bob Elliott, our trusty old Beau LX907/W, and the other aircraft and crew of 'B' Flight, left for Grottaglie on 1 November 1943. Grottaglie is near Taranto, on the inside of the heel of Italy. On 5 November, S/L Curlee, the 'B' Flight commander, led six aircraft against a German minelayer about fifteen miles off Trieste. One torpedo hit it, but I don't know if it was mine, and the *Ramb III* sank. We rotated back to Sidi Amor, while 'A' Flight spelled us off in Grottaglie. Then we switched again on the 14th. On 21 November we again went out to the Trieste area, but found the ships we were looking for in the harbour—so we did not attack. When bad weather prevented us from returning to Grottaglie, we landed at Foggia, returning to Grottaglie the next day. On the 24th we went looking for U-Boats in the Adriatic Sea, but none were found. We left the next day to catch up to the squadron that had in the meantime moved to Reghaia, Algeria, to the west of Tunisia.

Our squadron was now converting to rocket attacks; but I was grounded for a while due to a sinus infection that I picked up from a swimming pool

Murray Hyslop (R) with Andrew "Pat" Patterson from Regina at Sardinia, Italy. *M. C. Hyslop.*

in Egypt, so I did not start training with rockets until 29 December. I carried out six live-firing training flights with the rockets, but I never had a chance to use them in action. In the second half of January, we carried out fighter patrols, looking for Luftwaffe aircraft that were attacking the convoys coming through Gibraltar. These were all carried out over the waters between the Spanish coast and the islands of Ibiza, Majorca, and Minorca. My patrol on 25 January 1944 was my last operational flying.

At Reghaia I almost got to fly a Hurricane that we used as a squadron hack. Just before my turn to fly it, somebody crash-landed and it burned. Luckily the pilot was safe. At the time I happened to be squadron parachute officer, with a deficit of eight parachutes on our books. The Hurricane crash gave me a chance to write off the parachutes and balance the books!

In February and March, I did a lot of non-operational flying, as 39 Squadron moved again, this time to Alghero on the island of Sardinia. On 25 March 1944 I bade my unit goodbye. I made my way by C-47 back to No 5 Middle East Training School in Shallufa, this time as an instructor pilot. From July 1944 to November 1944 I flew almost daily at Shallufa, where I demonstrated torpedo attacks, day and night low-flying, single-engine flying, and deadstick landings. I also flew target-tug aircraft. While I still flew mostly Beaufighters, I had the chance to fly a Miles Magister, some Boulton-Paul Defiants, a Harvard, an Anson, a Blenheim, and a Wellington Mk XIII.

The Defiant, used at Shallufa for towing a target drogue, gave me a bit of trouble that I have not forgotten. Asked if I could handle it, I looked in the cockpit and said, "Sure, I can fly this." In reality I had never flown a high-performance single-engine aircraft. During the takeoff run, the torque from that Merlin surprised me. I went haring off the runway between two hangars a few hundred feet away, bouncing across the sand before finally getting into the air.

In October 1944, when I was giving a lot of one-engine-out instruction on Blenheims and Beaufighters, most of my students were South Africans. I did my last flight at Shallufa on 20 November 1944. Then I caught a boat to Gibraltar and thence to England. I was back in Canada in February 1945 and left the RCAF in October.

Ventura Lost

When Air Training Could Prove as Demanding as Operational Flying

ROBERT H. (BOB) FOWLER OC

During a lengthy and rewarding career in aviation, Bob Fowler has been awarded the McKee Trans-Canada Trophy, become a Fellow of the Canadian Aeronautics and Space Institute, been made an Officer of the Order of Canada, and was inducted into Canada's Aviation Hall of Fame. The story he recounts deals not with his days of aerial surveying or test flying but is from an earlier, formative time when he was completing his training to fly medium bombers with the RAF.

Learning to fly at Toronto's Barker Field with instruction from Vi Milstead (see "Flying With the ATA," later in this book), Bob had soloed before he enlisted in the RCAF in 1942 at the age of twenty. While he had no logbook to document his flying, he was able to produce a fistful of Patterson & Hill receipts to prove that he actually had the air time he claimed—much to the amusement of the recruiting officer. After mastering the Fleet Finch at No 4 Elementary Flying Training School and advanced training on Anson IIs at No 8 SFTS, Moncton, New Brunswick, he trained with an RAF OTU at nearby Pennfield Ridge where he picks up his story.

From the OTU, Bob went overseas to the RCAF Reception Centre at Bournemouth, England, and in May 1944, took Beam Approach Training on Oxfords, acquiring skills that would later prove extremely useful. His conversion training for NA B-25 Mitchell medium bombers was at Finmere, Bucks, and his operational training on the type at Swanton Morley, Norfolk. Bob's operational flying began with 226 Squadron of the RAF 2nd Tactical Air Force at Hartford Bridge, Hants. His experiences on low-level tactical bombing missions will make exciting reading for later publication. He flew forty-eight day- and night-missions to complete his tour and then did a six-month "rest" stint, instructing and ferrying Mitchells, Bostons, and Ansons in the United Kingdom and Europe.

After one year of law at the University of Toronto (1946), he returned to flying, piloting a Grumman Goose and a Consolidated Canso on magnetic survey operations for the Dominion Gulf Co. He then did similar work for Spartan Air Service using the Avro Anson V. In 1951, he flew a Lockheed P-38 Lightning for Spartan, a demanding assignment, which he describes in a companion Fifth House volume, *Skippers of the Sky*.

In 1952, Bob Fowler joined de Havilland Canada, retiring in 1987 as Chief Engineering Test Pilot. He had assisted in the certification of the Caribou and was first to fly the Buffalo, the Twin Otter, the Dash-7 and the Dash-8 prototypes. He also did the first air tests of the Pratt & Whitney PT6A and General Electric YT-64 turbo-prop engines. Retired, he became a technical consultant on accident investigation for DHC and private concerns.

O n the last day of August 1943, after completing the final four-month advanced flying training course at No 8 Service Flying Training School (SFTS) at Moncton, New Brunswick, I graduated with new RCAF pilot's wings. I was very nearly posted to the RCAF Central Flying School at Trenton, Ontario, to become an instructor. Before that could happen— through a happier combination of events—I was posted with three other Pilot Officer classmates, to No 34 RAF Operational Training Unit (OTU) at Pennfield Ridge, New Brunswick. 34 OTU was one of the few wartime Royal Air Force stations in Canada, and though I did not know it at the time, it was actually a unit of 2 Group of the RAF's 2nd Tactical Air Force. Complete crews were trained at Pennfield on the Lockheed (Vega) Ventura, which was then in use by the RAF in England mainly as a daylight tactical bomber by medium bomber squadrons of 2 Group.

Pennfield was situated on the north shore of the Bay of Fundy near Black's Harbour, New Brunswick, roughly forty miles west of Saint John on the highway to St. Stephen. No 34 OTU was a solid little British enclave staffed almost entirely by RAF personnel, right down to the batmen.

The four of us got off the bus from Saint John at the gate to Royal Air Force Pennfield Ridge, as proclaimed by a rather humble sign. After surveying the bleak landscape, someone said, "I wonder why they built an airport so close to that huge hill?" After a moment of thought, one of the others replied, "It probably helps pilots find the airport in bad weather."

It is astonishing to think that most of us were barely twenty-one, anyone

Bob Fowler, wearing helmet and goggles, leans on a Ventura's wing-root at about the time of the training incident he describes. *R. H. Fowler.*

Regards !
Bob Fowler.

a year or two older was called an "uncle." At Pennfield, I was checked out in the Ventura with its two 2,000 hp engines and a takeoff gross weight of thirty-two thousand pounds, after six short instructional flights totalling four hours and forty-five minutes. This contrasted sharply with the brand of training we had just completed—flying the Anson II for four months at the SFTS. It is a miracle there were not more Venturas lying about the airfield at the end of each day.

At Pennfield Ridge, for the first time in our airforce careers we were thrown together with other aircrew trades. Observers were trained in the dual skills needed for navigators and bomb aimers, and instead of a winged 'N' or a 'B' over their left pocket, they wore a gold-winged 'O,' irreverently termed "the flying arsehole." There were also wireless air gunners, who were trained both as wireless operators and air gunners, and "straight" air gunners, who specialized solely as air gunners. The normal four-person Ventura crew in the RAF used one of each.

Compared with the Mark II Anson with its 300 hp Jacobs engines, the Ventura seemed a big heavy machine, not a bit too small for its 2,000 hp Pratt & Whitneys. Holding it on the ground during takeoff until the airspeed indicator showed 110 mph convinced us we were in a completely different league.

After converting to the Ventura as a crew, events moved along at a steady pace. We quickly began to feel like old hands, throwing the "Vent" around with newly acquired confidence and respect.

At least 70 percent of the flying instructors at Pennfield were RAF, "Limeys," which enriched the whole experience. We got along extremely well. The majority of the other instructors were Canadian. Most had flown daylight- and night-bomber operations on RAF squadrons in 2 Group, and many were decorated. All had survived one or two tours of operations, mostly in Europe, and a few twitchy ones had done three. Where flying was concerned, they all seemed to have a fine appreciation of the things that mattered. Unlike SFTS, there was no spoon-feeding. In the pilot checkout phase, once the instructors had covered the main items at least once and felt you had a feel for the important aspects of flying a Ventura, they were gone. Off you went to train yourself with a hapless WAG along to handle the radios.

The weather at Pennfield Ridge was anything but predictable, and if the "powers that were" had not pressed us into every possible flying opportunity, we would never have finished the course on time. We didn't appreciate it at the time, but we were being well initiated into the sort of weather waiting for us in England.

One of our SFTS classmates, "Young" Lively, never got a chance to fly the Ventura. The first time he got into one with an instructor, it was immediately clear that it wouldn't work. Like Abraham Lincoln, his legs fit properly between him and the ground, but they were just not long enough to fit between him and the rudder pedals of the Ventura—and at the same time allow him the "luxury" of a view through the windshield. After a few days Lively was posted to Bagotville, Quebec, to do operational training on Hurricanes—poor Lively. From then on we tried coming down the stairs with both feet together, and any other therapy we thought might shorten our legs, all to no avail. Fighters would have to wait.

Lively was replaced on our course by a poised, good-looking pilot who was one of the first of our course to be sent off alone in a Ventura, and he quickly gained the reputation of being a very skilled pilot. One afternoon in the middle of the course, after my assigned flight had been cancelled due to a mechanical problem, I asked if I might go along with this new pilot and his crew to play with the mid-upper gun turret.

It was a new experience to be concerned about the members of one's crew as well as the aircraft we expected to operate when we finally went overseas. Every flight I had made in the Ventura had been from the left-hand pilot's seat. After some hair-raising fighter affiliation flying against a pair of "attacking" Hurricanes, I had been looking for an opportunity to go on a flight with another crew to operate the mid-upper electro-hydraulic gun turret. This way I could get some idea of the problems the gunners faced in order to defend us against enemy fighters.

The weather was sunny but cold, and my pilot friend and his crew were signed out to practise takeoffs and landings until the arrival of a snowstorm that was forecast to close Pennfield down by late afternoon. A few other Venturas were also signed out to do air work within sight of the airport until the snow arrived. The Ventura in which we were to fly had only one radio transceiver for tower communication, and the course needle of the magnetic compass was stuck at 254 degrees, rendering it useless. As a result, until these snags could be rectified, this aeroplane was restricted to takeoffs and landings at Pennfield.

We embarked on what seemed a perfectly innocuous event with no suspicion that we were walking into an experience we would be able to recall in stark detail for the rest of our lives. Prior to this flight, if I had the slightest idea of what was ahead, I'm sure I would have run in the opposite direction, without a backward glance.

Although it was prohibited, the mid-upper turret was an exciting place to be sitting while the aircraft was doing takeoffs and landings, and I had a fine time swinging the very responsive hydraulically operated turret around, bringing the reflector sight to bear on anything I chose as a target. I had evicted the crew's air gunner, who wouldn't have much to do while I was playing with his turret. He assured me before takeoff that he was quite at home between the guns, and said he would enjoy having a chance to look at the countryside around Pennfield.

On the third or fourth takeoff, we could clearly see a solid wall of snow bearing down upon Pennfield from the northwest. As I watched, I could see it was moving so rapidly that it was doubtful we would be able to get in any more circuits before the aerodrome would be shut down. Our pilot had been doing very nice three-point landings, which was the prescribed RAF technique for daylight landings. I could see why he had impressed those who had flown with him.

After landing, the pilot turned around and taxied back down the runway to its south end. I expected him to return to the parking area, but on the intercom I heard him say he thought he might just squeeze in one more takeoff and landing, and he asked the WAG to call the control tower for permission to do "…one more quick circuit." With no hesitation the control tower granted his request.

At the south end of the runway we turned around and roared off on a last takeoff. As we lifted into the air, I remember thinking that this pilot was obviously a solid, press-on type. The snow was close enough that if I was honest, I'm sure I would have called it a day—particularly with an unserviceable compass. After retracting the landing gear, and before we had gone much more than a mile or so, we were into the snow. I heard the pilot coolly say that he was "…going to do a 180 to the left to parallel the runway back to the airport."

After a few minutes we emerged from the snow into the sunlight. Pennfield was at our ten o'clock position on the left, and we were in a good position to complete the downwind leg and do another 180 to the left to the final approach heading.

I heard the pilot finish his landing checklist, and as he rolled out of the turn to line up with the runway, the view ahead was a little daunting. The grey wall of snow had almost reached the opposite end of the six thousand-foot runway, and we still had a good three or four miles to fly just to reach the airfield boundary. We were in a race with the snow, which was fast approaching from the other end, to see which of us got to the runway first. At 120 mph I remember thinking that we should be able to reach the approach end of the runway before the snow could work its way toward us from the other end. We were flying faster than the speed at which weather typically moves, but we were flying upwind and the snow was moving toward us—downwind. As we approached in the sunlight with the runway slowly coming closer, with nothing from the tower, we watched as it and the airport were swallowed up by the oncoming snow just before we too were enfolded in its embrace.

In the snow we could see nothing, but for some moments we seemed to continue the approach. Engine power was finally increased and as the landing gear and flaps were retracting, we climbed away from where Pennfield aerodrome had been moments earlier. Not knowing what plan the pilot might have, I stayed where I was. There would be plenty of time to leave the turret before we landed. After a while, the power was reduced and I was fairly sure we were flying level. Then on the intercom I heard a conversation develop about the compass—the one with the stuck needle.

With a little interest but not much thought, I got out of the turret and went forward. I stood at the rear of the radio/nav compartment that was just behind the pilot's seats, and plugged my headset into a jack box to listen to the intercom and radio talk.

A conference was in session concerning the arithmetic required to reset the gyro compass to our actual heading. The pilot, employing a common practice, had set it to zero when he lined up with the runway before each takeoff to facilitate the rectangular orientation of his takeoff and landing patterns. As a result, the gyro indication differed from our magnetic heading at least by the difference between zero degrees and the magnetic heading of the runway we had been using. A directional gyro is a very nice steady directional reference for turning or for accurately steering a course, but it knows *nothing* about direction until a pilot sets it to the heading indicated by a magnetic compass. The magnetic compass on the other hand knows *everything* about direction but is unwieldy to steer by due to a number of effects that cause its needle to wander about if the aircraft is disturbed by turbulence or normal pilot handling.

With the useless magnetic compass, different suggestions were being made as to what setting should be put on the directional gyro, bearing in mind that it had previously been set to zero on the runway before our last takeoff. They wrestled with the problem for a minute or two until someone

A Lockheed Ventura above a solid cloud cover mirrors the situation in which Bob Fowler and a crew from No 34 Operational Training Unit (OTU) found themselves—with their navigational aids mostly inoperative. *Air Ministry*

made the mistake of saying, "Isn't that right, Bob?" The simplest solution I could suggest was to turn the aircraft until the directional gyro indicated zero degrees, which was where it had been set on the runway just before our last takeoff. Then it could be manually reset it to the known magnetic heading of that runway—which did not require any arithmetic.

After the gyro was reset everyone looked happier, but we were still surrounded by an extensive area of snow with no idea as to how much of New Brunswick it covered. Significant fuel had been used doing the circuits, and the afternoon was beginning to fade.

A voice on the intercom suggested going to the Blissville radio range thirty-odd miles northwest of Saint John, and doing a range approach to the small airport there, so we headed for Blissville. We had learned some radio range procedures in the Link Trainer at Pennfield, but because no such radio facilities would be available when we got to England, only one or two beacon or range approaches were ever practised in the air.

We began the approach to Blissville, and during the letdown, someone said, "Look at *that!*" Through the snow we saw the grey top of a hill go by on the right, altogether too close for comfort. We turned away from the hill, and at the same time lost touch with the approach procedure. It was sensibly decided that the weather was too thick for a range approach, and engine power was increased as a climb was set up to a "safe" altitude.

Someone tentatively suggested to the WAG that he call Pennfield and ask if they could suggest an alternative destination where the weather was better. He tried this and said he didn't think the radio was working properly, but Pennfield came back on the tower frequency to tell us that they were closed in, but the weather was better less than 150 miles to the northwest at Caribou, Maine. When we heard this the observer, who was sitting with a map on his lap in the co-pilot seat beside the pilot, worked out a northwest-erly course to Caribou and gave it to the pilot. The observer had been doing his best to keep track of fuel and time, and he also tried to monitor the courses we were steering.

One or two weeks previously, I had flown with an instructor on a shop-ping expedition to the American airbase at Presque Isle, Maine. Presque Isle was south of Caribou, and neither was very far west of the Maine/New Brunswick border.

We flew on in the snow, but the windshield and windows stayed white and the weather showed no sign of changing. After almost an hour on instruments, the pilot began looking ahead through the windshield, and downward from his side window—possibly in the hope of making visual contact with the ground. His preoccupation with looking outside was affect-ing the accuracy of his course flying. He was holding altitude quite well, but the heading deviations increased to the extent that for periods of time we were well off the course that had been given to him by his observer, who occasionally pointed to the directional gyro in a tactful effort to restore his attention to it.

Again, I didn't envy the pilot. Our training to wings standard had not emphasized the fact that one must not lose visual contact with the ground without a clear understanding of the means by which it could be safely re-established. More to the point, as pilots, we had acquired no wisdom that told us what to do if we ever *did* lose visual contact with the ground in an aircraft that was not equipped with appropriate radios and a dependable magnetic compass, an admittedly rare possibility.

One other crew member had slipped into the radio/nav compartment, and quiet conversations erupted from time to time. One opinion expressed was that, " . . at least we have parachutes, we could always bail out." I remem-ber mumbling something to the effect that with street shoes, a battle dress blouse over a shirt and tie, and a wedge cap in my inside pocket, I was not fitted out very well to wander about the New Brunswick bush in early winter. I added that I for one would never leave the aircraft until the fuel gauges showed empty.

Our concerns grew as to where we were, and where we were going. We had not been able to tune the radio beacons at Caribou or Presque Isle. I had been watching the directional gyro from a distance, and it was difficult to estimate our average heading. With a useless magnetic compass, I had a feeling in the pit of my stomach that the directional gyro just might have a high drift rate, which in the time since it had been reset, could cause us to be flying in almost any direction. At our SFTS, it wasn't unusual during cross-country flights, where we were expected to regularly check the directional gyro against the magnetic compass, to discover that the gyro had drifted a good number of degrees in a fairly short period of time. The gyros were not quickly replaced due to high drift rates in order to impress student pilots with the need to regularly check and reset them to the magnetic compass that was the basic directional reference.

I didn't envy our pilot. He looked tired and was becoming a bit edgy. Neither of us had likely ever flown on continuous instruments for much more than an hour—or two at most. Every one of us in the aircraft was a rank amateur, and nothing in our training had prepared us for the ridiculous situation in which we found ourselves. Snow was down to the ground. We had a useless magnetic compass, and our radio equipment would only raise the Pennfield tower if we were close enough. At the SFTS we had only flown aircraft equipped with radios once or twice, and we had very little familiarity with the available in-flight meteorological facilities.

Our particular Ventura had been signed out only for the purpose of doing six or eight takeoffs and landings. The crew had not been given a detailed briefing of the weather outlook other than a warning that an extensive area of snow would be moving into the Pennfield area. I was at the advanced age of twenty-one. Our pilot might have been one or two years older, but no more. There were no "old hands" on board with experience to draw upon.

Rather abruptly, the pilot turned around, and after motioning me forward, he said he was getting tired and asked me to change places with him. With his crew clustered around, this seemed awkward. I didn't want to be injected into a situation where I was flying an aeroplane with a crew that was not mine. I told him he was doing fine and to hang on while we tried to get a line on something.

After a few more minutes, the pilot unsnapped his seat harness and parachute, and when his observer asked what he was doing, he said he had to "go back for a leak." The observer gave me a wide-eyed look. We both knew there was a relief tube under the pilot's seat, but it didn't seem the proper time to mention it.

The observer held the wheel awkwardly while the pilot climbed out of the left seat, and I slipped into it with an eagerness that surprised me. His parachute cushion was quite warm, and as I clipped on the parachute and seat harness, I felt a relief I hadn't expected, but I well remember thinking, "What the hell do I do now?"

Strapped in, I asked the observer what he thought was the average course we had been steering since we climbed away from Blissville. Palms up, he rolled his eyes toward heaven and said, "I don't have a clue."

At first, the only thing I could think of was to return to the northwesterly course on the gyro compass that the observer had given the pilot for Caribou, Maine, almost two hours earlier. That done, I wondered where that gyro heading might actually take us, particularly since the gyro had not been reset for so long. How long should we hold this course? The only things we knew for sure were that we didn't have much fuel or daylight left.

We were fairly high, so I came down to 6,000 feet, which was the highest spot-height listed on the observer's map. With less than three hundred hours of flying experience, it was the only thing I could think of, and it seemed to be at least a start. I asked the observer how long the remaining fuel would last. He came back with the gallonage, and said that at the existing cruise power it should last "more than an hour."

My thoughts told me that we couldn't bail out, but we couldn't just fly around until we ran out of fuel. The only thing we could try to do was to get the ground in sight, and with no navigational or approach radio aids, it could be more than a little dangerous.

Before I did anything else, I sent the air gunner back to ask the pilot if he would like to come up front and resume flying. A moment later the gunner came back and told me the pilot had said for me to stay where I was.

I asked the observer if he was sure that we were at the highest terrain height listed on his map. He confirmed that it was. I said that I was going to descend a thousand feet, and I set up a slow rate of descent. I knew that groping for the ground with no idea of where we were was a sure way to kill oneself; but with no compass, and faulty radios, I couldn't think of anything else. I looked at the observer, and the other faces for an idea, but all I got were

Bob Fowler at the controls of a Ventura. His right hand rests on the engine throttles. *R. H. Fowler.*

raised eyebrows and a few shrugs. I wondered if any of them fully appreciated the predicament in which we found ourselves.

I reduced the airspeed to have a little more time to react if we encountered anything in front of us that required a quick pull-up. I put down a small flap angle, and increased propeller rpm so that I could apply higher power if I had to pull up suddenly. Because I was flying solely on instruments, I asked the observer and the others to call out if they saw the ground or any obstacle.

After we had descended to our first target altitude without seeing anything, I asked the observer for the next lowest altitude tint on the map. After he gave it to me, I again did a slow letdown to that altitude. I remember thinking that our barometric altimeter setting was now probably inappropriate, but there was nothing we could do about that. Time and fuel were running out, and I had no better idea than to leave the altimeter setting where it was. The fact that nobody had any objection to what I proposed gave me a small dose of unjustified confidence.

As we descended through the next thousand feet, though we couldn't see anything, we noticed the light outside was becoming noticeably darker, particularly below us. I thought it might be from us being closer to the ground, or was it due to the waning daylight? As I slowed the rate of descent for the last few hundred feet, I was more than a little tense but tried to be a convincing fraud and appear calm. For the observer it must have been even more difficult. He was working with a pilot about whom he knew nothing, and at the same time he was knowledgeable as to what our apparent altitude meant relative to the altitude tints and contours on his map.

After a few more nerve-wracking letdowns, I felt we had run out of altitude for any further descent, and I was certainly not as relaxed as when I had bravely begun the first thousand-foot letdowns. Still alive, and not having hit anything, it seemed best to hold our height in the hope of seeing something of the ground. If it could be believed, the altimeter told us we were getting about as close as one could to sea level over New Brunswick without scraping the ground or getting wet. For all we knew we might have been letting down over one of the many bodies of water in, or adjacent to New Brunswick.

The observer and I were making a few speculations about our height above the ground when everyone yelled at once! I looked up from the instruments as we flew across a small opening in the cloud. For several seconds I could see the fuzzy tops of trees through the snow, not more than what looked, at best, a few hundred feet below. I called out our altitude and gyro heading to the observer and asked him to alert me if I got below that height if another opportunity came to sneak a glance outside. It struck me that I had become increasingly absorbed with catching any glimpse I could of the ground. After a few more breaks, we again lost sight of the ground, and I decided to treat our indicated altitude as ground level for the time being. At least we were over terra firma!

After we had lost contact with the ground, a few more flickering breaks occurred and I decided to do a slow 360 while maintaining the altitude at which we had stopped, in the hope of coming back over the breaks.

Maintaining a shallow bank angle, I commenced a turn to the left and held our altitude as accurately as I could. During the turn we had a few fleeting glimpses of the ground, but we held our height, and before we had turned through the complete 360 degrees, we flew across a good-sized hole where we could see the ground. This hole seemed larger, and as I straightened out on the original heading, I could again see treetops. I tried losing a few feet, and for a short time I kept the trees in sight while we flew level just above them. I had persistent thoughts of hills and power lines.

We stayed on the original course for a number of minutes flying through almost solid cloud and snow. For short periods of time we could fly one or two hundred feet higher and still get occasional snapshot views of the ground. There was simply no rule to apply, but we looked to be damned low. At best, forward visibility of the ground for these meagre periods could not have been more than a few hundred yards. We were sure the altimeter setting was in error as it showed us to be higher than we obviously were, but we had no idea as to how much the ground below us was above sea level. We had more fleeting glimpses of small clearings and open areas, but the visibility and lack of detail gave no opportunity to map read.

I began to think that if I could find a large clearing or a road I might be able to put the Vent down on its belly. I kept this to myself. Almost as though the thought gave birth to fact, we angled across a narrow road, and just as suddenly it was gone. I did a slow turn to recapture it. We crossed it again at a smaller angle, and with a quick turn I was able to stay parallel with it on my left. The consensus in the cockpit was that, "A road should lead *somewhere*, after all that's what roads are for."

The road became slightly wider, and we could occasionally see wheel tracks in the snow that mostly covered it. We crossed a smaller road, but decided we would stay with our original road because it seemed more prominent. After crossing two more small roads, we glimpsed fields on both sides, which looked so good that I again did a large 360 to have another look. There were no houses, but the clearings looked woefully small for a Ventura, so on we flew. In a matter of minutes, we came upon a few good-sized farm fields. I was about to begin another turn for a better look when we flew off the shore of what at first we thought to be a lake, but soon saw was a river. Now this was something!

Again I commenced a turn to the left, and after a few moments someone in the cabin said they had seen some lights on our right. Sitting on the left side of the aircraft, I had missed seeing them. My best view of the ground was from the left side, with the result that I usually did turns to the left. I continued the turn, and after a few moments, the fellows again said they could see some lights. I reversed the turn, and in moments, through the snow I saw a number of lights against the snow-covered ground. I adjusted the turn to bring us more directly over them.

As we came over the lights, I was surprised to see that we had found what looked to be a large town on the bank of the wide river where it made a big ninety-degree bend. The town even had a racetrack! Railway tracks went through the place that suggested a reasonable size. We speculated that it might even be a city. In the come-and-go visibility in the snow, the best we could see was intermittent fuzzy views of streets and houses on the ground in front us.

The observer said, "Caribou, Maine, is on a river."

It would be the most amazing luck if this was Caribou.

After a moment or two I observed, "That river has mud banks, which would normally be caused by a tide." After a little thought, the Observer agreed. "That's right," he said, "but Caribou is nowhere near a seacoast."

There are not very many large centres of population in New Brunswick, and we had a mind-set that we had flown far to the northwest. We were stumped to find anything on the map in that direction that made any sense. I speculated that if we ignored the fences we might be able to get down in one piece on the racetrack, which I immediately regretted—but it seemed to give us a lift.

While I was wheeling around the tops of the houses trying to hold altitude accurately, in the middle of the town I noticed what looked like one or two wooden RCAF hangars surrounded by wet pavement. All wartime wooden RCAF hangers were the same, and I knew that these were the standard variety. At least we were over Canada, but what would hangars be doing

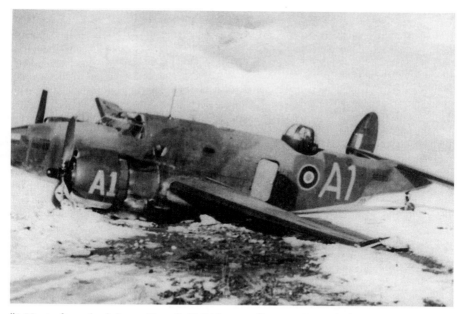

"A Vent after a bad day at Pennfield Ridge, NB," was Bob Fowler's description of this 34 OTU Ventura following a landing mishap. *R. H. Fowler.*

in the middle of a town? It very slowly began to sink in. The only place I remembered where there were hangars in towns was where they were used as drill halls or gymnasia! The last place in living memory where I had seen any RCAF hangars in the middle of a large town, was the place where I had trained for four months before I went to Pennfield, and that place was Moncton! We were looking at the RAF Personnel Reception Centre in the centre of Moncton!

I turned to the observer. "I know this place," I said. "It's Moncton!"

He looked at me with a grimace and echoed, "*Moncton?*"

He was now sure that this stand-in pilot had gone bonkers, and I can't say I blamed him.

"How could this be Moncton, that's only a short distance east of Pennfield?"

I said that was true, and gently observed that we had no idea where we had been flying for the last three hours or so.

I then said that I was going to look for my cousin Fred Ward's house that I had visited several times during my four-month stay in Moncton. In less than half of another circuit of the town, I located the house and saw Fred's back yard disappear beneath us. I now had no doubt as to where we were. At the same time, my mind rebelled at the thought that after the hours of flying we had done, of all places we had reached *Moncton*? We could have flown to Moncton several times in the past few hours.

I said this to the observer, who looked back at me forlornly and said, "There *is* a big bend in the river at Moncton, but . . ."

"I'm going to fly east from the town along that main road," I said, "and if we don't see an airport in less than five minutes, I'll bring you back and we'll land on the racetrack." I had no stomach for belly landing on that racetrack.

With a helpless shrug, and meagre enthusiasm, he stared at his map and said, "Okay."

I finished the turn to line up with the Lakeburn Road. As Moncton disappeared behind, we were again following a road, but this one had cars on it. The familiar bus ride from town was covered in minutes, and when the airport materialized, there was great hooting from the area behind the cockpit. We flew across the Moncton Airport and No 8 SFTS, both of which were behind us before I had a chance to say anything.

I wanted to get back to the airport on a heading that lined us up with a runway, so I turned left to fly back past the airport parallel to the main runway which I had seen when we flew across the airfield. After I was sure we had passed the airport coming back, I started a left turn back to it, and hoped the resulting racetrack pattern would bring us over the airfield on the original heading. It did, but the gyro heading made no sense, and we were too close to do anything.

I couldn't get lined up with a runway, but after a small turn to the right to parallel the longest runway, I reset the gyro to zero to simplify our orientation to the runway.

We were still forced to stay very low, and we regularly lost sight of the ground. I concentrated on an accurate but shallow 180 degree turn to the left. Flying very low in such poor visibility meant that extended turns had to be done carefully.

Again when the clock told me we had passed the airport on the return leg, before entering the final left turn, we performed the landing check, lowered the landing gear and approach flap. After straightening out on the approach heading, I slowed to the approach speed and waited for the airport to appear. The runway came up well to my left but we were too close and too low to do any aggressive turning to get lined up. Reluctantly, I increased power and we flew on past for another circuit. I looked at the fuel gauges and decided that, at this stage, if I had to do a dozen approach patterns, I wasn't going to lose the airport or try a risky landing from a bad approach.

As we passed over my old alma mater, I had a fleeting glimpse of people standing in the snow out in front of the RCAF control tower building. They were not waving at us. On the previous pass I noticed we were attracting the same kind of attention on the civilian side of the airport, and I remembered seeing people stopped on the sidewalks of Moncton who seemed to be looking up at something. I had a gnawing feeling that when this was all over I would probably be court-martialled.

When I turned onto the approach heading, I didn't like to think about how we would go about re-finding the airport if it didn't come into sight within the number of minutes I had allotted to the approach leg. I hadn't adjusted the return leg and final approach headings enough, as this time we were to the left of the runway, and too close in when it came into view. It was just not possible to get safely positioned for a landing. With an Anson, maybe—with a Ventura, never.

When I increased the power for another overshoot, I glanced at the fuel gauges to get an idea of how long this could go on. At least the needles were still moving. The observer noticed and said, "We are getting low on daylight too."

On the next try, suspecting the wind might be behind us on the final approach, when I punched the clock I added a little more time to the return leg to give us more distance for a sensible final approach.

The timing and headings of the circuit procedure were also adjusted in the hope of splitting the difference between the previous two approaches. On this our fourth approach (or was it the fifth?), I was hoping to have a bit more time for a close-in course adjustment. I reduced power. After slowly pushing the propeller pitch levers all the way forward, I put the undercarriage and approach flap down earlier, and slowed to the approach airspeed well before the runway came into view.

It worked. We were a little to the right, but there was enough time to select full flap and make a small adjustment to the left.

At the threshold I eased the throttles back to idle. As we crossed the edge of the runway, the airspeed was correct, but we seemed fast. This was the lowest weight at which I had ever landed a Ventura, and with the flaps still creeping down to the "full" position, we floated. Were we landing downwind? I didn't much care.

The feel of the wheels on the snow-covered pavement was wonderful!

While we were using up runway I noticed a few men running to the right side where some others were standing. I had landed on a runway under repair—and downwind! Using the brakes gingerly, the Vent finally came to a halt just before reaching the last few yards of the runway. The combination of a slippery snow surface, a large aircraft, and a tailwind made a runway that for four months I had thought was quite long for an Anson II, seem very short. But we were stopped!

The end of the runway was just visible over the nose, and turning around looked a bit tight unless we could let the right mainwheel go off the edge. Somebody said the ground should be frozen, which was not comforting. With the left wheel held stationary with brake (bad handling), I did a sharp turn to the left, and it was quickly clear that we could turn around without any trouble.

With all of 260-odd hours total flying time, including sixteen hours on J3 Cubs, I was back at my old SFTS. All I now had to do was successfully taxi the Vent to the RCAF tower building. The pavement was slippery, and I went so slowly that the crew thought we would never make it.

We parked on the apron in front of the tower beside a huge Curtiss C-46 Commando. We could almost park under its wing. For all its size, the Commando had only two engines, and I remember thinking that they were the same Pratt and Whitney R-2800 engines we had in the Ventura. After we were waved into position beside the Commando, a number of people congregated around us. I thought they were probably waiting to grab me. Things looked black.

The last time I had been on this pavement I was LAC Fowler, R.H., R-175475. It would be an understatement to say that I enjoyed parking the Ventura.

When I got the signal to shut down, I took a last look at the fuel gauges. With the tail on the ground, there wasn't enough fuel to move the needles. Somebody asked how many more approaches we could have completed before the tanks went dry. I didn't even want to think about that. The only thing of which I was sure was that we were actually on the ground. It seemed to have taken a hell of a long time to get to Moncton of all places!

All was quiet after the propellers stopped turning. I didn't want to miss anything on the shutdown check, and by the time I had unbuckled the parachute and seat harness, everyone had left the aircraft. A few heads were shoved through the rear fuselage door, and one of them with a very mature voice said, "The OC Flying would like to talk to the captain of this aircraft."

I walked aft and jumped to the pavement, almost into the arms of the Squadron Leader who owned the voice and introduced himself as the OC Flying.

He asked, "Are you the captain of this aircraft." I replied that, no, I was not the captain.

He stated that I had taxied it in, and I agreed that that was true.

He asked if I had landed it, and I replied that that was also true.

He then said he would like to have a chat with me in his office because he had to fill in the Air Traffic Control people on the details of our flight.

As we walked in, I told him I had received my wings at Moncton in August. For a moment he became almost friendly. "Well, we must have done something right." Only supreme self-control prevented me from observing that we had encountered a few things they had not covered.

During our chat, I learned that Pennfield had put out an alert to watch for three Venturas that had been unable to land due to a snowstorm. Two hours after the alert was transmitted, two of the Venturas, both flown by Dutch Navy crews had landed near Montreal, but we were unreported for two more hours after that, and Pennfield had become very worried.

The S/L asked why *we* had not been able to fly to Montreal where the weather was better. When I told him we had radios that were not working properly, and an unserviceable magnetic compass, he said, "They didn't mention any of that in the alert."

He asked me why I was flying the aircraft. I told him the other pilot had to relieve himself and, while I was doing the flying, we had found Moncton—which was true. He asked how long I had been doing the flying? I said I didn't know—which was also true. He then asked how we had found Moncton, and in as few words as possible, I told him. His were the second set of eyes to be rolled to the ceiling that afternoon. He then wagged his head a few times—in the "no" sense—before giving me a funny stare and left it at that. His parting remark was, "In case you are interested, Trans-Canada Air Lines did not get in this afternoon. You caused one hell of a stir in Moncton, and also with a lot of people who watched you trying to land here. I will say one thing—you have great patience."

That night there was an unexpected reunion in the officer's mess, with instructors I had known when I was a pupil, and a few others with whom I had trained before I attended the SFTS at Moncton, but who were now instructing there. I had gone through No 4 Elementary Flying School at Windsor Mills, Quebec with David Lewis, a good friend from Pittsburgh. I had known Don Douglas from Peterborough, Ontario, at No 3 Initial Training School in Victoriaville, Quebec. Steve Forbota and I had learned to march together at Manning Depot in Toronto—and others.

The snow continued until the next morning, and after it finally stopped, a Ventura arrived from Pennfield bringing a pair of instructors and a technical crew to prepare and ferry *our* aircraft back to Pennfield. I went back in the Vent that had just arrived, and the others returned later in the day in the other aircraft after it had been fueled and a new magnetic compass had been installed and swung. By then I had lost all interest in the gun turret.

On arrival at Pennfield, again I was taken in tow at the door of the aircraft by a Squadron Leader; this time C. R. Skinner RAF, DFC, and Bar, the Chief Flying Instructor of 34 OTU, and another senior instructor I had seen many times but did not know. We went straight to Skinner's office where he treated me to a very detailed chat. I learned that he had been talking to the people at No 8 SFTS in Moncton and was aware of most of the details of our flight. His last question was, "What do you think might have happened if you had not been in the aircraft?"

I guessed that the pilot might have burst his bladder.

Skinner spun around in his chair with his back to me, and for several seconds his shoulders jiggled and he made funny little noises until he took a deep breath, cleared his throat, and without turning around said, "Thank you, Fowler, you may go," and I went. No mention of our flight was ever again made while I was at Pennfield, and I was never court-martialled.

Over the years, I have often thought of that flight with the stuck compass. From a more mature perspective, I have wondered if my presence might have caused the other pilot to have been less relaxed than he might have been if I had not been in the aircraft. He might not have bothered to attempt the extra circuit, and even if he had, he might have had no problem getting into Pennfield, Blissville, Montreal, or Moncton, even if his bladder *had* burst. I will never know. I have never felt entirely at ease with the thought of what might have happened had our positions been reversed. I don't know how he spent the rest of his war.

But I do know that our getting away with such a grope for the ground— even without having to figure out the name of the town we found—was a one-in-a-million piece of the greatest of good luck.

During my training in Canada, and later in England, before and after I became involved in daylight tactical operations, like many other wartime aircrew I witnessed a number of flying accidents in which all or most of the aircraft occupants lost their lives. In a few of these instances, we were assembled for a briefing in which we were informed in great detail, of the circumstances which led to the accident and with particular emphasis on the error, invariably assigned to the pilot, which led to the accident. We were sometimes treated to heavy preaching on the course of action that *should*, or *might* have been taken which, of course, would have prevented the accident. Accidents which took the young lives of pilots who only a year or two previously had been riding bicycles—before they had any real experience, or had been in action—always seemed a sad waste.

I still wonder just where we went during the hours it took to make the thirty-minute flight to Moncton.

The RCAF's
"Flying Ground Crew"

A Different Kind of Flying:
Target Drogue Operation

MICHAEL J. COLLINS

Born in Dublin, Ireland, Michael Collins came to Canada as a child in 1928. His family began farming in what is now Clearwater Township near Barrie, Ontario. When he reported to the RCAF in May of 1943, he hoped, like most volunteers, to become aircrew. But, for reasons he will explain—again like many others—he was instead streamed for training as ground crew, specifically on General Duties (GD). He served at Lachine and Mont Joli (where he edited the station newspaper) in Quebec, and Centralia in Ontario. Although he applied for remustering as aircrew and was turned down, he nevertheless did manage to get into the air as a volunteer drogue-target operator. The flying time he would amass was equivalent to that of many operational aircrew. He flew in war-weary Fairey Battles, veterans of the Battle of France; and in obsolete Northrop Nomads, prewar army-cooperation machines obtained from the USAAF.

Although the importance of ground crew is widely acknowledged, their actual contributions, compared to pilots and other flying airmen, are largely unsung. Few stories have been written by or about their activities. An organization as large as the RCAF at its operational peak obviously included an immense infrastructure. In late 1944, while the RCAF had more than twenty-eight thousand aircrew overseas, over thirty-one thousand ground crew maintained their aircraft. Michael Collins's story is only one of a thousand such accounts that could be told by those airmen who did not have wings on their tunics.

After his discharge, Michael returned to farming but shortly thereafter sold his farm to become a civilian employee on the maintenance staff at Camp Borden (now Base Borden, near Barrie, Ontario). When he transferred to Transport Canada fifteen years later as a technical officer, he was foreman of all Base Borden cleaning staff. In the nine years preceding his retirement he was Duty Manager at Pearson (Toronto) International Airport. While residing in the Toronto area, both Michael and his wife obtained honors degrees in history and sociology from York University. Michael Collins has also had "some success writing short fiction, general articles and essays." His article appeared in the Winter 1998 issue of the CAHS *Journal*.

"**D**id you see that off the port wing?"

"No, not with the grass going by."

I was flying as a Drogue Operator, a crewman in a Fairey Battle, with a pilot who liked to make a long, low approach.

"I'm going around again. As we come in, look for a clearing in among the pine trees."

With the Battle's Merlin bellowing, we climbed away from the approach runway and rejoined the circuit. As we again came in to land, the pilot said, "Watch."

"You drive, I'll watch!"

Then I saw what he was talking about. In a clearing surrounded by scrubby evergreens, a group of airwomen were jumping up and down, waving at aircraft on the approach. They were sunbathing in the buff.

"Those're spruce trees, not pine," I told him.

"Farmer! Boy, that was something!"

We landed, turned off the runway at the taxi strip, and rolled to the Drogue Hangar area.

When World War II commenced, my friends were set to serve King and Country as aircrew—high adventure in the skies. But only one of us had the educational requirements to join the RCAF as a wireless air gunner. He died when his bomber crashed on takeoff.

The rest of us? Some joined the army; some joined the RCAF as ground crew. Me? Well, I stayed on the farm. "Producing food," said father, "is just as important as serving in the Armed Services." Besides, I did not have my Entrance Certificate, a prerequisite for joining the RCAF. We also had a large mortgage on our farm, (a thousand dollars was then a large mortgage) and he felt he needed my help to farm.

Father relented enough for me to join the local Reserve Regiment. I bargained with him to cut cordwood in our woodlot during the winter, and grow extra fall wheat to pay off the mortgage. Then I would join the RCAF. Cutting cordwood was slow work. Father figured that by the time I accomplished the woodcutting, the war would be over. I bought a four-foot Swede saw and that sped up the woodcutting. Between selling cordwood and extra bushels of wheat, the mortgage was retired.

When I went before the local High School Entrance Board, the members proved sympathetic toward a young man who had read more pulps of Great War air stories than he had Shakespeare. I was granted my high school entrance certificate. By then I was a Sergeant in the Reserve Regiment and a Regimental Signaller. I was adept with Morse code and the Aldis lamp. My weapons' training included machine guns. Joining the RCAF as a wireless air gunner seemed a certainty.

In the fall of 1942 I applied to join the RCAF. "Medically unfit for aircrew," said the RCAF medical examiner to me, but months later I was a crewman in drogue ships, flying several hours daily, helping to train air gunners. I was flying, not the way I had hoped and expected, but flying. I was offered General Duties or Service Police. I chose GD. I was certain that later I could remuster to aircrew. My reporting date was 20 May 1943.

Reporting in at Toronto, I was posted to Manning Pool in Lachine, Quebec, for orientation and Basic Training. Basic Training was more "Joe" jobs than training. I was seconded to the Bakeshop to do clean-up work. Thanks to the baker who, among his duties, included resting on the long worktable while he told me what to do, I learned all about mixing cake batter. Baking cakes, hundreds of pounds at a time, was not a skill I had expected to acquire in the RCAF. I also had a turn at painting—large doors with a one-inch paintbrush and window frames with a four-inch one.

Our Basic Training completed, I was posted to a Bombing & Gunnery School with a dozen other GDs, somewhere along the shores of the St. Lawrence River. On the way east in the train, an airman who appeared to know something about where we were going, said that German submarines had sunk several ships near where we were posted. A war on our doorstep? We had not heard about it!

Next morning, two blue-coloured RCAF stake trucks were waiting for us at the railway station in the small town of Mont Joli. Some of our group worked in the Men's Mess Hall, and some were assigned to the Turret Section, where gunnery trainees learned how to handle various types of gun turrets. The remainder, including myself, became grounds workers. The one-

and four-inch paintbrushes followed me from Manning Depot. Months later, I reached the heady rank of Aircraftsman First Class, and the only machine the RCAF had entrusted to me, besides the floor-model food-mixer of the bake shop, was a lawn mower. I remembered what father had said about growing food.

I did manage to get a flip in a Fairey Battle, a drogue ship. These yellow aircraft, with diagonal black stripes on the fuselage and wings, towed drogue targets. As we crossed the tarmac to their aircraft, the crew explained to me how target towing was done. I was grateful for the consideration they showed an AC1 flying for the first time. Ten days later, the same crew were killed when their Battle crashed. We were told that a glycol leak was the probable cause.

I also discovered that Drogue Operators were mostly GDs and that an aircrew medical was not required for that duty. I immediately requested a transfer to Drogue Flight. I was told to forget it. There were so many airmen ahead of me waiting to transfer that by the time they got to me, the war would be over. They did take my name but for me it was back to the grounds. I tried to remuster to aircrew after that, but with the same dismal results as before.

Then Drogue and Gunnery Flight had a series of non-fatal accidents and many airmen on the Drogue Flight list lost interest in flying. When I least expected it, I was told to report to Drogue Flight. Some GDs in that Flight worked in the Dropping Zone, retrieving drogues that were released from the drogue aircraft. I thought that was where I would be working. Instead I was given a tour of the Drogue Hangar with a Leading Aircraftsman as my guide. In quick order, I was shown where the Drogue Operators did repair work on the towing gear and the packing room where drogues were bundled and tied securely with light string. I was paraded through the Ready Room with its row of metal lockers. This was where the Drogue Operators kept their flying gear and where they dressed for flight. I saw the flight schedule board, where aircraft and crews were matched.

Then we crossed the tarmac and climbed into the rear cockpit of a Battle. I was shown how the short, metal-ringed drogue tie ropes were fastened to the drogues. The LAC explained and demonstrated how the metal-ringed end of the rope was threaded over the towing and release cylinder onto the towing cable and where the seven drogues were stored in the Battle, ready for streaming. Finally, I was shown how a drogue and cable were streamed out under the Battle's fuselage and how to control the towing winch with the brake handle. I had a quick look into the crowded rear cockpit of the other

Michael Collins with one of the Northrop Nomads used by the RCAF to pull
target drogues. *M. Collins*

towing aircraft, the smaller Northrop Nomad. The cable winch in both air-craft was directly behind the pilot's cockpit.

I was issued full flying gear, including a Mae West life jacket because training aircraft had gone down in the St. Lawrence River. I was shown how to keep track of my flying hours in my logbook and I was assigned a metal locker for my gear. I saw the daily weather report; as an ex-farmer I was interested in weather and would keep a tab on the reports.

That afternoon, fully accoutred, I went up in a Fairey Battle on the three o'clock line of five aircraft with my LAC guide. He streamed the cable with the first drogue, and after that I did the remaining four exercises. He told me what to do and corrected me over the intercom. Two-and-a-half hours later, when we landed and returned to the Drogue Hangar, I was pronounced a trained Drogue Operator.

The next day I flew in the rear cockpit of a Nomad for the first time. Then for the next few days I flew in the rear cockpits of Battles and Nomads, almost sweating blood as I learned what drogue operating was all about.

There were other things I had to learn about my new flying duties. I would be granted twenty-eight days annual leave, the same as aircrew. I would be paid seventy-five cents for each day flown. Drogue Operators wore no wing or any badge that indicated they were on continuous aircrew duties. If I asked to be relieved of flying duties there would be no stigma attached—but it meant a return to "Joe" jobs. Fortunately, experienced crewmen were willing to share their knowledge with a greenhorn. I found that the Drogue Operators were a tightly knit group, with the élan of aircrew. We were proud of our flying contribution to aircrew training.

As I've said, we used two aircraft types towing gunnery targets at No 9 B&G School: the Fairey Battle and the Northrop A-17A Nomad. The sturdier and larger Battle was more suitable for this work with a rear cockpit that afforded a comfortable working space. Its Merlin III delivered 1,035 hp. The Nomad was much smaller with a span of forty-seven feet eight inches com-pared to the Battles' fifty-four feet. You had to work from your cockpit seat as there was no room to move around. This two-seater aircraft was a cast-off US Army Air Force light attack-bomber, a relative of the RCAF's Northrop Delta and of the US Navy's Douglas Dauntless dive bomber. It had a P&W Twin Wasp of 825 hp.

Our drogue aircraft flew to a rendezvous south of the school. It circled at about 2,500 feet until it matched up with a gunnery ship. They then flew out over the St. Lawrence River at Metis Beach and followed the thirty-five-mile

After this forced landing, Nomad 3511 was soon repaired and back in the air.
M. Collins

gunnery range west to the outskirts of the city of Rimouski. As the two air-craft approached Rimouski—the trainee gunner having peppered the drogue (he hoped), the gunnery aircraft broke off the exercise. Both aircraft flew back to the B&G School where the gunnery aircraft picked up two new trainees and returned to the rendezvous. We flew over the DZ at about 1,000 feet and I dropped the fired-on drogue and streamed a new one. Our aircraft rejoined the rendezvous and matched up with another gunnery ship.

When we began a gunnery exercise, I streamed the drogue, cable, and release cylinder on pilot command. I let the cable unwind a few hundred feet from the winch, controlling it by the winch brake handle. This streaming was done as the gunnery and drogue ships headed out to the river range. Wind force broke the light string on the drogue and it streamed open at the cable's end. From then on, until the gunnery exercises were completed, I made my own decisions on streaming additional drogues but kept my pilot informed. When the pilot told me this was the last exercise, I dropped the drogue by sending the short tie rope, without an attached drogue, down the cable. Then I wound in the cable on the electric winch before landing.

The steel towing/release cylinder at the cable's end was eighteen inches by one and three-quarter inches. It was hollow and mechanized. An internal rod connected two projecting triggers, one at each end of the cylinder. When the metal-ringed tie rope, with the replacement drogue attached, slid down the cable and over the first in-curved trigger of the cylinder, the other reversed in-curved trigger also recessed. This released the streamed drogue from the cylinder. In the split second it took the metal ring to pass down the short distance of the cylinder, the other protruding trigger flipped back into place. The sudden snap of the ring against this second trigger opened the drogue, ready for another gunnery exercise.

Drogues were numbered with large painted-on figures. I kept a record of each gunnery exercise, the time it began and ended, the serial number of both the gunnery and the drogue aircraft, and the drogue we were towing. This record went to Gunnery Training, enabling them to check the trainee's hits on the target.

The gunnery ship generally flew out from the drogue a few hundred feet. If it flew too far ahead of the drogue aircraft most drogue pilots ordered more cable to be released since tracers zipping by fairly close could be disconcerting. Glycol leaks, engine problems, gear that refused to lower and lock into place, drogues that would not release (forcing you to drop the drogue and cable in the DZ), and towing cables over the tail assembly when pilots banked too sharply were routine. Fog or snowstorms that caught us miles from the safety of the School's runways were part of the day's work. By the time I had flown four hundred hours, the familiar farm smells had faded and the smell of hot oil and leaking glycol replaced them.

The other half of an aerial gunnery training team, a Fairey Battle with a gun turret in place of the rear cockpit. *M. Collins*

But there was variety in the air, planned or otherwise. I flew on many weather checks and on some test flights, testing large artillery type drogues to see if they were suitable for our work. When the town of Cabano, New Brunswick, put on a show for the homecoming of VC winner Major Paul Triquet, I was in a flight of three Nomads that shot up the town for the celebrations. I took a small part in the search for a downed Liberator bomber that had disappeared in a storm. The aircraft was not found until after the war ended. I had my share of low flying and that included the close-up acquaintance of the topography of the Shickshock Mountains of the Gaspé. However, the aircraft I crewed in, especially the Battles, flew with the steadiness of trucks. They got you into the air, they let you do your work, and they got you down safely.

As hours accumulated in my logbook, the unexpected did happen. I had pilots fall asleep and fly miles off the gunnery course. With one pilot I flew many miles toward Quebec City before I could awaken him. Fortunately, trimmed Battles could fly long distances safely before they decided to head toward the ground.

By 1943 and into 1944, some anti-submarine patrols were maintained along the St. Lawrence River and the Gulf, although it was known that only a few German submarines remained in the Gulf. A detachment of Eastern Air Command was based adjacent to our B&G School and they used our runways.

One day, as we flew down the Gunnery Range, my pilot saw a long, sleek form running awash in the river. He told me to drop the drogue and cable— we were going back to the School and alert Eastern Air Command! We didn't carry a radio as it had been long since removed for more pressing requirements. I had difficulty persuading him that the form in the water lacked a conning tower and was only a wandering Beluga whale.

On another flight when I streamed a cable and drogue, it jammed into the tail assembly of the Nomad. I tried to release it by working the winch, but I blew all the winch motor fuses including the spares. The drogue stubbornly refused to budge. The pilot was having difficulty flying the Nomad and he ordered me to bail out. I slid the coupe top back and reached forward to get my racked parachute. Suddenly the Nomad lurched forward. The drogue had blown free. The bail-out order was rescinded and the pilot told me to reel in the tattered drogue and the cable. We returned to the School, transferred to another aircraft, and finished our day's work.

I was in one mid-air collision. It occurred as we flew out from the rendezvous towards the St. Lawrence River. Our young pilots visualized themselves as fighter or bomber pilots, and not as flying drogue or gunnery, so they sometimes played games with their aircraft. One game was sliding the wing of their aircraft under the wing of another ship and flipping it over. As we flew out towards the St. Lawrence River, the game went sour and the wing tips of both aircraft shattered. This was the only time I actually put on my parachute.

Both aircraft returned safely to the School where we had to report to the office of the Chief Instructor—considered a man with little sense of humour. Our explanations were so similar he must have had doubts about their veracity. The CI, to be on the safe side of good order and discipline, gave the pilots extra Orderly Duty. The LACs, the two gunnery trainees, and myself escaped with looks from the CI that plainly told us that he didn't believe a word of what we had told him.

The Battle's V-12 Merlin engine was cooled by glycol and leaks could cause problems for the crews ranging from minor to total disaster. One morning I was crewman with the pilot whom, earlier in the year, I had advised that his pine trees were really spruce. As we took off, I smelled glycol. I ducked my head down and looked along the Battle's long inner fuselage. A mist of glycol was spewing up around my pilot who had his coupe top open and his head partially out in the slipstream to get fresh air. He started to say something but it was cut short when he knocked his intercom plug from the connector. I slid my coupe top back because the glycol fumes were getting to me. Still flying low, we joined the circuit. The pilot fired a red flare from his Very pistol, warning the Control Tower and other aircraft on the circuit that we were in trouble. We came around and he managed to line up our aircraft with the runway. The Runway Control truck fired red flares. The runway was not clear of aircraft. Over the pilot's shoulder I could see the panel's landing gear indicator glowing red. Our gear was neither down nor locked. Frantically the pilot worked the hand pump to lower the wheels. A crash tender and an ambulance raced down the taxi strip toward the runway that we were approaching. Red flares still arced upward from the Runway Control Truck. We crossed the School's perimeter fence, almost clipping the top strand of wire. I tightened my safety belt across my upper legs. I had seen what a cowling could do to your face when an aircraft stopped suddenly and you didn't. I sat and waited. If we hit the runway too hard we could be in trouble. The red light in the pilot's cockpit flickered and became green. The control truck's red flares were suddenly green. The tires hit the paved run-

The Fairey Battle, formerly an RAF light bomber, was also adapted for drogue towing. Michael Collins had flown in this machine only a few days prior to this forced landing. The lady seated on the wing eventually became Mrs. Collins. *M. Collins*

way. We had barely averted a wheels-up landing. When we reached the Drogue Hangar, towed there by a Farmall tractor, the pilot had to go to the Station Hospital. He had a large water blister on his left hand from pumping the gear down.

I flew as a drogue operator until 16 March 1945. The weather report for that day read icing above 2,500 feet. We flew above that height and found that the weather report was correct.

By then, the war in Europe was drawing to a close and the demand for aircrew had dwindled. Late in March I was posted to another station. Since this meant a return to "Joe" jobs, I applied for my discharge to return to farming. It was granted a few months later.

I stood on the Parade Square of the Discharge Centre between a pilot and an air gunner who was winged, well ribboned, and vastly outranking me. A Group Captain shook our hands and thanked us for serving King and country. I wondered just what my contribution to the winning of the war had been. No insignia on my uniform advised the Group Captain that I had flown with the RCAF's "Flying Ground Crew," to train members of the British Commonwealth Air Training Plan. While danger had been part of drogue flying, it was negligible when compared to the hazards that overseas aircrews faced daily. Nevertheless, some of our Drogue Operators had been injured in crashes and two Drogue Pilots and two Drogue Operators had been killed at the B&G School during the period of time when I was flying.

Despite the "not fit for aircrew" tag, I had made it into the air, logging almost eight hundred hours of service flying and helping to train twenty-five hundred men who became part of the aircrews that hastened the end of World War II. That, I thought, was something to talk about when you were old.

The large parade was dismissed. As I walked off the Parade Square my thoughts turned to my civilian occupation. I had adjusted from farming to flying, and now I would have to adjust back again. But other thoughts nagged. It seemed to me, just seemed, as I reached the edge of the Parade Square, that I smelled hot oil and leaking glycol.

Flying with the ATA

An Air Transport Auxiliary Pilot's Story

Vi (Milstead) Warren,
with Arnold Warren

Almost sixty-five years ago, the pilot of a light aeroplane playfully decided to give two Toronto high school football teams an unexpected thrill—and buzzed their field. Among the spectators was seventeen-year-old Violet Milstead. Ever since, Vi has been grateful to that unknown pilot who broke the law on a fall day in 1936. Then and there she decided that learning to fly would become the focus of her young life.

In the depths of the Depression money was scarce, and for flying lessons, non-existent. However, Vi was determined. She and her mother set up a wool shop and "like a miser," Vi saved every penny. Two nights a week she took ground school at Western Tech in Toronto. In the fall of 1938, a free introductory flight offered by Flyers Limited of Toronto's Barker Field introduced her to president and chief instructor, C. R. ("Pat") Patterson. While Patterson was one of the great aviation salesmen of the era, Vi needed no persuasion, "Just as soon as the earth began to fall away, I became alive in a way I had never before imagined."

Unexpectedly she faced another hurdle. After her medical, the doctor pronounced her fit and healthy but he had one concern: the length of her legs. Could she safely operate the rudder pedals of an aeroplane? Patterson had her sit in various aircraft, judiciously inserting extra cushions. Vi managed quite well. During her later ATA flying, only the Lockheed Hudson gave her difficulty. The necessary cushions forced her so tightly against the controls that breathing was difficult.

Vi took her first flying lesson on 4 September 1939, and on 20 December, received her Private Pilot's License. Four months later she acquired her Limited Commercial License. But Canada was at war and flying jobs, for pilots of limited experience, were few. Vi went back into the wool business and occasionally hopped passengers or delivered aircraft. In mid-1941, under Patterson's sponsorship, she obtained her Instructor's Licence and worked for Patterson & Hill. As a woman, she would not be lured away by the BCATP jobs available to male instructors. Among her students were Alan Wingate and Bob Fowler whose stories appear elsewhere in this book. Vi instructed until wartime gas restrictions closed down all non-BCATP flying schools.

After the war, Vi resumed instructing and married aviation writer and fellow instructor Arnold Warren. Together they worked for Nickel Belt Airways in Sudbury with Vi mostly instructing and Arnold flying in the bush. Very eloquently, Vi describes her love of flying, ". . I seem to be blessed with a temperament which has enabled me to delight in the challenges of flight, to love its freedom, its self sufficiency, its splendid loneliness, to marvel at the awesome beauty of skyscapes, to pity the earthbound—would they understand? Hardly. How could they?"

The month of January 1943 appears in my logbook as one lonely entry. On the 29th I flew Piper J-3 Cub, CF-BLD, locally. This flight closed my civilian logbook "for the duration." This left me very much at loose ends.

QUESTION: What was a girl to do?

ANSWER: What was there for a girl to do but fly?

QUESTION: How could a girl fly without aeroplanes, gasoline, and a job?

ANSWER: All these things were available with the Air Transport Auxiliary (ATA) in England.

This answer did not come immediately. It must have been in December when Jack Ball who had been flying with me at Patterson & Hill Aircraft told me about the organization. It was recruiting both men and women pilots and Jack was interested. We made inquiries. Eventually we both got there but it took months.

The Air Transport Auxiliary was a paramilitary organization of civilian pilots who, because of age or other reasons, were unfit for military service. Their principal work was ferrying military aeroplanes within Great Britain wherever and whenever required. Mostly, this meant flying fighting aircraft from factories to Maintenance Units where they would have radios and guns installed, from the Maintenance Units to operational squadrons and back

Vi Warren (Milstead) (L) with Pat Patterson and Marion Orr at St. Hubert Airport in the spring of 1940. Toronto Star *via V. Warren.*

again, when extensive repairs were needed. This released large numbers of military pilots for combat. ATA pilots were recruited, and the organization was administered by British Overseas Airways Corporation (BOAC).

Early in January, Jack Ball and his wife drove me to Montreal where Jack and I had interviews with BOAC. They must have been satisfactory because we were both soon notified that we had been accepted. At this time, I had approximately one thousand hours dual and solo in my logbook.

Marion Orr applied a little later and was also accepted. At some point, Marion and I were given a flight test in a Harvard at RCAF Station St. Hubert, Montreal. Since this must have been after we had been accepted by BOAC, the reason for the test is not clear to me now. Pat Patterson was there with a photographer who took the picture of Marion, Pat, and I with a Harvard in the background. This was the first flight for either Marion or myself in an aeroplane with so much power and performance, not to mention retractable undercarriage. I don't recall any problems with the aeroplane. It was a joy to fly and the RCAF instructor was satisfied with us.

BOAC seemed in no hurry to get us overseas. This may have had something to do with the difficulties of flying training in England during the winter. We were finally ordered to Montreal around 1 March and provided with accommodation in a very nice hotel. There we sat for almost two months—with a weekly trip to Dorval to report to BOAC. What did we do with our time? Being girls, we went shopping almost daily as we were on salary, and we had many things to pack in our steamer trunks when the time came to go. We saw a lot of shows. We visited in Toronto, but not often. We looked up every time we heard an aeroplane in the sky, which was often.

Marion and I had little opportunity to be lonely. Our hotel became the target for pilots visiting or passing through Montreal. I recall a visit from Jimmy Henderson, his wife, and two children, who arrived on their way to Nassau, Jimmy's Atlantic Ferry Command base at that time. A former student, with perhaps three hundred hours would drop in. He would be joining the North Atlantic Ferry Command and I would wonder how he would get along. Pilots from the Air Observers School at St. Jean would call when in Montreal. It was never dull. The waiting period ended in the middle of April. We were put on a train for New York, the first leg of our trip overseas. Marion had an aunt in New York and we spent a night with her. The next day we went on board our ship. According to my passport, this was 19 April 1943.

I can't recall the ship's name, but she was a very crowded, medium-size passenger liner. Marion and I were travelling first class courtesy of BOAC, but two American girls shared the small cabin. They may have been nurses. I suppose the trip across was a real adventure, but not of the kind likely to appeal to pilots. We were leaving the security of the American continent to cross the cold, inhospitable North Atlantic in a great wartime convoy, a convoy which would be the target of packs of German U-Boats which would do their best to sink as many of us as possible. Our destination was the embattled British Isles. For more than two weeks we would be continuously exposed to the possibility of disaster, but our role was entirely passive. All we could do about it was hope for the best. How different from a flying situation where a pilot can make decisions and take action.

The word "convoy" is a bit misleading. Except at the beginning and end of the trip, we never saw another ship, let alone any naval action. Nothing happened, at least nothing we knew about. Occasionally we heard noises—that was all. We plodded along day after day, allowed on deck only at certain times and never after dark. This was no great hardship as the weather was cold, wet, and miserable. No visiting between decks was permitted and we took our meals in shifts.

Eventually we landed at Avonmouth (the Immigration stamp in my passport is dated 9 May) and were promptly transferred to an RAF Holding Unit, which I think was at Hullavington. From the Holding Unit, we went to ATA Headquarters, White Waltham, for documentation and a thorough medical examination.

Perhaps I should explain here that while BOAC did the recruiting for the ATA, and theoretically had an overall responsibility for it, this appears to have been a device to provide some basis of legality for a paramilitary unit. In fact, the ATA was an entirely self-contained organization from its Commanding Officer down and it reported, not to BOAC, but to No 41 Group, RAF. It had its own administrative and operational staff supporting more than a dozen ferry pools spaced around the British Isles, pools varying in size from four or five pilots up to more than fifty. It had its own doctors, nurses, engineers, transport, training, and taxi aircraft; and of course, it had its own pilots.

The idea for the Air Transport Auxiliary was conceived in the months immediately preceding the outbreak of war. The plan was to recruit a group of already trained civilian pilots—ineligible for service in the RAF—for general communications duties such as the transport of mail, news dispatches, medical supplies, some VIPs, and ambulance cases—all in light training-type aircraft. Events overtook this plan very rapidly. As early as the end of September 1939, the ATA was being asked to ferry combat aircraft, a demand which never stopped growing during the war years. It became almost, but not entirely, the only function of the ATA. It created a need for an ever-increasing number of pilots, which meant ever-expanding training facilities. The development and growth of those facilities mirrors the development and growth of the ATA.

In the beginning there was no Air Transport Auxiliary school. Potential ferry pilots (men) were checked out at Whitechurch, and when the first women joined the organization on 1 January 1940, they were checked out at Hatfield, all in light training-type aircraft.

The demand to ferry service-type aircraft brought with it the requirement for conversion courses. The first of these was given to four men at the RAF Central Flying School (Upavon, at that time), in September 1939, and it is reported to have been somewhat sketchy. In June 1940 the first women were given conversion courses at Central Flying School on the Miles Master (roughly equivalent to the Harvard) and the Airspeed Oxford light twin.

In October 1940 an ATA school was established at Whitechurch but soon moved to White Waltham, where it shared facilities with an RAF Elementary Flying Training School. The EFTS vacated the field in February 1941, leaving the ATA with the necessary accommodation. Eventually there were about 150 training aircraft of ten different types.

Inevitably the ATA outgrew these facilities. In April 1942 the school was divided into an Elementary Flying Training School and an Advanced Flying Training School (AFTS). The former moved to Barton-in-the-Clay and the latter remained at White Waltham. Training ceased at Barton-in-the-Clay in the summer of 1943 and what became known as the Initial Flying Training School (IFTS) was formed at Thame.

For ATA purposes, aircraft were divided into class types as follows:

Class I – single-engine light types
Class II – single-engine service types
Class III – twin-engine light types
Class IV – twin-engine service types
Class V – four-engine aircraft
Class VI – flying boats

The IFTS at Thame did Class I and Class II training. The AFTS at White Waltham did conversion courses to Class III and Class IV, and the lecture courses for Class V. Flying Training for Class V was done elsewhere. The flow of pilots turned out by these ATA schools joined their predecessors ferrying combat aircraft. Their numbers grew until it was possible to say that every aircraft, British or American, seen in the skies over Britain had at some point been ferried by an ATA pilot.

Documentation and medicals completed, Marion and I were posted from White Waltham to the Air Transport Auxiliary EFTS at Barton-in-the-Clay. The first entry in my military logbook is dated 2 June 1943, *Miles Magister No 48, First Pilot F/O Cowan, 1:00 dual.*

Yes, I was an experienced flying instructor, and yes, I had about one thousand hours, but the check-out was very properly thorough, and in my opinion, not at all overdone. We started at the beginning of the book and worked our way systematically through to the end. By 22 June, when our training at Barton ended, I had 16:30 dual hours and 11:10 solo on the Magister, plus 5:35 solo on the Tiger Moth. While there, Marion and I were billeted in the town of Luton. ATA transport picked us up in the morning and took us home when the day's work was done.

From Barton we were posted to the IFTS at Thame and were billeted in Aylesbury. At first this was in an old house which had been furnished with army cots and other minimum equipment and turned over to a group of girls. Later, as the cold weather approached, we moved to a private home.

My first flight at Thame was on 25 June in a Hawker Hart, a big biplane which had been a prewar light two-seat day bomber. By the end of June, I had 3:10 dual and 3:30 solo in it. Training continued through July with the emphasis shifting to the all-important cross-country work. Our cross-country flying was done in the lower altitudes and we were never permitted to use our radios. Navigation was entirely by dead reckoning, calculation, and compass and map reading.

Map reading in Britain is a very different proposition from map reading in Canada. All surface features are compressed into a comparatively small space and our maps were four miles to the inch. It took some getting used to for pilots not trained in the British Isles. It is also an understatement to say that accurate navigation was essential with military airports, balloon barrages, anti-aircraft batteries, and other defence installations all over the place—along with a great deal of poor visibility.

There were two separate ATA units at Thame, the IFTS and No 5 (T)FP— (Training) Ferry Pool. We transferred to the latter unit at the end of July. During the first few days of August, I did my first ferrying, four short trips in training aircraft. On the 9th I had my first "taxi" flight.

The ATA taxi service was an essential feature of the work. ATA taxi pilots flew the ferry pilots to the airports where they would pick up the aircraft to be ferried, and if at all possible, would gather them up from wherever they might be at the end of the day and bring them home. There were no designated taxi pilots. The work was shared. Two types of aircraft were used for this important work—the single-engine Fairchild 24 (I had flown one at Barker Field) and the twin engine Avro Anson. My first taxi flight was from Thame to Cowley, to Cosford, to Thame in a Fairchild 24; two hours and ten minutes flying.

We did no flying between 9 and 27 August. In the interval we were given an intensive ground school course to prepare us for Class II ferrying. We learned about such things as hydraulic systems, retractable undercarriages, flap systems, braking systems (including pneumatic), different kinds of constant speed propellers and superchargers.

On 1 September, with ground school over, I had forty-five minutes dual and thirty minutes solo in a Miles Master. This aircraft had a Rolls-Royce Kestrel liquid-cooled engine of 585 hp and was an excellent stepping stone to the British fighters. On 2 September, I flew two hours and ten minutes in the Master. On the same day, I flew my first service type aircraft, a Hawker Hurricane. Formal training on Class 11 aircraft ended on 11 September. During those eleven days I had five flights in a Master, five in a Hurricane, four in a Harvard, and three navigation flights as second pilot on a twin-engine Oxford.

I should have mentioned earlier that when we graduated from IFTS at the end of July, we were issued with a numbered flight authorization card classifying us for Class I ferrying. My card was No W-111. This card would stay with me and be endorsed appropriately for further conversion courses to Class II, III, and IV aircraft, etc. I assume that mine was endorsed for Class II on 11 September. Later it was endorsed for Classes III and IV.

Along with the cards, we were issued with "chits" to purchase our uniforms. These were the same cut and style as the RAF officer's uniform, differing in the colour, rank insignia, pilot's flying badge (wings), and buttons. I quote from the *ATA Handbook*:

> "The uniform of the A.T.A. consists of:
> (a) Dark blue R.A.F. pattern uniform with such insignia and rank badges as are mentioned below according to the individual entitlements, and four black buttons of the A.T.A. standard Insignia.
> (b) Light blue R.A.F. pattern shirt and collar, regulation black necktie, black laced shoes or boots, plain black or navy socks.
> (c) Plain dark blue raincoat without rank badges, and plain black buttons.
> (d) Regulation greatcoat with rank badges on shoulders and A.T.A. buttons.
> (e) Dark blue field service cap with A.T.A. badge fixed to the front left side of the cap. Peaked caps, whilst permissible, are not to be worn on ceremonial occasions.
> (f) Gloves, which must be worn or carried, should be dark brown leather.
> (g) Regulation navy blue overalls for flying duties as issued, without flying badges but with rank stripes.
> The uniform for women personnel is exactly the same, but on ceremonial occasions skirts must be worn, with plain black stockings. Hair must not come below the collar, and shoes must be low-heeled."

Note: The only "ceremonial" occasions I can recall were funerals.

The ATA pilot's regulation flying badge was gold-coloured wings, worn RAF fashion.

In regard to rank, the ATA pilot was classed as a cadet until graduation from the IFTS. From there the ranks were Third Officer, Second Officer, First Officer, Flight Captain, Captain, Commander, Senior Commander, and Commodore. Rank was indicated by gold stripes and one-half (narrow) gold stripes worn on the shoulder. Third Officers had one gold stripe. Second Officers had one-and-a-half gold stripes. First Officers had two gold stripes, etc. Pilot personnel wore these stripes against a dark blue background.

My logbook reminds me that I was a Third Officer on 1 August 1943, and a Second Officer on 13 September. Later I became a First Officer. Likely this was after qualifying for Class IV ferrying.

On 14 August 1943, I started to work at No 5 Training Ferry Pool, Thame, as a Class II ferry pilot. By the end of that month I had ferried three Masters, one Martinet, one Tiger Moth, five Hurricanes, and flown four taxi trips in Fairchild 24s.

We (Marion and I) left No 5 Training Ferry Pool 10 January 1944, on posting to No 12 Ferry Pool, Cosford, one of two all-girl pools. The other was Hamble on the south coast. No 1 Ferry Pool at White Waltham, ATA Headquarters, was a mixed pool with both male and female pilots. The CO at Cosford was Marion Wilberforce who had been one of the "original eight" ATA girl-pilots in January 1940. Marion had been deputy CO of the first all-girl pool at Hatfield (before it moved to Hamble) from the time it was formed. She was the first and only CO of No 12 Ferry Pool, Cosford. Cosford is well north of the channel coast, roughly between Wolverhampton and Shrewsbury. No 12 Ferry Pool shared the field with a Spitfire assembly plant. Clearing this plant's production provided us with part of our work.

Marion and I were billeted with an excellent young family, Elizabeth and "Ridgie" Ridgeway. Ridgie was an RAF elementary instructor and later a fighter pilot. They had two children, a girl and a boy. I became godmother to the boy, Martin. Long after the war, my husband, Arnold, and I visited them in their home at Bridgewater.

We settled down to steady work as Class II ferry pilots. For example, from 20 to 31 January, I ferried one Hurricane, three Magisters, six Spitfires, one Reliant, three Swordfish, one Master, and had three taxi trips in a Fairchild.

Marion and I were separated at Cosford. I went to White Waltham for a Class III twin-engine course from 10 to 21 May. She was not at Cosford when I returned. She had taken home leave to which she was entitled and on her return was posted to the all-girl pool at Hamble.

Perhaps the most interesting and exciting time was the buildup for the invasion of Europe on 6 June 1944. As soon as I returned to Cosford from White Waltham on 21 May, I became very busy flying fighters to the south coast. We knew the purpose of the fighters. That was no secret. We didn't know when they would be used. Obviously it would be soon. The fighters I delivered were mostly Spitfires and all were painted with black and white invasion stripes on the wings. I suppose this was because the skies over the invasion beaches were going to be very crowded. The stripes made the aircraft both easy to see in the air and easy to identify.

The organization was excellent. As soon as we landed our fighters on the south coast airfield, there would be airmen at our wing tips guiding us to dispersal points. These might be in such unlikely places as among the trees of an orchard. I suppose this provided camouflage from enemy eyes, but the Allied Air Forces were in absolute control of the Channel at this time and I suspect it was mostly for some place to park the great numbers of aircraft being assembled.

They were thrilling, nerve-tingling days. Everyone was affected by the feeling of momentous events pending. When the great day came, the air belonged exclusively to the Allied Air Forces. We were grounded. We sat, listened to the news broadcasts, talked quietly, or moved restlessly about, and I suspect that most of us offered silent prayers for the boys on the beaches.

Class III ferrying was limited insofar as twin engines were concerned. About the only types covered were Oxfords and Ansons. I ferried the occasional Oxford, along with the usual single-engine work, and was able to take my turn on the taxi Anson. By the end of August, I had 7:15 dual and 44:15 first pilot on twins. On 5 September I was once again at White Waltham for my Class IV twin-engine course. This was on the Lockheed Hudson and the Albermarle. It lasted until 28 September. Then I went back to Cosford for the duration.

The ATA's method of "bringing along" its ferry pilots and increasing their type capability was fantastically successful and that adjective is justified by results. It was also utterly baffling to military pilots and engineers accustomed to Air Force procedures for qualifying pilots on new types.

Let me try to explain: the formal part of my Class II (single-engine service type) training ended with the Hawker Hurricane. Nevertheless, I went on to fly about fifteen different marks of Spitfire and such performers as the

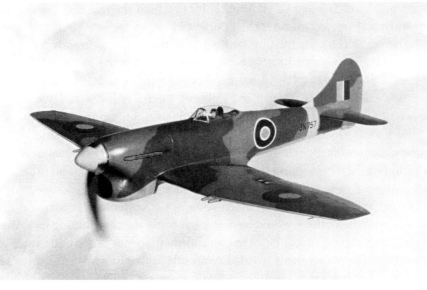

One of the RAF's most potent fighters was the Hawker Tempest. Vi Warren delivered several of them. *Air Ministry*

North American Mustang, the Vultee Vengeance, the US Navy's Vought Corsair, and the Grumman Wildcat. I also flew the much more powerful Grumman Hellcat, the Hawker Typhoon with its Napier Sabre twenty-four-cylinder H-type engine developing almost 2,400 hp, and finally—the ultimate—the Hawker Tempest with the same huge engine, this time developing more than 2,800 hp.

In September 1944, I completed Class IV training (twin-engine service type) on the Lockheed Hudson. I went on to fly Wellingtons, Whitleys, Blenheims, Bostons, Mitchells, and many others. These included that very challenging pair, the Bristol Beaufort and Beaufighter. Lastly, and most fondly remembered, I had the opportunity to fly the de Havilland Mosquito fighter-bomber.

This progression from type to type without further training was made possible, in part, by the ATA's policy of feeding the individual pilot with aircraft types of higher performance as she demonstrated ability. (No pilot was a specialist. They tried to make every pilot as versatile as possible.) Mostly it was due to a remarkable series of ATA-produced publications.

The first of these was *ATA Handling Notes*. They were white covered books—one for each type of aircraft—designed to enable the ferry pilot to deliver safely a type of aircraft that he or she may never have flown before. All marks of an aeroplane were included in one book which was kept strictly up to date. The information in all the books was arranged in exactly the same order and produced in the same style. Mechanical details such as cockpit controls, undercarriage retracting gear, and the fuel system were given first. These were followed by instructions for starting the engines, preparation for takeoff, takeoff, cruising, landing, etc. It included carefully written instructions on emergency action to be taken in the event of such things as hydraulic failure. These books were available on loan to pilots from the Engineering Library at each Ferry Pool. We drew them and studied them in our spare time, especially for types we might be flying in the near future.

Then there was *Ferry Pilots' Notes*, a blue-covered pocket-book issued on loan to us and retained as long as we remained in the service. It did not replace the *ATA Handling Notes*, but contained all the information on each aircraft in abbreviated and well organized form—on one easily accessible card.

With a little experience, it became a simple, routine matter to climb into the cockpit of a new type of aircraft, get out the *Pilots' Notes*, find everything in the cockpit, check engine starting procedures, takeoff and climb procedures, figures on cruising, and approach and landing. Then I would start the engines and go. We were told not to try to remember this data. We were expected to look it up in the book. However, Air Force personnel unaccustomed to working with the ATA could not understand how this was possible. They took a well-justified pride in the challenging and demanding aircraft they flew on combat missions and could not understand how a pilot who had not spent many hours studying it and being trained on it could get into one of their aeroplanes and fly it. There were such queries as:

"Have you got much time on this type?"

The question might be asked as I started to climb into, say, a Beaufighter, in the tone of a man who finds it difficult to believe what he is seeing. It would be accompanied by a very doubtful look.

"No. I've never flown one before."

"Never flown one before?" in an outraged voice. "Then what makes you think you can handle it?"

"No problem. It's all in my book."

"In your book! Good God, girl, you can't fly this aeroplane from a book!"

"I can—from my book."

Let us recognize right here that ferrying an aeroplane safely and efficiently from point A to point B was much less demanding in several important respects than flying the same aeroplane in combat.

We, in the ATA, were pilots. We could fly, and all aeroplanes are fundamentally the same. We had learned how to handle big, powerful engines, different kinds of constant-speed propellers, hydraulic systems, etc. We had available all the performance data for every type of aeroplane—temperatures, pressures, power settings, airspeeds. We could take off, cruise, and land with the best of the boys—perhaps even a little better than some. Their job was to fly the aeroplane in combat—taking off and landing were merely a means to this end. Our job was limited to flying the aeroplane, and we worked at it.

The aeroplanes we ferried were never loaded down with bombs and ammunition and we were required to fly them—within narrow, carefully defined performance limits. There was, for instance, the ATA airspeed established for each type of aeroplane. It would produce the most economical cruising in terms of range and fuel consumption, and the power settings for it were right there in our notes. As I said, the system worked, and worked beautifully, but we really couldn't blame the Air Force boys for finding it hard to understand.

It has probably occurred to the reader that our ferrying program required

Vi Warren (Milstead) at five-foot-two and 115 pounds after climbing down from a Mosquito fighter-bomber that she has just flown from Prestwick, Scotland. *V. Warren.*

a lot of planning and organizing. It did, and the person most visibly involved in this was the Operations Officer. This officer and her staff were among the earliest arrivals at the pool each morning. It was her duty to plan the day's work for the pool, a formidable task, in accordance with the following aims:

a) to move every aircraft to its ultimate destination with as few intermediate stops as possible and by the shortest route;
b) to return all pilots to base the same day, if possible;
c) to apportion the work among the pilots so that flying hours, experience, and advancement in types would be even and fair.

The day's program for ferrying would have been received over the telephone the previous night by a Night Duty Officer from Central Ferry Control for all Ferry Pools. The Operations Officer would have this in front of her. She would also have before her a list of ferry pilots available for duty and their categories, and this would be supported by an intimate knowledge of the development and type-capabilities of each one of them. (Assigning pilots to new types was done in consultation with the CO and her assistant.)

Planning the day's ferry flights and taxi trips to move as many aircraft as possible, in existing weather conditions, and in accordance with the above objectives, was a responsibility I would not have cared to undertake. Our Operations Officer at Cosford was Vivienne Jefferies, an English girl. After the war she teamed up with one of our American girls, Virginia Farr, to run what they call the V-2 (Virginia and Vivienne) Ranch in California. I had a very enjoyable visit with them there in 1952.

When we reported for work in the morning we would find one or more ferry chits in our mail box, or the chits might be handed to us by the Operations Officer. The chit was our authority to collect the aircraft and its equipment. It gave full details of its present location, its mark and type, and its destination. It included a form of receipt for the aircraft, which the ferry pilot was required to give to the authority from whom she collected it; a signal of delivery to be sent to Central Ferry Control immediately after arrival at the aircraft's destination; and a report sheet on the state of the aircraft as she found it.

With chits in hand, our next stop was the Meteorological Office. The ATA had its own Met Service which had been built up during the war to suit the special requirements of ferry pilots whose flying was strictly VFR and without use of radio. Once the pilot was airborne, he or she had no one to help with decisions if encountered bad or unexpected weather conditions. The exacting task of the Met Service was to reduce to a minimum the number of occasions on which the weather she encountered was unexpected. This was a real challenge in the British Isles.

The problem was complicated immensely by the fact that weather tends to arrive from the west. There is a vast area of ocean west of the British Isles from which ships in wartime were not permitted to radio weather information for obvious reasons. The weather information needs of ATA pilots were different from those of the military pilots. Ferry pilots required detailed weather information over a comparatively small area. All Ferry Pool Met Offices presented this information in two standardized forms.

The first was forecasts. Three-hourly synoptic charts were displayed and forecasts for the standard routes flown by the Pool were written on a chalkboard. Met staff were available for individual briefings.

The second was actuals. Maps of the British Isles were covered with transparent plastic on which was shown, in coloured chalk, any area in which conditions were below ATA visibility minimums of eight hundred feet (height) and two thousand yards (distance). In addition, a chalkboard showed actual conditions at a large number of airfields around the country. The individual pilot made his or her own "go, no-go" decision, taking into consideration the weather, the type of aircraft, and the route. Each pilot was required to sign a book in the Met Office certifying that the met information necessary for the flight had been obtained. It all worked remarkably well; but, when dealing with the weather, no system could be perfect. Sometimes we had anxious minutes—or hours.

For instance, I took off from Cosford one morning in a Warwick, which I recall as a great, lumbering twin-engine bomber. I was to deliver it to Kinloss, a Ferry Pool in the north of Scotland, on what turned out to be my longest ferry flight of two hours, forty-five minutes. I had, incidentally, brought the same aeroplane into Cosford from Beccles, a flight of one hour and ten minutes, two days earlier. The trip north was my second in the type.

Immediately after takeoff I encountered very poor visibility, so poor that I would have returned to Cosford if I had dared. I didn't. I couldn't see enough to risk it. The weather was supposed to be improving somewhere ahead so I kept going. There was nothing else to do. The visibility was worse in the Midlands where great quantities of industrial smoke mixed with the vapour in the air. I knew that my course would take me quite close to an en route Ferry Pool and I would have landed there if I could have found it, and if I could have seen enough to make an approach. I could do neither.

The Warwick and I were well into Scotland when the weather changed. The visibility improved quite rapidly and I was happy again. Obviously I had flown from one air mass into another. I eventually landed at Kinloss and parted company from my Warwick.

Air adventures tend to be like that. You run into difficulties, or you get yourself into difficulties. You get out of them and there is nothing much to tell, or you don't get out of them, and someone else does the telling.

After visiting the Met Office, we moved on to Maps and Signals. This was Operational Intelligence. All flights made by ferry pilots came under the category of "non-operational flying in wartime," and in order to fly around the country without getting into, or causing, a great deal of trouble, it was necessary to pay attention to the rules and regulations for non-operational flying. Among the reasons for these rules were the following:

a) to avoid interference with, or confusion among, the active and passive defences of the country;
b) to avoid the risk of false air raid alarms;
c) to avoid the risk of being shot down by our own defences.

The ferry pilot needed current information about the condition of airfields to which he or she would be flying and their local regulations. The pilot was also very concerned about such things as the location of balloon barrages, anti-aircraft installations, practice ranges, and other defence installations. There were areas which could not be entered without advance Routeing because Fighter Command reserved the right to "shoot first and ask questions afterwards" in the case of unidentified aircraft. At the ATA Ferry Pools, the officer responsible for issuing all this information was known as the Maps and Signals Officer, and his or her office was the pilots' Routeing Room.

Balloon barrages protected sensitive areas from low-level air attack and this included aircraft factories. A flight into a factory to pick up a new aeroplane, one of our most frequent assignments, invariably meant approaching through an established corridor in a balloon barrage. This was a thought-provoking operation under conditions of low ceiling and poor visibility with the balloons hidden in the overcast conditions. A visit to the Routeing Room before takeoff to get the most up-to-date information on such things was a must.

I don't remember hearing of any accidents resulting from failure to visit the Routeing Room but there is a story told about one of ATA's most famous girl pilots.

One morning, when ceiling and visibility were both low, she was given a chit to pick up a four-engine Stirling from a factory which was surrounded by a balloon barrage. There was, of course, a corridor through the balloons, a corridor which could be closed rapidly in the event of an air raid alert, and which was subject to change—but not without notice. That morning, for some unexplained reason, the girl failed to go to Maps and Signals for the latest information.

She flew the taxi Fairchild and approached the airfield through the corridor she had used before. She landed, picked up her Stirling, and left by the same corridor. Later she learned that the corridor had been moved. It was not where she had thought it was. She had flown the Fairchild into the airfield and taken the Stirling out of it through the balloon barrage, and without hitting a thing.

With routes and all pertinent information marked on our charts, our last stop was to study the taxi sheet which was posted in a convenient place. From it we would learn who would pick us up, and approximately when. It was always comforting to see in black and white the plans that had been made to bring us, eventually, back home.

The following are typical operations:

On 9 February 1945, I had a taxi flight Cosford to High Ercall, twenty minutes. I ferried an Avenger II, High Ercall to Worthy Down, forty-five minutes. I flew a taxi flight, Worthy Down to Speke, one hour forty-five minutes. I ferried a Vengeance IV from Speke to Hawarden, fifteen minutes. I ferried a Mosquito VI, Hawarden to Cosford, twenty minutes. An unusual feature of that day's work was that I was the taxi pilot on the two taxi flights. Another taxi pilot would have been available to carry on.

On 24 February, I flew by taxi aircraft Cosford to Ansty. I ferried a Mosquito VI, Ansty to Hullavington, thirty-five minutes. I taxied an aircraft, Hullavington to Brize Norton. I ferried a Spitfire VIII Brize Norton to Cosford, thirty minutes. I ferried a Spitfire IX Cosford to Lynham, thirty-five minutes. I ferried a Spitfire IX Lynham to Lichfield, forty minutes. I taxied an aircraft, Lichfield to Cosford.

At the end of a long, hard day, it was a pleasure to see the taxi Anson waiting for you with a familiar figure at the controls; to take a seat among a group of girls from your own Pool amid an exchange of good-natured nonsense; and take off for home. It was all very normal to us. A girl once remarked, as the taxi Anson droned along, "I suppose the people down there look up and say, 'There go our bomber boys to blast the enemy.' What would they say if they could look inside and see a woman up front flying the thing, and six more women sitting in the back, knitting?"

Sometimes the flights could be dovetailed so nicely that there was no need for taxi service. For example: on 30 March, I ferried an Oxford from Cosford to Prestwick, Scotland (terminal of the North Atlantic ferry flights), one hour fifty minutes. I carried a Flight Engineer (a girl) with me in the Oxford for the next trip, which was to ferry a Dakota (my first) from Prestwick to Kemble, two hours. I left the Flight Engineer at Kemble to be picked up by taxi aircraft and completed the day's work by ferrying a Typhoon from Kemble to Cosford, twenty minutes.

So far I have said nothing about "enemy action." In fact, I saw almost none. There was plenty of evidence of it, especially in the south, and our ferry routes often took us there.

My twenty-fourth birthday came in October 1943 while I was at No 5 Training Ferry Pool, Thame, just north of London. A group of us from the Pool celebrated the occasion at the Savoy Hotel in London. During the celebration there was an air raid alert and I suppose we were expected to head for shelters. Instead, we all rushed outside to see what was going on. There was a fantastic pattern of searchlight beams weaving around the sky. Anti-aircraft guns were making a great uproar and producing a splendid display of fireworks. It was very exciting, but no bombs fell near us.

After the allied invasion of Europe in June 1944, enemy aircraft intrusions were few. Buzz bombs and V-2s kept us a bit thoughtful before their launching sites were found and blasted. I was never near the spot where one landed—for which I am thankful.

The spring of 1945 is much too long ago for me to remember any details that are not called to mind by my logbooks and other documents, but I am very sure that we knew the end of the war was approaching. The steady, triumphant advances of the Allied armies into Germany from the west and the east made it inevitable. My last flight in wartime was 4 May to ferry a Typhoon from Lichfield to Milfield, one hour.

I cannot recall much about V-E Day, 8 May. No doubt I reported for flying as usual, learned that there was no flying to be done, and with some of the other girls wandered back to the village. I saw no wild rejoicing and dancing in the streets such as were reported, for example, from London. For one thing, there were few young people in the villages of England to dance in the streets. I believe that most people were doing the kinds of remembering which would give them quite other inclinations.

My next flight was 10 May, two days after the war in Europe had ended: a Beaufighter from Weston to Cosford, fifty minutes. The following couple of weeks were very busy but now pilots were resigning and Cosford closed 24 May. In the period 1 May to the closing of Cosford, I ferried seven Spitfires, three Barracudas, two Typhoons, one Mustang, two Hellcats, two Tempests, four (taxi) Fairchilds, one Hurricane, five Mosquitoes, three Beaufighters, one Beaufort, two Warwicks, one (taxi) Anson, two Wellingtons, and one Westland Welkin.

I am proud of that Welkin. It was a rarity. I think there were only a few of them made. On 15 May I flew it from Yeovil to Cosford, fifty minutes. I recall

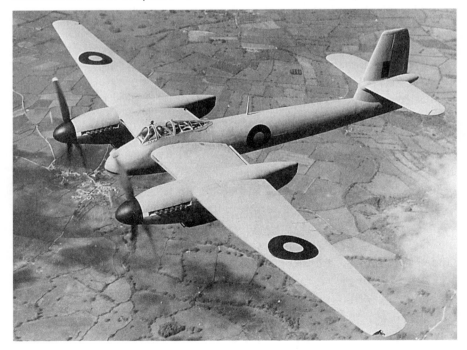

Among the rarest aircraft ferried by Vi Warren was the Westland Welkin, a high-altitude interceptor development of the Whirlwind that never saw operational service. *Westland*

it as a high performance, Mosquito-like twin. No doubt production was stopped—or never started—because the end of hostilities was near. While on this subject perhaps I should say here that during my service with the ATA, I flew twenty-nine different types of single-engine aircraft and seventeen different twins. This does not include the different marks or models of the same make. For instance, I flew fifteen different marks of Spitfire. There were a number of different marks of many military aircraft. I have, for example, three marks of Mosquito in my logbook and a number of other Mosquitoes not identified. There must have been about six.

When Cosford closed, I was posted to No 1 Ferry Pool at White Waltham. Just west of London, White Waltham was nearer to the Channel by many miles, and its pilots, at this time, were picking up aircraft from the continent. I made four trips into Europe during the first three weeks of June. On 9 June, I flew a taxi Anson to Operational Field B56, wherever that was, and from there to Brussels. In Brussels we were provided with accommodation in an interesting old home turned into a hostel. We had one day and two nights to see the city. On the 11th I flew an Auster back to England from a place called Cortrai, two hours and thirty minutes—a long "sit" in an Auster.

On the 14th I was back in Europe ferrying an Anson from B55 to England. On the 16th I brought a Mosquito out of Europe from B77 to Hullavington. On the 19th I ferried another Auster from B55 to Odiham. This concluded my trips to Europe.

In one respect my career in the ATA ended in style. My last three deliveries were a Tempest, a Mosquito, and a Spitfire. On 20 June, I ferried a Tempest from Langley to Aston Down. On 21 June I ferried a Mosquito from Leadesden to Hullavington. Also on 21 June I ferried a Spitfire from St. Athan to Chilbolton. This closed my ATA logbook. It shows 39:00 hours single-engine dual; 388:50 single-engine pilot; 18:25 multi-engine dual; 146:30 multi-engine first pilot.

In these pages I have talked almost exclusively about girl ferry pilots. That is because I was working, except for the last few weeks, in an all-girl situation—girl pilots, girl flight engineers, girl Met Officer, girl Operations Officer, and girl CO. Now I must point out that, while there were approximately eight hundred pilots in the ATA, about seven hundred of them were men. Only about one hundred of them were girls.

In these days, as we hear much about women's lib, it often seems to me that the Air Transport Auxiliary, way back in the years of the Second World War, was one of its greatest manifestations. We girls worked on an equal footing with the men, doing what had been thought to be strictly men's work.

In terms of aircraft deliveries completed, the object of the exercise, the girls held their own. According to some figures they more than held their own. The female wastage rate—those who left the service for various reasons—was understandably a little higher (still less than 5 percent higher), but their safety record was better than that of the men. While 8.1 percent of the men were killed on duty (158 fatalities), the figure for the girls was only 4.9 percent.

Fifteen girls were killed during the five years the ATA was in operation. One of them was Jane Winstone, a lovely girl from New Zealand. She was my roommate after Marion left, and she was my friend. She joined the ATA partly because her fiancé was flying with the RAF. He was killed before she reached England. Jane was taking off from Cosford in a Spitfire, lost control almost immediately after takeoff, and crashed. The cause was probably engine failure. She was the only fatality among the Cosford girls.

Four of us girls from Cosford accompanied Jane on her last journey to White Waltham. We left her there in a lovely churchyard in a plot reserved for ATA personnel. I undertook the sad task of writing to her parents in New Zealand. I treasure in my files their gracious reply.

Most of the ATA girls were English. The remainder came from the United States, Canada, occupied Europe, South America, Singapore (an English girl), and New Zealand. The motto of the Air Transport Auxiliary was "*Aetheris Avidi*, Eager for the Air." It was apt. During the war the ATA flew 415,000 hours, delivering more than 309,000 aircraft.

In the last days of June 1945, with the war in Europe well over, the ATA was winding down. I expressed a wish to return home and tendered my resignation. It was accepted. There were final medical examinations and other formalities. They took a long time. Eventually the ATA allocated me to a hostel in London to await embarkation. I waited and waited. I was still waiting on 10 August when Japan accepted terms of surrender and the whole, long war—six full years of it—came to an end on 10 August, a date which would go down in history. There I was, alone in London with nothing to do. I could not just sit there.

I would describe myself as a lonely soul, and in a sense, this is true. I like people. I enjoy being with them. I have many good friends, a few of the "everlasting" kind. I love a party whether I am attending it or giving it, but I have always found it difficult to take the initiative about such things. Left to myself, I am anything but gregarious.

Vi Warren (Milstead) in December 1939 from the photograph on her pilot's licence. *V. Warren.*

Although this is true, on that so-special day I had to do something.

By this time I had been away from my native Canada for considerably more than two years. My work, my usefulness in England, was ended. I was waiting to go home. I wanted to be home. The next best thing that special day was to meet with other Canadians and I made what was for me an uncharacteristic decision. I went, by myself, to a big old home in London which had been turned into a meeting place for RCAF officers. I was, of course, in uniform.

There I met—or perhaps I should say, there I was found by Jack Riley. This was the same Jack Riley who, a couple of years later, would take over as chief flying instructor for Leavens Brothers Air Services Limited at Barker Field when Arnold and I moved to Nickel Belt Airways in Sudbury, the same Jack Riley who, still later, married Molly Beal. Jack, a boisterous Irishman and highly sociable, tells of finding this little person wearing wings and with Canadian badges on her shoulders, standing by herself.

The waiting ended a few days later. I was assigned to a ship, embarked at Liverpool on 18 August, and sailed for home. There were three ATA girls from the United States on the same ship and they were good company. I have no record of their names but they were inveterate bridge players in need of a "fourth," and they did their honest best to teach me the game. I still don't play.

According to my passport I cleared Canadian Immigration in Halifax on 26 August 1945. I was back home in Toronto by the end of the month.

"Queen-One Cleared for Takeoff"

An AOS Pilot Recalls a Memorable Night Flight

ALAN G. WINGATE

Alan Wingate learned to fly at Barker Field on the outskirts of Toronto, paying for his lessons from the salary he earned working on the construction of Anson IIs at de Havilland's nearby Downsview plant. (Elsewhere in this book his instructor, Vi Milstead, describes her subsequent overseas experiences flying with the ATA.) Leaving de Havilland, Alan Wingate completed the rigorous training, including seventy-eight flying hours, given to would-be staff pilots for the civilian-operated Air Observer Schools (AOS), then being set up across Canada as part of the massive British Commonwealth Air Training Plan. He was based at No 9 AOS at St. Jean, Quebec, flying Avro Anson Is and Vs to train RCAF navigators.

Required to plot courses over hostile territory to a blacked-out target in the dead of night, the air observer was a key member of any bomber crew. He also aimed and dropped the bombs—and manned a gun if necessary. In March 1942, with the need to master more sophisticated navigational aids as bombing was stepped up, it was decided that tracking the aircraft's position was work enough. A bomb aimer/gunner was added to each crew and the term "air observer" was abandoned in favour of "navigator." The navigator and pilot worked as a team, the former providing directions that the latter followed to the best of his ability. Upon them depended the safety of the entire crew. Trust was implicit. Relying upon such skills as astro-observation, when stars were to be seen, the navigator undoubtedly filled the most mentally exacting of aircrew positions. The vast majority of Commonwealth navigators obtained their training in Canada. Ten Canadian AOS would graduate some thirty thousand navigators. An

AOS pilot had also to be a competent navigator. Should a crew became hopelessly lost—following a trainee's instructions—it behooved the pilot to bring them safely home. While not instructors, AOS pilots were expected to comment on student performance and attitude. The navigation-training flight described took place in September 1943. By combining events from several different flights, it typifies such exercises.

Before each flight, aircrews are posted on the briefing room blackboard. Pilots, navigators, and wireless air gunners (WAGs), all assemble in the pre-flight briefing room. On this occasion, the information we receive includes detailed meteorology conditions and a warning of lingering air mass thunderstorms north of our route. Our crew of two navigation students (LAC Jessop and LAC Shakespeare), our WAG (Sgt Bastien), and myself leave and walk along in front of a line of fifty Mk I and Mk V Ansons, parked wing-tip to wing-tip on the dimly lighted tarmac. We locate old *Queen-One* (Q-1), our assigned aircraft for tonight's flight, and climb aboard. Our aircraft has been inspected by a PUI (pilot under instruction) who assures me that she is in airworthy condition. After I complete my own brief outside checks, I enter the Anson by the rear starboard door and move forward to the business end, checking that the battery cables are properly connected and that all of our chest-pack parachutes are correctly secured in their storage locations. The crew settle into their seats. Other aircraft are coming to life with engines running.

With all switches off before starting, the engines are turned over by hand (pulled through) to avoid the hydraulicing of oil which may have seeped into the lower cylinders, and which would result in damage during the start. Using verbal and hand signals to communicate with the engine-starting crew, I flip the big, old-fashioned brass magneto switches at the top centre of the windscreen. They hand-crank our two Cheetahs into noisy life. Some initial vibration smoothes out as all of the plugs come into action. Engine instruments read normal and all flying controls work smoothly with the control surfaces moving in the right direction. The flying instruments act as they should; we are ready to taxi out. Our radios are on, checked for signal strength, and tuned to the St. Jean tower frequency. I call the tower and receive clearance to taxi to the runway in use, No 06.

It seems strange that we are taking off to the northeast even though the upper winds are from the opposite direction. However, winds on the ground are calm and we will be using the longest and most convenient runway in the humid air with the temperature reading a warm twenty-seven degrees centigrade. We move out and taxi to the left along the tarmac in front of other aircraft still preparing to leave.

At the end of the tarmac a ground mechanic collects L-14 forms with each pilot's signed acceptance of his aircraft. We proceed to the engine run-up position at the beginning of the runway in service; we are one of many Ansons waiting, ready to go. The tower clears one machine for takeoff about every sixty seconds. As each Anson climbs off the runway, another receives clearance to leave.

The run-up of each engine to plus two-and-one-half pounds boost with static rpm of 1,850 is normal, as are left and right magneto drops of a few rpm. The oil temperatures and pressures are within limits. The oil pressure gauges on some of these aeroplanes are out on the engine nacelles and must be checked at night by the use of a flashlight—"torch" in a British aeroplane. All checks completed, I set the altimeter to airport height of 136 feet above sea level. Then I set the directional gyro to the compass heading, uncage the artificial horizon, and check for normal position. I will reset the horizon once again when we are in level flight; the directional gyro will be reset to correct for recession every fifteen minutes during the flight. I have the engines at fast idle. I switch on pitot heat just in case there is some moisture lingering in the pitot head from earlier wet weather conditions.

As I watch a white tail-light recede and rise off into the darkness, I speak into the hand-held microphone, "St. Jean Tower: *Queen-One* is ready for takeoff." From my large rubber-cushioned headset I hear, "*Queen-One*, you're cleared to position." The controller's voice is discernable through the atmospheric crackle and static that is ever present on the low-frequency two-way radios of the Second World War era. On a hot and humid summer night, this condition is aggravated by electrical storms still in the vicinity.

I taxi *Queen-One* to position, lining up ready for takeoff on No 06, St. Jean's longest (2,765 foot) diagonal runway. Our climb out will take us directly over the 1943 city of St. Jean de Iberville, Quebec (now St. Jean sur Richelieu). The Anson's differential air brakes, operated by moving the rudder pedals with air pressure controlled by a lever on the front of the quadrant below the throttles, hiss slightly as I straighten the aeroplane on the runway. It is a dark night; I switch on the Mk I's hand-adjustable landing light briefly, to check for skunks, foxes, or other possible obstacles in my path. I dislike using the landing light for takeoff; there is too abrupt a transition, once airborne, from glare to sudden blackness when the light is shut off. Later on, use of the landing light would become mandatory.

"*Queen-One* is ready for takeoff," I say into the mike. From my headset comes, "*Queen-One* is cleared for takeoff; the wind is calm." It is 21:20 local time.

I release the brake's air pressure and move the two throttles steadily forward. Alternately, I walk one ahead of the other as needed to keep the aircraft straight on the runway—until the speed increases sufficiently for the Anson's big rudder to become effective. Then I open the throttles to full-power position against the stops—beyond the stops is a "through the gate" emergency position. We feel pushed back into our seats slightly as the two mighty Cheetahs spring to full power. The boost gauges both read maximum plus two-and-one-half pounds of boost with the automatic mixture control in its full-rich setting. The propeller rpm is 1,900, and 1,800–1,900 is normal with our fixed-pitch props. I press the control column forward slightly to lift the tail to takeoff attitude. At 85 mph I gently bring the control back a little. Without any sensation of doing so, we leave the dark and virtually invisible runway. Outlined only by the flare-path, it disappears beneath us as I lower the nose, accelerating to our safe single-engine climb speed, 90 mph. It has been a typical, almost effortless Anson I departure.

By turning the rugged folding crank on the right side of the throttle quadrant, I adjust the elevator trim-tab to lessen the slightly forward control column pressure. Some rudder trim is also needed, so with my left hand, I reach for the small knobbly rudder trim-tab control located over the side cockpit window and wind forward sufficient to take the rudder pressure from my left foot. In case of an engine failure this little control becomes extremely important; a lot of turning would be needed to help move the rudder fully over to the side of the live engine, keeping the aeroplane straight.

We maintain a steady climb. The second navigator, LAC Shakespeare, occupying the co-pilot's seat for this flight, has the unenviable task of winding up the undercarriage using the large folding hand-crank on the lower left-hand side of the pilot's seat. I must unlock our lowered wheels with a lever on the other side of my seat before Shakespeare can start the 140 awkward turns—using his left hand—to bring the gear fully up to the locked position. Sometimes a kindly pilot will take pity and finish cranking the wheels up himself. For him, using his right hand, it is actually easier. Even with the undercarriage fully retracted, the wheels will still project slightly, a fortunate feature in case of a wheels-up landing.

Alan Wingate in his "office," the cockpit of an Avro Anson Mk V of No 9 Air Observer School (AOS) at St. Jean, Quebec. *Via A. G. Wingate*

The flare path disappears beneath our nose as we climb away from the runway. The transition to complete darkness requires that I switch from visual flying to reliance on the flight instruments clustered together on a cushioned panel directly in front of me. The standard pattern on most British military aeroplanes is, from top left to right: airspeed, artificial horizon, and rate of climb. Bottom, left to right, are: altimeter, directional gyro, and the Reid and Sigrist slip and turn (turn and bank).

We climb at a steady 500 feet per minute with airspeed now 100 mph. I've brought the throttles back to normal climb power and I move the automatic mixture control to auto-rich with the boost readings on both engine gauges at plus one-and-one-half pounds. All engine readings are okay, double-checked for our ascent to our operational altitude. Since we are one of twenty-five aeroplanes still in our traffic zone, I fly *Queen-One* about 80 percent instruments and 20 percent visual. The other machines, visible only by their navigation lights, are spaced out in a large ascending spiral up to 6,000 feet.

During our initial climb, the red warning lights of the Singer Manufacturing Company's tall smokestack had loomed up ahead and then dropped down to pass beneath us. We cross over part of the well-lighted industrial area of the city, noticing the long dark area that indicates the path of the Richelieu River between St. Jean and Iberville. We recognize the lighted bridge between the two communities and then, to port, the brightly illuminated dam north of St. Jean. As well, in the darkness to port, we are able to pick out the barely visible shapes of the 1,250-foot-high Rougemount and the 1,350 foot Mount St. Hilaire before we start our first turn to the left at about 900 feet ASL.

We continue to climb in a wide circle around the airport to our planned operational height of 6,000 feet. At that height, we will set a westerly course on the first leg of our exercise. The wheels are now fully wound up and locked. The red U/C warning lights are on with small night shields over them to cut the glare. With the gear down, they will be replaced by green lights. Two curious little knobs, a second warning device, have retracted like snails into their respective tubular hiding places, later to reappear when our undercarriage is again down and locked for landing. Thirdly, should we fail to heed these two warning devices, a loud horn will sound if the throttles are closed with the gear not down and locked—rudely waking us to that realization. Now I am getting ahead of myself.

At our cruising altitude, I level the aeroplane prior to our starting point in order to establish cruising speed, synchronize the fixed-pitch propellers with the throttles, and move the mixture to auto-lean for economical cruise and thus maximum endurance. The boost is set at minus one-and-one-half pounds for normal cruise, oil temps are okay and the oil pressures are checked once again with the essential flashlight. Indicated airspeed is 120 mph.

LAC Shakespeare disappears to the back of the cabin to assume his duties as second navigator assisting Jessop. The latter has been busy since the time of our pre-flight briefing. Boarding the aircraft he immediately began making entries in his navigation log and arranging his charts and equipment along with an assortment of astronomical tables, manuals, and almanacs on his work table behind the pilot. He has his Mk III navigational computer and at his desk there is a duplicate flight panel with an airspeed indicator, an altimeter, and an outside air temperature indicator. He is required to enter into his flight navigation log all headings and other pertinent information affecting the entire flight such as: time of takeoff, time to height, visibility, outside air temperature, and any unusual circumstances which may affect his performance. By using the forecast winds obtained at our pre-flight briefing, outside air temps, and true airspeed; and by applying the local magnetic variation and compass deviation, he determines the initial compass heading to our first turning point.

The very busy Jessop hands me a slip showing the compass heading, to be set over the station, to our first destination, the tiny village of Killaloe Station, 204 miles to the west, up the Ottawa Valley. I set *Queen-One* on course—along with twenty-four other aircraft in our flight, all presumably on the same heading for the same destination. There are approximately fifty Ansons out tonight. Strangely, on this relatively clear but still humid evening in September 1943, we will see very few of the other aircraft, and such sightings will only be passing navigation lights. Like other faint objects in the dark, they are better seen if one looks slightly to one side and not directly at them.

We clear from St. Jean tower control over to "Company," our home base radio operation. The winds at six thousand feet, we are advised, are southwest at 20 mph.

Sgt Bastien has by now fully reeled out the trailing antenna and is busy working the monster radio and transmitter located at his post, the second seat back of the pilot on the port side, just aft of the navigator's position.

He has been keying back flight information by Morse code to our ground station (Company radio). He will supply radio bearings for position lines and other required data to the navigators throughout the trip. He will also receive and relay information from base to the pilot with respect to weather changes, recalls to base, or other instructions affecting the safety of our aeroplane and her crew. During an earlier flight with me, Sgt Bastien was involved in just such an emergency in Anson 6359 (*'Z' for Zebra*) one night when we had to make a single-engine forced landing at Ottawa's Uplands Airport.

I set Jessop's compass heading, 284 degrees, on the P-6 compass located ahead of my knee at the bottom centre of the instrument panel, just left of the throttle quadrant. He comes forward to check my compass setting, to make sure that the luminous grid wires line up with the luminous north/south needle and that the grid ring is locked in position. He also checks that I have put north on north. Some pilots will try to trip up a student by putting a reciprocal heading on the compass—to see if he catches the error. That is something I never do. The poor student has enough to worry about without losing confidence in his pilot.

Here we are on this smooth, dark night heading for our first turning point. All is tranquil and I sense the two navigators moving about in the subdued light from their desk lamps. The black curtain at my back, separating us, shields me from the cabin lights and their reflections in my windscreen. I turn my instrument lights almost off for better night vision, the luminous instrument dials supplying ample light once my eyes adjust to the dark. Outside there are just the port and starboard wing-tip navigation lights showing. I can't see my tail light, of course—hope it's on. Ahead—easily mistaken for stars, or visa versa—I see one or two white tail lights. There are times when I see no indications of other aircraft at all. Today's airliners are flooded with light and powerful strobes; our training aircraft were not. Even TCA's Lodestars were very difficult to pick out at night. All is so smooth, and with cotton in my ears and my headphones still on, I experience a kind of peaceful coziness, a sensation that occurs only on a dark night, never during daytime flying. Looking back at our airport in the distance, I can see still more of our Ansons taking to the air.

Off to port I see flashes from Canadian Colonial Airlines' row of bright rotating beacons—in a line from Burlington, Vermont, to Montreal's Dorval Airport—that CCA pilots follow at night. The vast lights of Montreal glare up a few miles to the right and off to port are the distant, much fainter lights of Massena, New York, and Cornwall, Ontario—long, dimly glowing streaks near the horizon.

Far ahead, up the Ottawa Valley and over the Laurentian Mountains, bright pink lightning flashes. The clouds have the appearance of huge lanterns. With each flash there is a corresponding click in my headset that I continue to wear. Along with the cotton in my ears, it deadens the sound of the engines and the wind noise from the unsealed windows of the cockpit area. The big, beautifully lit clouds are no doubt all that remain of the storms that another crew and I encountered earlier in the day in Anson 6491 (*Donald-One*). The afternoon's flight had been wild, bumpy, exciting—and a bit scary. Co-pilot Hagenston and I both returned from that three-hour-and-twenty-five-minute trip thoroughly soaked from a typically leaky Anson I cockpit and from sweat. Flying in rough, wet weather was hard work.

I shine the flashlight on both oil pressure gauges to check the oil pressure. Then I adjust the throttles to re-synchronize the propellers, reset the directional gyro, and check all the other gauges and instruments. Then I observe the lights and revolving beacon at Dorval. I watch carefully in all directions for air traffic that may be approaching the airport. Since the WAG isn't operating the radio, I use the pilot's remote control panel on the cockpit roof to

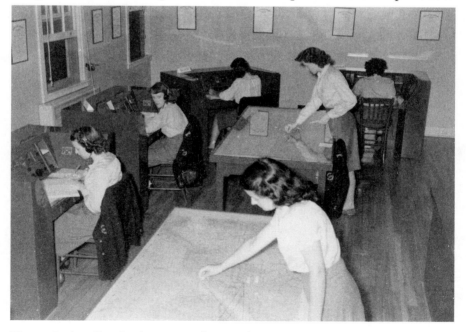

The station's radio-plotting room where civilian women employees kept track of aircraft on training flights. *Via A. G. Wingate.*

161

tune in the Dorval radio range and listen briefly to an 'A' quadrant signal, and then to the Dorval tower for traffic. There is little to hear. I tune in CKAC and hear the Andrews Sisters singing "Rum and Coca-Cola." Then I return the radio to the sergeant.

I catch sight of the St. Eugene EFTS coming up at the two o'clock position. There are Tiger Moths flying night circuits. Their navigation lights rise in a line from the light-outlined runway, follow a square pattern, and then seem to float back down onto the runway. Suddenly I spot a large bright orange-yellow light flaring up some distance ahead. I can't determine just how far it is—too remote to identify, but I can't take my eyes away from it.

Pendleton airport seems to approach from ahead and then pass to starboard. There are lightning flashes, fairly close, to the right. Then a long horizontal streak of light materializes in our path. It is Ottawa, and we should pass almost directly over it. The bright orange light on the ground is becoming closer and more intense.

Jessop hands me a heading change for Killaloe, based on new winds he has determined from establishing a fix with radio bearings supplied by Sgt Bastien. I alter the compass and bank to the new course as Jessop checks our new heading, 287 degrees.

The intense flames are almost below us. They come from an unfortunate farmer's barn complex, which at this time of year was likely torched by the spontaneous combustion of damp hay. Even from our height we see frantic activity on the ground, with people and animals rushing about—a sad sight. Had we been lower and off to the right, we would have felt a bump from the rising thermal.

We've been on course for fifty-seven minutes. The streak of light, which was Ottawa, has now expanded to become a carpet of illumination. Several searchlights create glowing shafts that wander lazily about the sky. I look at the SFTS Harvards far below, circling Uplands airport and remember my relief the night it offered a safe haven for my sick Anson, 'Z' for Zebra, a few weeks ago.

We pass along the north edge of Ottawa's bright lights, over the outskirts of Rockcliffe. The lights of Almonte and Carlton Place are off to port and Arnprior is detected approaching almost on our path. I must use some trim as one of the crew is doing a lot of moving about. A few sparks fly back from the exhaust collector rings. By chance, one catches momentary sight of them as they whisk away and fade in the dark. They are never seen in daytime.

On a future night flight, I will have the starboard engine provide a fine display of sparks when the exhaust collector ring partially disintegrates. One crew member will be all set to jump until I spoil his fun by pointing out that there is no reason to panic. I persuade him to settle down and return to work. We would complete that particular flight uneventfully—except for the blue flames that continued to shoot harmlessly from the damaged exhaust system at the rear of the cowling.

During a night flight in smooth air, once everything is in equilibrium, there is little for the pilot to do except keep his machine straight on its heading with an occasional small push on one or other of the rudder pedals. But if one has a crew which must move up and down the long cabin while working, keeping an Anson level at a constant altitude demands more effort. The pilot must continually adjust the elevator trim to compensate for changes in the centre of gravity. Like most aeroplanes in level flight, the Anson has a tendency to hunt—alternately climbing and descending slightly—only noticeable when flying alongside another aeroplane. The need for all this trimming does serve to keep the pilot awake. It is very easy to doze off. A change in engine and wind noise can also waken one abruptly—to find that the machine is wandering up, down, or into an unintended turn. It is better to keep busy.

There are always the fuel gauges to watch, especially important as we approach two hours in the air, which will happen over Killaloe. We always use the two outer wing tanks for takeoff and for the first half of the flight. In the case of a pump failure, fuel flow would be better. In a panic situation, changing to the two inner wing tanks could be a chore in a Mk I Anson. The fuel cocks are operated by four knobs in slots on the far side of the cockpit from the pilot, who must leave his seat to change the tanks. The trick is to change them and regain your seat—and the aircraft's heading and attitude—if a crew member has changed the centre of gravity by moving from the front to the back of the Anson's long cabin.

Back to our flight. Over the Gatineau Hills, close to our starboard side, there are still some brilliant lightning-filled CBs (cumulonimbus clouds), and I notice that the propeller tips are making visible rings of bluish pink light, St. Elmo's fire. It is a strange sight. Sgt Bastien calls my attention to the sparks dancing about on the front of his radio and transmitter. The two navigators don't notice the phenomenon because they are too busy. This is the last electrical display we will see tonight—the clouds are dissipating as the evening progresses—but not before they provide one final show of sparks along the bottom of my windscreen.

We are approaching Killaloe, barely visible in the distance. There is little aerial perspective on a dark night and it is difficult to judge distance accurately. A dim light close by may be mistaken for a bright distant one—a moving car's headlights or the powerful light from a train on the horizon may be taken for an airborne light close at hand. As previously noted, one may observe a white light ahead and dismiss it as a star, not realizing that it is another aircraft's rear nav light, maybe too close for comfort. Killaloe is small, with scant lighting. This night it could be mistaken for other nearby clusters of lights, unless one is able to identify the indistinct outline of Golden Lake alongside the village. Since the Killaloe airport is not used at night, no lights mark it.

Our navigator has positively identified the village and his expertise has brought us directly over it. We have reached Killaloe Station in one hour and fifty-nine minutes at a ground speed of 105 mph. Now is a good time to change tanks to the inners, while we are circling and climbing to set course for our new destination. I undo my seat belt, set everything to fly right, leave my seat, and move over to slide the fuel cock controls to their new positions.

The Canadian-built Anson V, typified by RCAF 12206 (*Queen-Three*) on the strength of No 9 AOS, was the mainstay of Canadian Air Observer Schools. *Via A. G. Wingate.*

They work smoothly—no sweat. Back in my seat, I buckle up again; nothing has changed, *Queen-One* is flying just as I left her, but there is always that moment of anxiety when the tanks are changed, until one knows that the engines will continue to run smoothly. *Queen-One* doesn't miss a beat.

Jessop gives me the new compass heading, 116 degrees, to Napierville two hundred miles east and close to our home base. At Napierville we will carry out a simulated bombing run over the camera obscura, instead of dropping practice bombs as at our regular LaPrairie range. Jessop assures me that our ground speed on this leg will be 135 mph and our estimated time to target will be one hour and twenty-nine minutes.

For our easterly course, we climb another 1,000 feet to separate ourselves from those aircraft still coming to Killaloe. I observe several sets of green and red navigation lights in the darkness and flash my landing lights momentarily, receiving two flashes in return. At 7,000 feet I level off, return the engines to cruise rpm and boost, return the mixture to auto-lean and synchronize the propellers. I turn gently onto our new heading a few moments before passing over the village. Jessop records the precise time and comes forward to check the compass heading. Satisfied, he returns to his desk. More red and green lights approaching below us trigger the customary landing light flashes.

Almost immediately I spot the lights of Eganville directly ahead and farther to the east the brighter lights of Renfrew—which we pass to the north in just sixteen minutes. We *are* moving faster on this down-wind course. A landing light comes on straight ahead spearing through the slight haze. I acknowledge with my own. Away to port on the Quebec-side of the Ottawa River toward Shawville there are no lights to be seen. The earlier lightning-filled clouds have been replaced by total blackness north of the river.

I become suddenly aware of a change in air pressure and the unfamiliar sound of rushing air. Our navigator is practicing his training in astro navigation on this leg of the exercise, by opening the astro hatch and using his sextant to shoot some stars for position lines. I glance around the black curtain to be certain that he has fastened the ship's safety cable to his parachute harness. Anson Is with opening-top astro hatches are equipped with safety cables to prevent the loss of the navigator should a sudden downdraft or other severe negative G-force be encountered. Jessop was fastened to the aircraft okay. He would have to be quite skinny to go through the hatch—but anything is possible.

I should add here that I never allow my crews to fly without their parachute harness properly fitted. In the event that we have to abandon the air-craft in flight, there would be little enough time to grab the chest packs from their stowage containers and clip them on before jumping. The harness can be uncomfortable, but better that than suffering an extremely painful descent and likely death due to a sloppily worn harness.

For a while there is a lot of crew movement back and forth in the cabin. Constantly I have to re-trim to maintain level flight and keep pressure off the controls. Such pressure can be very tiring. At this stage, I've little to do but sit there checking gauges and looking outside. With low windowsills, large sliding side windows, and a Plexiglas roof, the Anson has excellent cockpit visibility and this is easy to do.

Sometimes during a flight, a crew will receive a code "BBA" which is a sig-nal to return immediately to base because of weather deterioration or other flight security reasons. We receive no such signal tonight. In one instance when I received one, I was already on my way back, on the final leg of the exercise.

I notice from trim indications that someone has gone to the back of the cabin. This is a long flight, and obviously one of the crew has had to use the rather awkward relief funnel by the back entry door. I can't imagine how a lone pilot in flight was expected to use this facility. I never tried.

We pass Renfrew, Arnprior, and Ottawa in relatively quick succession, and I spot all that remains of the poor farmer's burned out barns, which we saw ablaze earlier. Now the fire's remnants look like nothing so much as the remains of a large wiener roast or marshmallow-toasting fire. From this same location, I had once observed a landing flare accidentally dropped over our bombing range about one hundred miles ahead at La Prairie.

The navigator has just given me a time to correct our heading by two degrees to starboard and waits while I make the compass adjustment. A lit-tle bit of rudder is sufficient to move our nose for such a small change of direction. I spot another of our Ansons not far to starboard. With our head-ing altered in his direction, I will have to watch him. Our aircraft are con-verging, and his red light appears to be coming closer. If I feel we are too close I will slow down and pass behind him. He is in fact a bit ahead of us and we will pass astern with no action necessary. I'm glad to have something like this occur if only to keep me alert. Before this happened, I had thought that our port light was blinking off and on—but it was just me dozing off for a second or two.

Ottawa is long behind us and we are coming up on Alexandria which seems to slide smoothly under us, then Lake St. Francis is to our right with Massena, New York, just visible at three o'clock about twenty-eight miles south across the St. Lawrence River. There is a prisoner of war camp there with searchlights that they play on us whenever we fly over them and tease them with our landing lights. Valleyfield is approaching and will pass under us. Another slight heading change from Jessop will take us directly over Napierville. Shakespeare, our bomb aimer for tonight, is already down on his hands and knees pushing himself into the nose compartment for our run over the target. As we begin our run, the bomb aimer calls on the intercom for "bomb-doors open." I repeat, "bomb-doors open," as I reach over to the bomb door handle and move it to the open position.

Shakespeare continues to give me directions, "rrright," or "left, left," or "steadeee," to line us up on the target with the bomb-sight, using the wind directions supplied by our navigator. I make all of the corrections with the rudder, just skidding the plane slightly, as the slip-and-turn shows. The camera obscura down there somewhere in the darkness will record and plot our flash from the No 10 flashbulbs in the bomb bay, activated by the bomb aimer's bomb release switch. Sometimes, as I've said, landing flares also get dropped—for which there is hell to pay. Fortunately for us, there is only the hazy flash of the bulbs and the smell of wood burning. This is scary the first time one experiences it—in a wood and fabric aeroplane. However it is only the bulbs' anti-shatter coating which melts and smokes a bit.

Our bombing run completed, I turn toward St. Jean, put the mixture into auto-rich, bring the throttles back, and trim for a quick ear-popping letdown from 7,000 feet to the St. Jean indicated circuit height of 1,136 feet, in a distance of about ten miles. I keep a bit of power on although there is little danger of chilling the engines on a warm night. I've easily picked out our revolving beacon from those of Colonial Airways and St. Hubert airport farther north, ours being the dimmest. There is no need to use radio aids tonight, as we occasionally do to find our way home; the visibility is well over fifteen miles.

I call the tower and ask clearance for *Queen-One* to join the circuit. I'm told that we are number five and cleared to the circuit for Runway 29, our shortest at 2,600 feet. The wind is 5 mph from 260 degrees. There will be a slight crosswind component from the left but nothing to concern us. All the crew are securely fastened in their seats and once again Shakespeare, who has quickly wriggled uphill and backward out of the nose, is in the now folded-down co-pilot's seat. After descending to the north from Napierville to our circuit level, all the while keeping an eye open for other traffic, I turn right to join the downwind approach to the circuit fairly far to the west of the airport. I've already checked with Sergeant Bastien that the trailing antenna is fully reeled in and secured. With its heavy lead weights, we don't want to lose it on the boundary fence or to wallop one of the cows in the field on our approach path. The undercarriage has been wound down. One can hit the crank and it will almost coast down on its own. I make sure that it is down and locked and I will likely do this several more times before we land. Those little green knobs have popped out of their tubes, the red U/C warning lights are off, replaced by the green ones. The U/C warning horn does not blow when I close the throttles, so I'm sure the wheels must be down and locked.

The mixture is moved to full rich, all gauges are checked, fuel level is sufficient, air pressure is okay, and speed is reduced to 100 mph. The aircraft is trimmed for slow flight. There is no carb heat to check on a Mark I. Carb ice is eliminated by hot oil continuously circulated through a jacket surrounding the carburetor's throat. Our relatively simple downwind check completed, I report, "*Queen-One* downwind." The tower acknowledges that I'm

With its four hangars and neat rows of aircraft, No 9 AOS at St. Jean, Quebec, was typical of RCAF British Commonwealth Air Training Plan stations. *Via A. G. Wingate.*

number three in the circuit and I'm cleared to the crosswind. Turning left into the crosswind, I cut back the power to let down to 500 feet above ground, or as the altimeter shows, 636 feet above sea level, before turning final approach. I select flaps-down and pump on fifteen degrees of flap using the big hydraulic pump lever behind the right side of my seat. I use my throttle hand, which is very busy during the final stages of the landing. I turn final and inform the tower, which responds, "*Queen-One*: check wheels down. You are number one to land behind the aircraft now touching down." "Wheels down," I acknowledge, reduce my speed to 80 mph, and pump on more flap to about thirty degrees. The landing light has been on all during final, although sometimes I don't use it and never in ground fog.

Speed over the fence is back to 70 mph. I bring the nose up to an almost three-point landing attitude as I watch the lights at the beginning of the runway pass under us. The flare-path on both sides appears to rise to meet us. The throttle is off, the left hand is back on the control column, and the right hand is still ready with the throttles in case they are needed. There is a slight thump and a tire sound like a dog's bark as we make contact with the runway and the wheels suddenly come up to speed. We hear a slight rumble and feel the runway's surface as we coast along, gradually slowing down. We are slow enough at the end of the roll out that, at the taxiway, I let the aircraft gently coast around to the right, with some help from the air brakes. The tower clears us to the tarmac parking area to park alongside those who have already returned. The flaps are pumped back up; one is fined if they are not fully up for taxiing. The busy right hand must now control the brake's air pressure again. However, on the ground, that is the hand's sole function for a while.

Taxiing a Mk I is not simple, but it is much better if one has long arms. The pilot taxiing must wrap a left arm around the control column bringing it back against his chest to keep the tail on the ground while at the same time stretching his left hand over to work the centrally located throttles. His right hand is mostly occupied operating the air pressure control lever on the front of the throttle quadrant. It in turn controls the air pressure to the differential air brakes worked by the rudder pedals. It is harder to describe than it is to do.

I make it to our parking spot and swing the aircraft around into line. We are back home again, wing-tip to wing-tip. The landing light is off, pitot heat off, throttles closed, idle cutoff pulled to stop the engines, and magneto switches down to off. All is quiet except for the low conversation of the crew as we pack up to leave *Queen-One*. I close the fuel cocks, shut off the master switch, disconnect the battery cables, and follow the boys out, shutting the door after we jump to the ground.

We walk along the tarmac toward the hangars, avoiding other aircraft taxiing to their parking spots. We say our goodnights as Jessop and Shakespeare head to their classroom for de-briefing. Sgt Bastien has already gone ahead and I proceed to the pilots' locker room, stopping along the way to report no snags on *Queen-One* to the crew-chief.

The locker room is full of conversation mixed with the sound of pilots whacking themselves in the belly to release their chute harnesses. We use the British harness with the quick-release gizmo in the front at the level of one's diaphragm. A turn of the safety catch and a whack on the fastener releases all catches simultaneously. Hence the term "quick release." This is excellent if one is ditched in the sea. I don't believe the American forces ever adopted it.

After stowing my belongings in my locker, I head over to the Sergeants' Mess to grab a bite to eat before my trip into town. It is around 2:00 A.M. when I pick up my bicycle and clear myself out at the guardhouse. With only my trusty flashlight to show me the way, I set out on the dark two-mile ride into town. There is only a solitary street light at the edge of town to give me something to aim for and keep me aligned on the straight road. The light also assures me that I am still upright on my bike; I can't see the black paved road beneath me. How one can stay vertical riding a bicycle in total darkness without any sight references—and no instrument panel—has always remained a mystery to me.

The *Tirpitz* Raid

The Famed Dam Busters Disable One of Germany's Mightiest Battleships

DONALD A. (DON) BELL DFC

Because of their spectacular success in May 1943—breaching the Mohne, Sorpe, and Eder dams with purpose-designed bouncing bombs dropped from modified Lancasters—617 Squadron RAF became known as the famed "Dam Busters." Subsequently, 617 specialized in dropping 12,000-pound Tallboys (like the bouncing bombs, a brainchild of Sir Barnes Wallis) with pinpoint precision on targets such as submarine pens, heavily strengthened to withstand normal bombing. The Lancaster was the only aircraft of its generation capable of carrying such loads.

When twenty-five-year-old Don Bell tried to enlist as RCAF aircrew in January 1941, he was rejected because of injuries from a motorcycle accident ten years earlier. Three weeks later, not mentioning the accident, he tried again and was accepted. Following the usual Trenton stint, he was sent to Initial Training at Victoriaville, Quebec, where a flair for math earned him a posting to No 7 Air Observer School (AOS) at Portage la Prairie, Manitoba. He learned bombing and gunnery at No 3 B&GS at MacDonald, and then astro navigation at Rivers, both in Manitoba.

Don Bell arrived at Bournemouth in the United Kingdom in February 1942, and was posted successively to an Advanced Flying Unit at RAF Millom and to an Operational Training Unit (OTU) at RAF Eastmoor. His operational flying began with 158 Squadron RAF on Halifax Island. However, when his pilot had difficulty coping with a four-engined aircraft, his crew was reposted to 425 Squadron RCAF, flying Wellington IIIs out of RAF Dishforth, Yorkshire. The last fifteen trips of his forty-mission tour were flown from North Africa against targets in Italy. During his subsequent instructional OTU stint, he teamed up with pilot Bill Duffy and assembled a crew of volunteers to join 617 Squadron, considered an elite unit specializing in near suicidal missions.

After several successful missions with "Duffy's Mob," including the collapsing of the Saumur Tunnel, Don was awarded the DFC in July 1944. For a change, Duffy and Bell occasionally flew a Mosquito on target marking (pathfinder) operations. When Duffy was killed on a practice flight, Don joined Nick Knilans' crew, just in time for the adventure he recounts.

After the war, Don Bell remained in the RCAF as a navigator on photographic Lancasters, surveying northern Canada. During the Korean War he guided RCAF North Stars from Washington State to Japan and Korea. In the early 1950s, on an exchange posting to the United Kingdom, he came across his old CO, Willie Tait, then commanding RAF Waddington. S/L Don Bell retired from the RCAF in June 1963 to join a Toronto brokerage. His story appeared in the Summer 1980 *Journal,* based upon a May 1978 Toronto Chapter presentation. Don Bell died on 30 November 1992.

I would like to tell you a true tale of high adventure in the air and in a foreign land, which not only made history but which also had a happy ending.

In October 1936, the keel was laid at Wilhelmshaven, Germany, for *Tirpitz*, sister ship of *Bismarck*, the second of the great German battleships that were the largest ever to see war service in the Western world. At 43,000 tons, the *Tirpitz* displacement was only slightly less than that of the American *Missouri* class later built for Pacific operation.

The resistance put up by the *Bismarck* when she broke into the Atlantic in 1941, and in particular her sinking of HMS *Hood*, dramatically affected British naval planning. Three battleships of the latest *King George V* class were considered necessary to offset *Tirpitz* in home waters. She exercised a dominating influence over British naval strategic thinking. The Admiralty dreaded that she might break out into the Atlantic as a commerce raider.

As early as August 1940, Winston Churchill exerted pressure on the top naval and air brass, the First Lord of the Admiralty, the First Sea Lord, the Secretary of State for Air, and the Chief of Air Staff, for air attacks against the two German battleships before they were commissioned. He realized their ability to seriously change the whole balance of sea power and consequently the course of the war.

Handley Page Hampdens of Bomber Command made the first two attacks on the *Tirpitz* at Wilhelmshaven in the fall of 1940. Initially using

F/O Donald Bell in 1942. Don served for twenty-three years in the RCAF, retiring with the rank of Squadron Leader. *Mrs. A. Bell.*

200-pound armour-piercing bombs, and later attempting to run magnetic mines underneath the hull during her fitting out, both attacks were unsuccessful. The techniques and technology of aerial bombardment needed much development before they could seriously damage such a well-protected vessel.

Nevertheless, a total of nineteen attacks were made against *Tirpitz* prior to August 1944—by every force, using every idea and technological development that seemed to have a chance of success. Several times in 1942, Bomber Command attacked with new four-engined Handley Page Halifaxes. The Royal Navy tried to bring battleships to bear, used the Fleet Air Arm repeatedly, tried human torpedoes (code name Chariot), and then specially designed midget submarines. The Russians even claimed an attack with bombers in February 1944, although German and other records studied after the war show no evidence of any such attack.

The human torpedo attack, which had been planned with close help from the Norwegian underground, failed almost within striking range of the *Tirpitz*. The torpedoes broke away from the fishing boat, which was towing them in rough water, and were lost. The Charioteers scuttled the fishing boat inshore and headed for Sweden on foot. Four days and four nights later, one party crossed into Sweden, but the other encountered a border patrol and the charioteer, Evans, was wounded and captured. He was hospitalized by the Germans and nursed back to health and strength. Then, on the direct orders of the German High Command, he was shot. Such brutality only enraged those hot on the trail of *Tirpitz* and increased the ferocity of the air attacks.

Although the sum total of all the early attacks produced only minor damage to the great ship, this in no way detracts from the skill and valour of the men who pressed home those raids. In fact, it is reported that W/C Guy Gibson expressed relief when he learned that the special mission which he had been selected to lead in 1943 was to be against the big dams in the Ruhr and not the *Tirpitz*—a deadly and almost impossible target.

That target was made increasingly difficult as the ship was moved away from danger, farther and farther up the coast of Norway. By 1943 she was anchored at the top of Norway in Alten Fiord, not far from the border of Finland, well beyond the range of British bombers. In addition, batteries of radar were installed, scanning to the west and southwest, to give warning of approaching aircraft and to direct some sixty anti-aircraft guns. Finally, the entire fiord was ringed with smoke pots that could cover the whole area with smoke in three minutes.

With her destroyer screen, other German capital ships such as *Hipper* and *Lutzow,* and strong air support, *Tirpitz* comprised a fleet-in-being astride the convoy route to Murmansk, necessitating coverage for every convoy by the British Home Fleet. This left the British Isles undefended and effectively tied up the Home Fleet. It placed the British Admiralty in a demoralizing quandary. When the number of convoys carrying arms and food to the Russians was reduced, the Russians repeatedly threatened to sue for peace, so the Admiralty was obliged to jump right back into the frying pan sending more supply ships and increasing efforts to neutralize the *Tirpitz* threat.

Tirpitz was photographed as she lay at anchor in Alten Fiord. The original 35-mm negative was taken covertly by a Norwegian underground agent, Torstein Raaby of *Kon Tiki* fame, from almost under the nose of a German guard detachment. It reached the United Kingdom within twenty-four hours, revealing the exact location of the *Tirpitz*. The agent was a Norwegian miller whose mill backed onto Alten Fiord. From the inside, he gouged a hole into the stone wall of the mill and took his photo, right in the middle of an armed camp. Discovery would have meant death or worse.

This grainy photograph of the *Tirpitz* moored in Alten Fjord, taken secretly in 1943 by Torstein Raaby of *Kon Tiki* fame, initiated the raid by 617 Squadron in September of the following year. *Via Mrs. A. Bell*

Sir Barnes Wallis was the British scientist and inventor who designed and built the bouncing bombs which were used by 617 Squadron, the RAF's famed Dam Busters, to breach the big power dams in the Ruhr in 1943. Wallis had a restless mind, full of new and practical ideas. He had been designing for Vickers since the First World War, creating the R-100 in the 1920s, the most successful British dirigible. In the 1930s he invented the geodetic form of aircraft construction, applying it in the Wellesley, which captured the world's non-stop distance record; and the Wellington bomber, probably the most rugged aircraft ever built.

Although he was going against the tenets of the experts in every air force in the world, Sir Barnes's studies and experiments showed that the bomb required to win a war must be capable of destroying power sources, viaducts, submarine pens, and coal mines. It had to be streamlined, huge, and dropped from as high an altitude as possible to attain maximum terminal velocity.

After the bouncing bombs, which destroyed the big Ruhr power dams, Sir Barnes went back to his drawing board with renewed vigour and in the spring of 1944 brought out his perfectly streamlined 12,000-pound bomb, code-named "Tallboy." Its needle-sharp nose comprised five feet of hardened nickel steel, capable of penetrating twenty feet of reinforced concrete when dropped from 20,000 feet. With a finned tail, it was a precision weapon, designed to fly like an arrow.

The Dam Busters (617 Squadron) had been switched from low- to high-level bombing early in 1944. Equipped with a special precision bombsight, they followed a gruelling daily program of high-level daylight practice bombing from 20,000 feet. An average of three direct hits out of every ten bombs released—the rest being near misses—was achieved and maintained. Sir Barnes's Tallboys were being produced at the rate of thirty a month in the United States and seven a week in the United Kingdom. They all came to us, beginning to arrive just before D-day. We first used them the night after D-day to collapse the Saumur Tunnel under the Loire River. The Tactical Air Force destroyed all the bridges over the Loire at first daylight so several crack German divisions were stranded in southwest France during the critical period of the landings in Normandy.

The next few months, as the bombs arrived, we destroyed hardened targets which had previously been secure—submarine pens and V-1 and V-2 sites. The Tallboy's enormous success was limited only by the small number available. It was quite a change for flyers trained to preserve their aircraft, to be instructed to bring Tallboys back if for any reason they could not be put on the aiming point, even though landing might well weaken or collapse the undercarriage.

By late August 1944, A/C Sir Ralph Cochrane, the Air Officer Commanding (AOC) of the group in which we operated, had decided that we could sink the *Tirpitz* with our Tallboys if only we could reach her. He obtained permission from A/M Arthur Harris, the Chief of Bomber Command for the Dam Busters, to make the attempt.

When I arrived back on the squadron from a short leave, after burying my pilot from my Lancaster and Mosquito tours, I was invited to join a prize crew consisting of personnel who, for one reason or another, had no crew but wanted to get the *Tirpitz*. Nick Knilans, our pilot, was an American in the RCAF who had been selected for the RAF Dam Busters. His crew finished after two tours, but he wanted the *Tirpitz*. While in the squadron, he had switched over to the USAAF on the understanding that he would be left with the Dam Busters. Thus, his was the only khaki uniform on the station, amid a sea of air force blue. He had a DSO for three tough Berlin trips, bringing back dead and wounded crew each time.

Larry Curtis, our wireless operator and the leader of the wireless section

F/O Donald Bell (extreme right) with the crew of his 617 (Dam Busters) Squadron Lancaster. This machine still has its mid-upper turret, which was removed for the *Tirpitz* raid. *Mrs. A. Bell*

on the squadron with over one hundred trips, was English. "Taffy" Rodgers, the bomb aimer, was Welsh, and "Paddy" Blanche, the rear gunner, was of course Irish. The last two both lost their crews when they did not fly with them on a fatal night. The flight engineer was a young, clean-cut Englishman with the least experience in the crew.

As a preliminary step, all our aircraft were fitted with new improved Mk 24 Merlin engines, just then entering operational service. The United Kingdom was searched for a supply of Wellington bomber overload tanks. To install these in the fuselage of the Lancaster, it was necessary to remove and re-install the rear turret. In an effort to lighten the aircraft, the mid-upper turret was removed and the hole faired over. Even the armour plate around the cockpit was taken out, along with anything else detachable, including the Elsan sanitary toilet. But, with fuel for twelve hours of flying, we would need the Elsan. It was re-installed. The Lancaster's all-up weight with overload fuel tanks and a Tallboy would be seventy thousand pounds—five thousand pounds over the maximum for the aircraft. Avro sent up two engineers to advise on the modifications and to monitor takeoffs; but we still had problems. Even with the overload tanks and a departure from Lossiemouth in Scotland, the return distance was too great. And what of the smoke screen at Alten Fiord?

Things began to fall into place when word came that we were to fly to Russia, to a place near Archangel on the White Sea, for refuelling and rest. This would permit us to attack *Tirpitz* from the northeast, while the German radars were all scanning to the southwest. We should be able to surprise them and beat the smoke pots. The flight to Russia would be low level so that German radar would not pick us up and spoil our surprise party.

The aircraft of neighbouring No 9 Squadron had also been modified and fifteen of these were to augment the No 617's eighteen aircraft for a total of thirty-three machines. Larger numbers would help confuse the defences. Most of the No 9 Squadron aircraft carried Johnny Walker wandering mines, designed to rise from the seabed and sink back a number of times, exploding on impact—hopefully under the ship. Two Liberators were also to make the trip, carrying ground crew and aircraft spares.

Preparing for the flight, the navigators ran into an unusual problem. In all of the western world there were no air maps covering the area east of Finland. We eventually located some old First World War army maps which showed the White Sea coastline on an odd scale—and nothing else. Our destination was Yagodnik. We were given a latitude and longitude and an assurance that we would receive radio homing assistance in finding Yagodnik, somewhere in that vast hinterland of northern Russia.

The weather, as reported by the reconnaissance Mosquito based at Murmansk, was poor. Nevertheless, on 8 September, we all climbed into our heavily laden aircraft and started up, only to receive a cancellation signal before the first aircraft was ready for takeoff. The weather picture continued to deteriorate and this procedure was repeated on two subsequent days. On the fourth afternoon the weather report was appalling, by far the worst yet. As we started our run-up we were mentally prepared for the operation to be scrubbed. Zero hour arrived and the first Lancaster—with all four Mk 24 Merlins straining under emergency power—lumbered down the runway and lurched into the air, just high enough to clear the breakwall at The Wash, on the English coast, three miles away. Still there was no white Very flare to signal that the operation had been scrubbed. Aircraft followed aircraft in rapid succession. Nor was there any recall by wireless as we flew up the North Sea so we made the logical assumption that the weather report had been proven wrong. All our aircraft got off and the Avro engineers were reported to be smiling as they left for their factory.

We turned to parallel the Norwegian coast, and I remember the blazing sun hanging over the Orkney Islands only to sink slowly into the North

Atlantic. Then we flew into utter darkness, without any aids to navigation—no radar, no astro, no beacons, no wireless, no visual pinpoints, and no bearings. It was catch-as-catch-can with whatever might turn up. We could see nothing but haze as we crossed the Norwegian coast without a position check, the total overcast above us contributing to the blackness of the night. Using the radar altimeter which had been installed that day, the first one I had ever seen, I was able to plot the highest points we crossed over Norway, and establish our track as some ten miles south of the planned one. I got exact groundspeed and position checks as we crossed the Gulf of Bothnia and clearly saw the curvature at the top end of the gulf with lights blinking from bordering house windows. They were the first lighted houses I had seen in three years, but this was neutral Sweden.

Morning came over Finland. We were frequently flying in low cloud and I remember picking out a conspicuous former frontline from the Russo-Finnish War but it wasn't on my map so I couldn't use it. As we flew on it became apparent that the weather report had been correct and weather had not improved. Fog, drizzle, and cloud were right down to the deck. As we approached our ETA (estimated time of arrival), pilot Knilans let down to fifty feet on instruments. We were right in it, with the tops of evergreen trees frequently sticking out of the clouds around us—but no airfield and no radio assistance materialized.

We had been up twelve hours and had only a twenty-minute reserve. With no alternate airfields, our options were running out along with our fuel. We turned back on a reciprocal course to an area over the White Sea where we last had had some visibility. Coming out of the cloud fifteen minutes later, we decided that things looked a bit more open to the south. As we flew south over the White Sea I noted that our twenty-minute reserve was gone—we maybe had ten minutes left in tanks reading empty.

Should we jettison our precious bomb to give us a chance to ditch? The bomb aimer prepared to jettison. Then a piece of White Sea shoreline showed up on our left with two moored Russian cargo vessels and a patch of ground beyond. "Hold the bomb and prepare for crash landing!" We had no time to reconnoitre the open patch—apparently a narrow clearing running inland a short distance. We would have to come in low and slow over the Russian ships, touch down near the shore, and use all of the short distance available. I should explain that flying over any ship was always at your peril because they invariably fired on you even when they knew you were friendly. This was one of my worst moments.

We pumped out Very light flares, hoping to indicate our distress, as we scraped over the mast of a ship to touch down on soft grass. We raced ahead with brakes squealing all the way into the far corner of the clearing, where we stopped with one wing pressing against a tree. The soft ground had helped to slow us down. We had been airborne twelve hours and thirty minutes, the last ten minutes on "empty tanks." Two engines cut out before we could shut them down.

We couldn't see much with our nose in the trees but soon another Lancaster came in on a different angle and stopped short of the trees. It continued to drizzle, and except for the grass, we were surrounded by a sea of yellow mud. We stayed in the aircraft, which seemed a very nice place now that we were down. Unfortunately, all bombers leak badly. Gradually we grew wet and cold as well as tired, hungry, and thirsty.

Eventually a Red Army jeep, with the American white star painted red, drove up. They inspected both sides of our aircraft from a respectable distance, being careful never to be directly in the line of fire of our rear guns. Accelerating sharply on their turns, they threw up mud as they skidded around, probably a training manual procedure for reducing vulnerability. The jeep drove off, but now we knew our presence was known. As it turned out, that was all they did know. With no idea who or what we were, we could have been from outer space for all the information they had.

We noticed that we were near a large one-storey log building, either a military hospital or convalescent centre. A number of men wearing light blue dressing gowns braved the drizzle to get a look at the strange black things that had dropped in on them. Crutches, slings, and bandages were prominent among our visitors—who stayed at a safe distance.

Then another jeep bearing a pennant (the local commandant, no doubt) drove straight to our aircraft door, while a second jeep stayed at a distance. We got out and went forward to meet the two Russian officers and a young woman in uniform. She, it turned out, was the interpreter; but she spoke no English. Obviously we had them surprised and confused. Having a USAAF pilot in American uniform helped the identification, but probably increased the confusion. My Canada badges mystified them. I suspect they had never heard of Canada. Later I realized that they would find a name in English as unintelligible as I would find one using the Russian Cyrillic alphabet.

Finally it was indicated to us that we were to follow an army officer who led us through the mud to an elevated boardwalk. We all had trouble walking on it as every third or fourth board seemed to be loose or broken.

Stepping on the wrong boards, we kept going through into the mud. The Russians had no such problem. We arrived at a smart-looking, one-storey, log building that was flying the flag of the USSR. We took the building to be the town hall.

They put us in a large room with the walls covered by huge portraits of the Bolshevik leaders. Despite the drizzle and our wet battle dress, we were all very thirsty, probably in consequence of all our sweating as we strove to get down. We kept asking for water, in English of course. We were overjoyed when a Russian in a white jacket appeared carrying a tray of full water tumblers. Paddy Blanche was served first and he threw the whole tumblerful down his parched throat. Then he turned white as a sheet and sagged to the floor, unconscious. The tumblers were full of neat vodka, Russian hospitality! They continued to surprise us. We were served a meal featuring a bowl of delicious meaty soup and sour black bread—which I enjoyed although some didn't.

By the time an English interpreter showed up, the commandant had been told by his headquarters who we were, and Yagodnik had been notified where we were. Apparently the early-arriving aircraft got into Yagodnik before the weather closed in, despite the lack of the promised radio-homing assistance. Some, like us, barely made it. Six crash-landed in swampy terrain, but the crews survived. We learned that we had landed at Onega City, a fighter strip last used in the Russo-Finnish War.

Willie Tait, our squadron commander, was flown over in an ancient Russian biplane to assess our situation. The biplane looked like a coffin, he said. It flew like one and he was afraid it would become one!

Both crews at Onega were quartered in what was possibly VIP quarters—neat, clean, log bungalow-type buildings. Our only complaint was about the sentries pacing around our buildings who wouldn't let us go out. The interpreter explained that Russia was a vast country and they didn't want us to get lost or have anything happen to us. We were warned not to attempt to get shaving kits or anything from our aircraft. The guards had orders to shoot anyone approaching them. We sure didn't need to worry about the safety of our Lancs!

In the morning a Russian DC-3, with the American white star painted red, landed with a small supply of one hundred-octane gasoline, enough to get us over to Yagodnik. We were very pleased to find our Lancaster—still bearing the heavy bomb—had been turned completely around and was now ready for takeoff, facing toward the White Sea. We had seen no tractors, and being curious, I asked, through the interpreter, how they had managed. "He say manskies," she replied, "many manskies." Noting the two huge holes in the mud and the deep skid marks behind the tires, I checked the cockpit, and sure enough, they had moved the aircraft 180 degrees by hand with the brakes still on. I'll bet they used a lot of manskies!

It had stopped raining and we were anxious to reach Yagodnik for a noon briefing on the latest weather report from Alten Fiord. The other Lancaster went first, turned right over the White Sea, and cleared the treetops on a direct line for Yagodnik. Then we bumped across the field with the big Merlins on emergency power. We lifted off at the water's edge and began the turn for Yagodnik. When Knilans called for 'wheels up,' the flight engineer unaccountably selected 'flaps up.' Quickly, he corrected his mistake—but it was too late! The aircraft mushed. We hit the trees that the other Lancaster had cleared nicely. Churning along, some five feet below the treetops, we cut a swath for several miles through a Russian evergreen forest. Paddy Blanche's surprised voice from the rear turret reported trees jumping up behind him. But those Mk 24 Merlins on emergency power saved us—our sturdy Lanc eventually pulled clear of the trees.

Our glazed nose, pitot head, and bombsight were gone and the cockpit windscreen was shattered. In order to see, Knilans had used one hand to protect his face. The bomb doors were torn off but the bomb was still there. My maps all blew out via the rear turret. A sliced-off tree branch, three feet long and two-and-a-half inches in diameter, travelled through the aircraft and was found back by the main door. Later we mounted it on the wall of the officers' mess at Woodhall Spa where it remained for many years, captioned, "Believe it or not!" The starboard outer radiator—filled with pine cones and needles—quickly overheated, forcing us to cut the engine. It appeared that our *Tirpitz* attack would be a non-starter. The flight engineer was still with us, but we considered pushing him out the open nose.

We landed on the grass field at Yagodnik late and with extreme difficulty. Some of the controls were jammed and the airframe seemed twisted. The briefing was in progress, and I caused a stir when I rushed in straight from our machine. Apparently my tousled hair was full of pine needles and other debris, and my face was caked with dried blood. My haste was unnecessary because Alten Fiord was clouded over and the attack was postponed another day.

Our support people, aided by the Russians, were to make an effort to rebuild our aircraft using parts from one of the Lancasters that had crash-

The Tallboy from Donald Bell's Lancaster rests on the ground at Yagodnik, Russia, while the aircraft was being repaired. With no crane available, it was lifted back into the aircraft solely with the brute power of "many manskies" from the Russian Army. *Mrs. A. Bell.*

landed nearby. To repair our bomb bay it was necessary to drop our bomb on the field, where a photograph was taken. It was the first non-official picture of the Tallboy, a secret weapon. The photographer felt he was safe breaking British regulations since the violation was taking place outside the United Kingdom. Back in England, a specially designed heavy-duty loading crane raised the Tallboy into the bomb bay. How would the Russians reload our Tallboy out here on the airfield without a crane? Why, with "manskies," of course—as many as could get an arm under it. It didn't seem possible, but they did it with *many* manskies!

We were all up early the next morning, 15 September, hoping for a better day, and we were vindicated. The sun was rising in a clear sky, and when we rushed to the airfield there was our aircraft, cleverly patched-up and repaired. Our maintenance NCOs, directing Russian mechanics and sheet metal workers, had worked all through the hours of darkness under floodlights. A pile of scrap parts and sheet metal as high as our aircraft stood beside her. We now had the nose, bombsight, and other parts taken from the Lancaster, which F/L Wyness, the commander of 'A' Flight, had crash-landed just across the river.

A third piece of good news arrived with the reconnaissance Mosquito from Murmansk, which flashed in to a landing to report clear and cloudless conditions over Alten Fiord.

We had been running up our aircraft in anticipation, and the force now reduced to twenty-seven aircraft—eleven with Johnny Walker anti-shipping mines and sixteen carrying precious Tallboys—was ready for takeoff. The Russians, who had been quite impressed by our aircraft, our bomb, and our unbelievable arrival without loss of life, turned out in force to watch us lift off the bumpy grass field. To avoid detection, we flew low and in a gaggle led by Willie Tait, climbing slowly as the terrain rose.

Over Finland, the force had a scare when we found ourselves over a large German air base. The runway lights were on, but we could see no aircraft on the ground. We concluded that one or two squadrons of fighters were in the air nearby. Without a mid-upper turret and with front and rear turrets armed only with relatively light .303-calibre guns, we felt vulnerable without our customary cloak of darkness. And we were. We could have been decimated within thirty minutes of the *Tirpitz*. What scared us was the thought of our attack being foiled—as had been so many others—just short of our goal. But no fighters appeared and there was no ground fire. If they were looking for us, they should have stayed at home!

Ten minutes from Alten Fiord, we opened up the Mk 24 Merlins to emergency power. The aircraft quivered as we raced for the target, each aircraft fighting to achieve maximum altitude before the two-minute straight and level bombing run. This was the minimum requirement of our bombsight if we were to put our Tallboy down the funnel. It had been decided that any altitude over 10,000 feet would produce sufficient velocity for the Tallboy to penetrate the armoured steel-clad decks. The best aircraft reached the highest altitude—11,500 feet.

Ahead, Alten Fiord lay quietly in the sun, like a picture. We picked out the black matchstick at her anchorage under the cliff just as white plumes of smoke began vomiting out from hundreds of smoke pots on both sides of the ship and around the edge of the fiord. We had achieved the surprise that was so essential. The flak guns on the heights began firing immediately and our gaggle ran steadily through the black curtains produced by exploding AA shells. They were fused for our altitude initially, but they would probably change the fusing if they brought no one down in the first minute. Then the guns on the *Tirpitz* opened up so gun flashes piercing the enveloping smoke marked the target aiming point.

With a clear view of the target, the first three Lancasters, led by Willie Tait, had a good bombing run. Unfortunately, one of the three had a hung-up bomb that could not be released or even jettisoned. A heavy landing at Yagodnik had jammed it into the airframe. For the next three aircraft, which included us, the target was obscured by smoke for five to ten seconds before the moment of release. The next three aircraft estimated the middle of the ship from the gun flashes and used them as an aiming point. The remaining seven aircraft did not drop their Tallboys. Since a second run would have been useless, they were brought back to Yagodnik, in hopes of another chance that never came. Although our starboard outer engine was overheating badly, Knilans waited until after the bombing to shut it down. We came back on three engines, the last to reach Yagodnik—for another engine-out landing on bumpy grass.

How successful had we been? Had we been foiled by the smoke? Only the

In this spirited painting, artist David Coulson, GAvA, has captured the first critical moments of 617 Squadron's daring attack on the *Tirpitz*. *Courtesy 617 Squadron Association*

185

first two of the nine bombs had been perfect drops. Our training accuracy was three direct hits in ten, which would be one hit in three and a third bombs. With only two perfect drops, we could have failed. But three bomb aimers, following the target down the bombsight drift wires during their bombing run, had seen a direct hit on the forward deck of *Tirpitz* by the first bomb down—dropped by Willie Tait's bomb aimer Danny Daniels, a Canadian.

The Russians were disappointed to see seven Tallboys brought back. They viewed conservation of bombs or ammunition as a western capitalist plot! Nevertheless, later in the day they went ahead with a little ceremony, held on the *Ivan Kalyev*, the river steamer on which we had slept the first two nights. Suspended fifteen feet in the air over the entrance to the ship was a twenty by three foot white banner bearing the inscription in big red letters, "Welcome the glorious flyers of the Royal Air Force." Against this impressive setting we lined up and were each presented by the political commissar with an enamelled red star emblazoned with a gold hammer and sickle. Although the commissar wore no rank, he apparently outranked everyone.

We punched holes in our battle dress and mounted our prizes. The first crews back to England did the same with their best uniforms and wore the star to London. Then came the order from Air Ministry drawing attention to a paragraph in *King's Regulations (Air)*, which stated: "The wearing of unauthorized foreign decorations or emblems is strictly forbidden." They gave no advice as to what to do about the holes drilled in good 5A Blues.

The Russians made a fine effort to entertain us. They brought in a bunch of bullet-headed young men to play a game against the RAF soccer players in our group. One afternoon they took us by motor launch to the brick and stone, European-style city of Archangel—at the latitude of Churchill, Manitoba. I bought a desk blotter at a hotel with rubles drawn from the RAF Liaison Officer in Archangel to be charged against my pay account. The equivalent cost in Canadian money worked out to about twenty dollars. It was the only thing for sale that I could find in the city, and I figured they might have a hard job catching up to my pay account. They never did.

One evening they held the equivalent of a mess dinner, beginning with a small glass of vodka, raw fish (in cubes on toothpicks), a large bowl of red borsch—which was delicious—and roast yak. There was also Caucasian red wine with which we first toasted the King and then the Secretary General of the USSR, Joe Stalin. The Russians toasted the RAF and we toasted the Red Army, Yagodnik, and the day after they paved the runways!

The *Ivan Kalyev*, a steamer moored on the Dvina River at Yagodnik, Russia, where Donald Bell and his fellow crew members were billetted for two nights. *Mrs. A. Bell.*

We moved off the *Ivan Kalyev* after two nights because of bedbugs and the stench of raw sewage—none of the plumbing worked and hadn't for a long time. We were delighted to find what was probably the biggest outhouse in the world nearby. It had a capacity of 150 holes each side, back to back. And it was clean, being scrubbed continuously by two elderly women—one on each side—who never left, never stopped, and never finished.

Our new quarters were bunks in a large heated building, which was built underground. The entrance was cut into the side of a sand dune, and we were accommodated with Russians in various types of uniforms. Except for the bedbugs, it was quite good. The bugs, which didn't seem to bite the Russians, sure gave us a working over. An eye would frequently be swollen shut from a bite, which is serious when your business is flying, but the Russians all seemed to think it was hilarious.

One morning I was endeavouring to make conversation with a Russian naval pilot through an interpreter. Looking out over the White Sea at a Catalina flying boat moored offshore with the American white star painted red, I remarked, "American Catalina?" The interpreter shook her head, became quite solemn and said, "You are wrong. It is a Soviet aircraft made in the USSR at Plant 34 in Gorki." Gorki was a new industrial city near the Ural Mountains. She also gave me the name of the Soviet designer. Then, without a smile, the two departed and I got the message. They had been warned of western capitalists claiming that everything was theirs. By identifying the Catalina, the DC-3, and the jeep as being American, we put ourselves in that ugly capitalist category about which they had been warned. Not only would they disbelieve you, they would politely dislike you. Frequently they pointed out that Russia was fighting the greatest war in history and needed all the help she could get. Russia would win, and when she did, it would be good for all those countries that had helped her, provided that they had helped enough! Several of us had similar enlightening experiences.

Our wireless operator, a veteran of over one hundred Bomber Command ops, announced that he would not be flying back with us, but would fly as a passenger in another aircraft. Obviously he thought we weren't going to make it. This was to be his last operational flight and I can now understand his concern. Since leaving England, we had had a series of close calls and they seemed likely to continue. Our aircraft had a bent airframe, was difficult to control, and the starboard outer engine needed a major overhaul, not just the minor tune-up it could be given at Yagodnik. On a flight of maximum duration we couldn't go far on three engines. Instead of being concerned that a very experienced officer chose to cease flying with us, we were so gung-ho that we felt affronted. We dismissed his defection. Good riddance! We would return without radio or wireless contact—who needed it?

We took off late on 17 September, the second-last aircraft to leave, without weather or wind forecast. We plotted a track over the Baltic, avoiding defences, but our route was otherwise as direct as possible to our Lincolnshire base. After some hours, all on instruments, we began to ice up rather badly. Since we were going to have to come down to try and get under it, Nick wanted a position. Having nothing to go on for navigation, I took a dead-reckoning position placing us over the Baltic, midway between Sweden and Germany. It came as a shock to break out of the cloud over a very busy street in a big, brightly illuminated city with flashing neon lights and high buildings all around us. While Stockholm made a lovely pinpoint for me, we weren't welcome. We climbed back into the icing cloud in a sky full of accurate flak. Over the Baltic we got under the icing and flew across northern Denmark right on the deck, producing a lot of wild AA fire several thousand feet above us.

In ten hours we were over Woodhall Spa in England, our home base. But there was one last shock, most of the United Kingdom was under fog with zero visibility. We were diverted to Lossiemouth in Scotland, which was still open. If we had asked for another wireless operator back at Yagodnik, he could have picked up British weather and the diversion two hours out and we could have gone directly to Lossiemouth. Instead, we had to endure another hour of increasing fatigue as we fought the aircraft. We were relieved to get down at Lossiemouth. One of our Lancasters, carrying an extra crew from one of the aircraft that had crash-landed in Russia, did not arrive and was never found.

The next day we flew back to Woodhall Spa, where our aircraft was towed away for scrap. We stripped off all our clothes in the courtyard and burned them before going into the mess for a good bath and clean clothes.

Meanwhile, at Alten Fiord, the Murmansk Mosquito sighted the *Tirpitz*, still afloat. The Norwegian resistance reported that she had been hit at the bow and the front main 15-inch gun turret was gone. This was, in fact, the truth. Willie Tait's bomb had struck fifty feet back from the prow, pierced the armoured deck, and exploded as it emerged well below the water line on the starboard side. The German official report, which was found after the war, would have set the minds of the British to rest. It was estimated that repairs, if they could be carried out without interruption, would take at least nine months. However, on 23 September 1944, at a conference at which both the Commander-in-Chief and the naval staff were present, it was stated that it was no longer possible to make *Tirpitz* seaworthy again. On 15 October she was moved to Tromso Fiord, two hundred miles down the coast, where she was berthed, resting on a shoal so that she could not be sunk. With her AA defence batteries, smoke pots, and anti-torpedo nets, she was to act as a defence battery, protecting Germany's Norwegian flank.

The British Cabinet had no knowledge that she was seriously stricken. A good stock of Tallboys had accumulated by late October, and on the night of 29 October, thirty-one Lancasters, all carrying Tallboys, flew to Tromso Fiord, just within range of Lossiemouth. Low cloud blew in from the sea and covered the fiord just as they arrived. One of our pilots, Carey, had two engines shot out and jettisoned his Tallboy but made it to northern Sweden before crash-landing. His crew was flown to the United Kingdom by the Swedes before their crashed aircraft was discovered. (International law calls for internment for the duration of the war of bomber crews crash-landing in a neutral country.) The other Tallboys were all brought back to Lossiemouth.

Time was rapidly running out. By 27 November Tromso Fiord would be in a zone of total darkness until spring, and British Intelligence reported that two German fighter squadrons had moved to an airfield thirty miles from Tromso, an obvious defensive preparation which gave the operation a suicidal aspect. Nonetheless, on 12 November, thirty-two Lancasters, all carrying Tallboys, again flew from Lossiemouth to Tromso.

This time they found good bombing visibility. Although the smoke pots had been moved down from Alten Fiord, they had not been primed, and did not work. *Tirpitz* tried to conceal herself with her own smokescreen, but it was too late. The bomber gaggle had reached 14,000 feet to clear a mountain. The attack was much like the earlier one at Alten Fiord, even to the fact that Tait's bomb aimer, Daniels, again scored a direct hit, followed by a number of others and many near misses. *Tirpitz* listed to port increasingly as the bombing went on until she reached an angle of seventy degrees. Then there was a violent explosion that blew one of the fifteen-inch gun turrets forty feet from the ship. She rolled to port and capsized. Although the order had been given to abandon ship, there was not enough time for most men to get out. Of the 1,700-man crew, 1,000 were drowned, 87 were rescued by cutting holes into compartments in the ship's bottom where they were trapped. No fighters appeared, although the *Tirpitz* defenders called frantically for them throughout the attack.

Congratulations poured into the Dam Busters' base in Lincolnshire from the King, the war cabinet, Air Marshal Harris, the Chief of Bomber Command, Sir Barnes Wallis (the inventor of the Tallboy), Air Commodore Cochrane commanding 5 Group, the Royal Navy, Prince Olaf of Norway, and even from our allies and former hosts, the Russians. Willie Tait, who was ever after to be known as "Tirpitz Tait," was awarded the DSO, his fourth, to go with his two DFCs.

The next morning Commanding Air Officer, Air Commodore Cochrane, presided over the 5 Group daily conference. He glanced at his minutes and reported brusquely, "Last night's operations—successful—*Tirpitz* sunk. Now, about tonight's operations ..."

Night Intruder

Flying Alone and Unseen Deep Into Occupied Territory

GEORGE E. STEWART

"**D**ear God, please make it last long enough for me to get my free flying lessons." So thought seventeen-year-old George Stewart of Hamilton, Ontario, in the summer of 1941, as Ansons from a nearby Service Flying Training School flew low overhead. George immediately presented himself at a recruiting centre—only to be told to wait until his eighteenth birthday. To have any hope of becoming a pilot, he must upgrade his education by taking a special twenty-six-week pre-enlistment course. Of the sixty who began the course, only fifteen graduated, George among them. He enlisted on 11 March 1942.

Serious training began at No 6 Initial Training School (ITS) in Toronto. An aptitude for blind flying—as simulated by the Link Trainer—earned him a posting to No 12 Elementary Flying Training School at Goderich, Ontario, where he flew Tiger Moths. "Simply fantaaaastic!" he recalls. After seventy-five flying hours, George was posted to No 9 Service Flying Training School at Centralia, Ontario, on Canadian-built Avro Anson IIs.

At Bournemouth in England, given a choice of assignment, George opted for "intruding on Mosquitoes," fully expecting to be sent to a heavy bomber squadron. He was surprised and elated when posted to an Advanced Flying Training School on Blenheims, for Ops with a Beaufighter unit. If he did well, he might fly Mossie intruders. Needless to say, he did well. He began by ferrying a Mosquito to join 23 Squadron RAF in the Middle East. After following 23 around the Mediterranean, he found it over-populated and returned to the United Kingdom by sea. Eventually, he did join 23 Squadron, but in England.

The de Havilland D.H. 98 Mosquito that George Stewart so much enjoyed was the most versatile aircraft the Allies possessed. A light bomber built entirely of wood, it had the power and carried the bomb load of a medium bomber. Capable of 400 mph, it could outrun enemy interceptors—making defensive armament unnecessary. It excelled as well in the long-range reconnaissance role. Its potential as a night-fighter was obvious, and de Havilland quickly developed a radar-equipped fighter variant with devastating fire power. Such was the machine in which George flew the mission he so vividly recalls—one of fifty similar night-intruder sorties.

As the war wound down, George got in even more Mossie time at No 36 Operational Training Unit in Nova Scotia. In 1948, finding civilian life tedious, he jumped at an unexpected opportunity to resume his love affair with the Mossie. Chiang Kai-Shek had purchased Mosquitoes to equip his Nationalist Air Force in their fight against the Communists. George flew to China to train pilots.

In 1974, he became the Canadian Warplane Heritage's check pilot introducing others to Second World War aircraft. Thirteen years later, when Kermit Weeks (owner of an aviation museum in Lakeland, Florida) purchased a flying Mosquito in England, George, as co-pilot with George Ayrd, ferried this rare machine across the Atlantic. With 1,030 Mossie hours, George Stewart has more flying time in the Mosquito than any other pilot in the world. His story was published in the Winter 1976 *Journal*.

Thirty-two years (in 1976) have gone by since I was engaged in Night Intruder Operations over enemy territory during the Second World War. So many years can do a lot to erase or dim memories, both the good ones and the bad. However, I have kept many notes and records that were made at the time and they are sufficiently complete to make 1944 seem like yesterday. Come back in time with me and share some of the experiences as we do an actual sortie together.

We are stationed on an airfield in England close to a small Norfolk town called Pakenham, at an even tinier hamlet called Little Snoring. My navigator, Paul Beaudet, and I are an experienced Mosquito crew with 23 Squadron RAF, which shares this base with another RAF Intruder squadron, No 515. Our base commander is G/C "Sammy" O'Brien-Hoare, DSO and Bar, DFC and Bar, and our commanding officer is W/C "Sticky" Murphy, DSO and Bar, DFC and Bar, Croix-de-Guerre and Palm, and Czech Medal. Sammy Hoare pioneered our work in World War Two and Sticky Murphy made a name for himself dropping off and picking up undercover agents, flying Lysanders into occupied France, and landing after dark without lights. Paul and I have done thirty-eight trips since we started operating on 12 July 1944, and now we wake to a lovely November day, ready to return to work after a day off. We are flying the British-built de Havilland Mosquito Mk VI fighter-bomber, armed with four 20-mm cannon, four .303 machine guns, and two 500-pound bombs. The aircraft are painted the traditional grey/green camouflage and also sport stunning black and white invasion stripes on the under surfaces of wings and rear fuselage. Our exhaust stacks are shrouded to make us less visible to enemy night fighters. We are equipped with "Gee" boxes which, by a grid system, make it possible for us to determine our exact position over blacked-out Britain and to a lesser degree just inside enemy-held territory. We also carry a small black box called IFF (Identification Friend or Foe). When we switch it on, our radar "bashers" can recognize us by our distinctive blip. This is so secret that we have a destructive charge ready to detonate and destroy our IFF, if there is any risk of the aircraft falling into enemy hands.

George Stewart (L) with his navigator, Paul Beaudet, after collecting a new Mosquito to be ferried to the Middle East. *G. Stewart*

George Stewart at the controls of a Mosquito. *G. Stewart*

Canadian airmen operated on a two-tour system. In night intruder work, the first tour would consist of thirty-five sorties, followed by a period usually as instructors on operational training units, or in operational planning at group headquarters. A second tour of twenty-five trips would round out our operational obligation and then we would be eligible for a posting home. Paul and I did our first tour in eleven weeks and we were still raring to go, so we applied for and were granted an extension to our first tour of fifteen trips. By being very quiet about it, we thought we would be able to sneak in an extra ten sorties without anyone noticing. Then we could say that we had done our two tours and so would get back home sooner. This plan didn't work. As soon as we finished the extra fifteen, we were off operations. Now let's get on with today's trip.

It is 4 November 1944 and Charlie, our batman, has just come into our Nissen hut with cups of tea. "Good morning, gentlemen," he says. "It is now 7:30 and we are having a nice day." Tea is a ritual by now and it certainly warms you on a cold morning in an equally cold Nissen hut that is always chilly and damp. With no running water, we wash in basins and put on our battle dress ready to cycle over to the officers' mess about a mile away. I hear the sound of our flight commander's jeep starting so I dash outside to ask him (F/C Griffiths) to please be sure that Paul and I are on the roster for tonight's flying. As a general rule of thumb, we operate two nights in a row, then have a night off, with a week's leave every six weeks. Paul and I have decided that we would rather do three nights on, then one night off. We've found that we are a bit edgy on the first night, not edgy, but alert on the second night, and except for being a bit tired we are fine for the third night's work.

Six or eight of us cycle to the mess just in time to enjoy our ersatz scrambled eggs and sausages as well as lots of tea with toast and jam, all generously mixed with conversation about last night's flying. Was there any "joy" (damage to the enemy), or anyone missing, etc.? Our day has begun. The notice board in the mess has briefing time posted for 14:00 hours so there are a few unrushed hours for comfortably fitting in all we have to do. The CO and flight commanders have left for our flight offices. Eventually we all mount our trusty bikes and follow them.

The aircraft status report is drawn up, showing which aircraft are available today, and which ones are, for any reason, unserviceable. Our flight commander has listed beside the aircraft registration the names of the on-duty crews, and Paul and I note that we are again assigned Mosquito PZ448 (YP-J), which happens to be our own regular kite. We are happy! Our aircraft has been topped up with fuel, oil, glycol, and ammunition. Since we didn't fly yesterday, we prepare to do our traditional NFT (night flying test), a short hop to give us the feel of the aircraft that often reveals some little snag that can be fixed up before our Op. The Mossie is such a delightful aircraft to fly—a pilot's dream (mine at least)—that we jump at any excuse for taking her up.

These few minutes of happy romping around in a Mosquito are among my best memories, flying for the sake of flying. We very often get into mock dogfights with Thunderbolts, Spitfires, Havocs, or anything else we can find. I remember closing in on an American Flying Fortress for a bit of formation fun. Imagine my surprise when Paul tells me to look to my right. There, large

Little Snoring, Norfolk, England, in November 1944: the men of 23 Squadron RAF pose with one of their Mosquitoes. George Stewart is perched on the aircraft's nose. *G. Stewart*

as life, is another Fort. It must have looked hilarious to see we three nuts in such an unbalanced formation.

We prepare the aircraft for the night's work and check that the parachutes are correctly positioned and ready to snap on. This done we make our way back across the field for lunch or briefing called for 14:00 hours. All aircrew and others involved—meteorology and intelligence bashers as well as flight commanders and COs—head for the squadron intelligence library and briefing room behind station headquarters. The on-duty aircrews wait in the intelligence library until the planning is completed. Usually there is a lot of speculation about where tonight's raid will be directed, plus the expected amount of armchair "quarterbacking."

The orderly officer has just opened the door to the briefing room, and that is our signal to file in. It is a large room, something like a classroom, with a slightly elevated stage at the front. On the wall behind is a large map of Europe. The target board—just off to one side of this stage—is covered, as expected. S/L Charlie Price, our senior intelligence officer, mounts the podium and a hush fills the room. "Good afternoon, gentlemen. Today's briefing will now begin. Will you please close the door, orderly officer, and I will call the roll?" He calls the names of each crew operating tonight. "Sir," we answer when he says "F/0 Stewart and F/0 Beaudet."

Charlie retires to the back of the stage, and with his pointer, indicates which target our heavy bombers are pranging tonight, how many are being used, and their routes to and from the target. He explains the tactical purpose of the raid—the demolition of certain industries or the demoralizing saturation bombing of a large city. He advises us of other groups supporting the raid, such as Pathfinders. Then he explains how we are to be deployed. Our aircraft will be used to patrol enemy night-fighter aerodromes near the target and on the way to and from the raid. At last the target board is uncovered, and we look for our names, then our target, and finally our patrol times. Charlie reads each one out and makes certain that the crew concerned understands clearly their job, their target, their patrol time, and their armament—whether or not they are carrying two 500-pound bombs. "Stewart and Beaudet, you are to patrol Ardorf aerodrome from 20:15 hours until 21:15 hours and you will carry bombs. If you have time, take a look at Marx and Varel while you are in the area. Is that clear?" "Yes Sir," we reply.

The meteorology basher has his turn, telling us about tonight's winds and weather—usually we have lots of both. He tells us what moonlight we can expect and gives us an idea of weather at base upon our return. We are warned about very strong winds.

Charlie Price has now asked W/C Murphy to say a few words: "All right, chaps, you know what you are expected to do: get cracking, use your heads, and don't stick your necks out. Be sure to keep a sharp lookout behind and watch out for that wind to change direction and strength!"

"Gentlemen," Charlie continues, "we will now synchronize our watches. Half a minute before 14:56. I'll begin counting at ten seconds to go—ten, nine, eight, seven, six, five, four, three, two, one. 14:56—good luck, chaps!"

Mass briefing concluded, Mosquito crews pair off to plan their own particular sortie. Each operates independently of any other. My navigator, Paul, has started to spread out his maps, trip log, Dalton navigational computer (really a visual calculator, not to be confused with computers as we know them today), and Douglas protractor. My job is to draw flying rations, enemy colours (flares) of the period (ESNs) if they are known, so that we can fire them from our Very pistols if needed for deception. These are nicknamed "sisters." I also draw escape kits containing small compasses, German aircraft cockpit checks (on rice paper), concentrated food portions, first aid materials, and pills to keep us awake should we need them, as well as water-purifying tablets.

I pull out the files on Ardorf, Marx, and Varel aerodromes and note their layouts and memorize where their defences are marked, as well as station buildings and ammo dumps. I note, too, the heights of nearby obstructions

This de Havilland Mosquito fighter-bomber coded YP-E (RAF PZ2187) is one of the 23 Squadron machines that George flew on many of his intruder missions.
G. Stewart

as well as the main function of and the type of aircraft used there—night fighting Ju 88s. I also obtain our phony passport pictures and negatives. Paul has by now drawn in his routes to our target. I note that we will cross the Dutch coast at Noord Egmond at 1,500 to 2,000 feet, diving and weaving from 3,500 feet. We are going to cruise at 240 mph indicated airspeed, starting out at 6,000 feet over base, steering 102 degrees magnetic. Our true airspeed works out to be 260 mph, and with this wind, our groundspeed will be 310 mph. Therefore we will fly twenty-three miles in four-and-one-half minutes to the British coast where we will dive quickly to 500 feet over the English Channel and head for Noord Egmond, 134 miles (thirty-one minutes) away, with a groundspeed of 262 mph.

Weaving over the Dutch coast, Paul and I will cruise on to our target, varying height from about 2,000 to 4,000 feet, keeping a constant lookout behind for any Ju 88s or Fw 190s on our tail. Our next turning point is on the Leda River, southwest of Emden. Then we turn north into the patrol area just above the Jade Canal, which leads into Wilhelmshaven. If Ardorf isn't lit or is hard to locate, we may have to continue on to the north coast, pinpoint our location, and backtrack to our target. We add up the anticipated times, including this latest possibility, and find that we have seventy-five minutes. Subtracting that from our slated time on target of 20:15 we must be off the ground at 19:00 hours. Our trip is planned, and all we have to do is to fly it!

Paul puts his gear into his locker and we cycle over to the mess just in time for tea at 16:00 hours. Since we will miss dinner at the regular sitting because we are leaving so early, we gorge ourselves with tea, toast, and cake—just delicious!

Comfortably seated, we don our red goggles to adjust our "visual purple" for night vision. We relax for an hour of reading or chatting. At a time like this we can't help but speculate on what this sortie could mean—joy (hacking down an enemy aircraft), death, or a cold jump into the night and a very uncertain future. It is a disconcerting sensation to consider that we might be shot down and just dissolve into the night, or sink into the Channel or North Sea without anyone seeing us go, leaving no trace behind. Sitting in the mess waiting to leave, we feel somehow chilly and alone. Our beds down at our hut seem warm and enticing.

It's kind of strange, this feeling before doing a trip. We know that a Mosquito will be patrolling Germany tonight with us in charge. Somehow, however, it doesn't seem quite real. We have a detached feeling. It won't be us out there but others who take over our bodies on such occasions. We sort of shed our souls and minds and mentally tuck them into bed until our return, when happily they reunite. And there is nothing we can do about it.

While we don't dread what's to be done—it is fascinating work and can be a lot of fun and very exciting at times—that twitchy feeling is felt now more than on the actual trip. Our job is a lonely one and the fact that we will likely be the only British aircraft within maybe one hundred miles makes this feeling more intense. We are lucky tonight because we have such a short time for such reflection before going out to our aircraft. To all outward appearances, we, the aircrew here in the mess, are very offhand about the whole thing. The impression we may give is that we couldn't care less. Not so!

"Well, Paul," I say, "It's 5:45. We'd better get down to the aircraft." Hopping on our bikes, we cycle to our locker room, stopping off at the intelligence section to place our valuables in little bags and collect Paul's navigation equipment, rations, and so on. We ride on, with Paul bitching about how awkward it is to carry his stuff and ride a bicycle. At our lockers by our flight office we crawl into our escape boots and don our Mae Wests. I sign out and we pile into the 15-hundredweight van (3/4-ton truck) that takes us around the perimeter track to our dispersal area and our aircraft, YP-J. I walk over to Chiefy's office and sign the *L 14* and then return to the aircraft.

In the cool darkness, it's like a world of our own because it all seems so unreal, so quiet, so private. By this time, as I've tried to explain, a certain amount of anxiety has crept into our souls and down our respective spines. It often has the effect of making us a bit high-strung and cranky. It causes us to shiver slightly, even though we don't feel cold. We don't talk much.

Now we come to the much-practised ritual that precedes every operation. For good luck, we walk back to the tail of the aircraft and christen the tail wheel with urine! With fifteen minutes to go, we climb aboard, telling the ground crews to douse their flashlights because they will spoil our night vision. We strap in; our boarding ladder is removed, collapsed, and handed to Paul. He snaps it into its place on the door after the door is closed and latched. The external starting batteries are plugged in, the engines are primed, and we are ready to start. These few minutes before starting drag like hours. Eight minutes before takeoff, I yell, "Contact starboard!" and we start our engines. With both Merlins going and the radio heating up, we feel much better and our anxieties fade away.

The ground crew have unscrewed the undercarriage locks and removed the starting batteries. They wave us out to the perimeter track where we follow the blue lights around to the takeoff position. After a quick run-up and cockpit check, I flash our downward recognition light to signal that we are

The all-wooden Mosquito possessed a distinctive silhouette. Nose armament distinguished the fighter bomber variant while Mosquito bombers carried no defensive armament. *De Havilland via G. Stewart*

ready to go. A green light flashes from the control tower so we line up and take off. All signals before an op are visual only, so that the enemy can't tell from radio chatter when we depart. It's very black outside and we don't feel comfortable until we have 1,000 feet under us. The aircraft feels loggy with full 50-gallon drop tanks plus the added weight of two 500-pound bombs. It is 19:00 hours, and as we climb and turn to set course over the field, I flash "dot-dot-dot-dash" (V in Morse code).

The time is 19:06, and at 5,000 feet over Haisborough Light on the British coast we alter course slightly for Noord Egmond. Diving to 500 feet, I switch off our navigation lights. It is fascinating to see the bright phosphorescence in the water below us. On a dark night like this, it really shows up!

"Four minutes to go, George," says Paul. This is my signal to climb quickly to between three thousand and four thousand feet. Once across the coast, I am ready to dive and weave our way across the Dutch countryside that is just ahead. Almost as soon as we climb, we can hear enemy radar scanning us, insect-like in our earphones. It imparts a nervousness all of its own. Diving and gently weaving, we are safely across, levelling off between fifteen hundred and two thousand feet. The scanning has stopped and we set course for our next turning point.

Flying over enemy territory, seeing the odd rotating beacon and distant searchlight, is almost a physical sensation. As we pass over the Zuider Zee, we can see the riding lights of many small fishing craft. Our landfall is coming up on the east coast of the Zuider Zee and we alter course for our previously mentioned turning point on the Leda Canal. We now rely upon waterways as landmarks because everything else below us is pitch black.

"Look back, Paul," I say as I pull sharply up and Paul scans behind for enemy aircraft. (On one trip, we did spot a Ju 88 when we did this.)

"There is Zuidlaarder, George. We are right on track," says Paul. "Let me know when you see the Dortmund Ems Canal." Soon we are there and shortly we arrive at the turning point on the Leda River. I hum a few bars of "Isn't This a Lovely Way to Spend an Evening?" and Paul makes a rude comment. "Okay, George," he says. "Steer 005 and look out for the Jade Canal." "Right, Paul, have another look behind."

Five minutes later, over the Jade Canal, we see ahead of us in the distance the landing pattern of lights (visual Lorenz) that the Germans use to guide their aircraft in for a landing. Right on the money at 20:15 hours, it is Ardorf nicely lit up to welcome us. "Okay, Paul, load up a 'sister' just in case we need it." I dive the Mossie to 500 feet so that we can look up and see any aircraft silhouetted against the gloom. Parallel searchlights challenge aircraft on the downwind leg with one holding and the other dipping.

"There goes an ESN (*sister flare*), Paul. Someone is on the downwind leg." We race around the circuit and see some navigation lights on final approach. Turning my gun safety switch to firing position, we close in on him as he turns on his landing lights. I get in a quick shot when he silhouettes himself against his own light. A Ju 88! Strikes appear all around his nose area. By now he must be very low. Suddenly, the whole field is plunged into total blackness.

Paul and I speed up and around the airfield again. Imagine our surprise, when looking up, we see another aircraft on the downwind leg. I pull up sharply and overshoot his tail. I execute a sharp wing-over and close in to fire a quick burst of cannon, noticing strikes all over the starboard wing and cockpit area. Pieces fall off. It is a Heinkel He 111—a bomber—and huge sparks are trailing behind him as we pass. We see him no more.

Hanging around the area we are challenged by the searchlights. We fire off a sister and the lights are doused. "There goes their visual Lorenz on again, Paul," I say.

Our patrol time is coming to an end and I turn away. Quietly we climb to 6,000 feet, ready to dive back in to bomb. Very often they will switch off all lights as we increase power to climb—they know what's coming. Okay, we're there now with our bomb doors open and our bombs armed. We roll into our dive, aiming at the runway—5,000—4,000—3,500. We ease out of the dive at 3,000 feet and release our bombs just as the searchlights reach up to grab us. We weave and skid gently out of their rays, looking to see our bomb strikes.

We notice that there is an extra string of lights beside the main flare path, and a lot of activity at the upwind threshold of the runway. Must be where our Ju 88 went in. Our bombs burst right on the runway. All lights are doused as we weave and dive away from the airfield to set course for home.

"Okay, George, steer 293⁰M. We're going for a Gee fix in the North Sea. ETA twenty-two minutes and seventy-six miles away against a headwind." This I do. Now we can both relax a bit.

At 21:35 hours we reach our invisible destination and Paul says, "Okay, George, alter course to 263⁰ M." "OK, Paul, look behind." We are headed for the British coast, 204 miles and sixty-one minutes away. Fatigue has caught up with me and I ask, "Paul, hang on to this for a bit while I rest my eyes, will you, please?" He reaches over and flies with his left hand as I lean my head back to rest. "Cats-eye" intruding requires tremendous concentration and is very tiring. I sometimes wonder anxiously, as I lean back like this, if I will be alert enough to land the aircraft safely. I am so tired. We will start to accumulate a film of salt on our windscreen that will further reduce my vision.

We are now forty miles from the British coast, near enough to make our initial radio contact. As Paul turns on our IFF, I say, "Hello, *Largetype*. This is *Cricket 34*, identifying, and my cockerel is crowing (IFF turned on)." "Roger *34*," they reply, "*Largetype* out."

Ten minutes later, as we cross the coast—a most welcome sight—I transmit, "*Cricket 34* drying my feet and changing frequencies."

"Roger, *34*. Goodnight."

"Goodnight, *Largetype*, and thank you. *Cricket 34*—out."

Now is the time to call base (Little Snoring), turn on my navigation lights, and turn my IFF off.

"Hello, *Exking*, *Cricket 34* drying my feet, clear to the circuit."

"Hello, *34*, you are clear to the circuit. Call overhead at 3,000 feet."

"Roger *Exking*, *34* out."

England is very black at the moment and it seems so unlikely that in all the darkness below an airfield can suddenly light up.

"George," Paul says. "We are just coming over base now."

"Hello, *Exking*. *Cricket 34* over base at 3,000 feet. May we have the flare path lit, please?"

"Roger *34*. *Exking* out."

I descend quickly to 1,500 feet on our downwind leg: drop the undercarriage; check my fuel, rpm; radiator flaps open; then turn smoothly to port on final, keeping my airspeed at 150 mph all the way around. Five hundred feet above ground, full fine pitch, I drop my flaps, trim off the control pressures, and adjust power to hold 140 mph and a nice sink rate. With the threshold of the runway coming up quickly, I allow my speed to slacken to 130 as I cross it. Then, throttling right back, I hold off and we sink gently to touch down with the tail wheel low—not a three-pointer, but much smoother, and I am always in control. Turning off at the end of the runway I call, "*Cricket 34* clear. Goodnight, Cobbt," to which our controller replies, "Roger *34*. Goodnight, old chap."

I taxi along the perimeter track to our dispersal area, where our everfaithful ground crew has been standing by for our return. Our marshaller waving his illuminated wands guides us into position.

With brakes on, engines at 1,000 rpm, radio off, rad flaps closed, I pull out

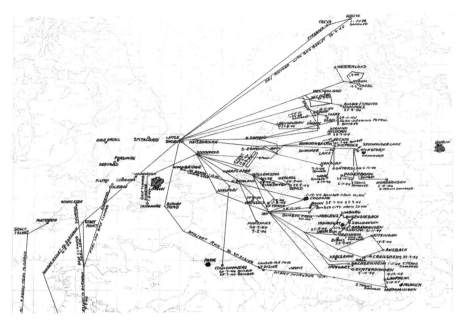

Following each mission, after checking with his navigator's log, George Stewart drew in the night's flying on this map, which covers an extended tour from July to December 1944. *G. Stewart*

the idle cut-off knobs, and—when both props are stopped—gas off, switches off, throttles closed, and all lights off. Paul opens the door, hands down our ladder and prepares to disembark. "Chocks in place," the ground crew says. "Any joy?"

"A bit," I reply. "Brakes off."

Paul is now climbing down the ladder and the gyros are still humming as I unstrap and remove my helmet. "Ouch!" My bloody ears hurt from the damned earphones pressing against them for so long. My face is tender and perspiring where my oxygen mask has been touching it. What a relief to get it all off. My bottom is now feeling the effects of sitting on a most uncomfortable dinghy for so long, and as I climb down, my circulation starts up again. I've been longing to stretch and I do so as soon as I get out, taking a much savoured deep breath. I head back to re-christen our tail wheel before the 15-hundredweight arrives to take us back to the flight office and our lockers. Glad to be back, we are feeling slaphappy with fatigue. We laugh at anything and everything as we chat with our ground crew and then with the other crews. Paul and I put our gear into our respective lockers and then we mount our bikes and cycle back to the intelligence section for debriefing. Paul, as usual, complains bitterly about his bulky navigation bag being so bloody awkward to carry on a bike.

With a cup of hot tea and a cookie, we relax, waiting to be debriefed. All at once the world seems a better place. The intelligence officer motions Paul and me over to a seat and we tell him all about our trip as he makes notes. This concluded, we hand in our escape kits, retrieve our valuables, and head for the officers' mess, where, with the other crews, we have a most welcome meal of eggs, bacon, toast, and tea. There is a lot of chatter as we linger over this treat. Then delicious fatigue creeps over all of us and we gradually break up and bike back to our huts and our beds—tired, but relaxed and happy.

The Phantom Auster and Other Stories

Recollections of a Royal Canadian Artillery Air Observer

W. B. (BILL) HAGARTY

F lying light aircraft in an active war zone—aircraft normally used for pilot training and recreational flying during peacetime—would seem a hazardous assignment, and it was. Air Observation Post (AOP), "seat-of-the-pants" operations, were an important, if unsung, aspect of wartime flying in aid of ground forces. AOP pilots were the "eyes" of the army—specifically the artillery—contributing as significantly as did the pilots who flew photo-recce Mustangs and ground-attack Typhoons. Their aircraft, the Auster, developed from the ubiquitous American Taylorcraft and powered by Lycoming or de Havilland engines, was a sturdy machine of simple steel tube and wood construction with fabric covering.

As the son of a distinguished senior artillery Officer, joining the Canadian Army was a logical choice for Bill Hagarty. He left the University of Western Ontario in 1942, in his freshman year, to enter the Royal Canadian Artillery as a nineteen-year-old lieutenant. Receiving his gunnery training at Gordon Head, British Columbia, and Petawawa, Ontario, he was posted overseas to England in 1943, where he took advantage of an offer made to artillery officers to train as AOP pilots. He was sent to No 22 Elementary Flying Training School, RAF Marshall Field, Cambridge. He amassed one hundred hours on Tiger Moths before moving to Andover for AOP training and conversion to the British Taylorcraft Auster, which he flew for a further one hundred hours. Completing his course with the rank of Captain, he and his fellow graduates flew their Austers directly across to Lille, France. There he performed transport and communications duties before joining his unit at Breda in the Arnhem area of Holland in March 1945—where he begins his story.

Later, on leave in England, Captain Hagarty was privileged to have his father, Col W. G. Hagarty DSO, a regimental CO with the Royal Canadian Horse Artillery, as a passenger in his Auster. Leaving the Service, Bill Hagarty returned to University to obtain a law degree, setting up practice in London, Ontario. Bill's story appeared in the Spring 1994 issue of the CAHS *Journal.*

In Holland, 'B' Flight, my flight, was transferred from Breda to Nijmegen to be attached to the 5th Canadian Armoured Division. After spending a few days beside the Maas Kanaal near the main road into the city, we finally selected a farm down river, near the village of Ewijk, as our base. Not far away was a tall, thin, and white church spire, which made the site easy to spot from the air. There was a fairly flat field with some tall poplars here and there along the sides. Inland, to the southwest, was a very large marshy area. We set up our living quarters, such as they were, under the apple trees just behind the farmhouse. The wind direction was usually such that we took off between poplar trees toward the marsh.

The forward areas and infantry positions, as pointed out to them by an artillery officer from Divisional HQ (headquarters), are marked on an old map that recently came to light—just as they were given that day in 1944. Starting on the left at a place called Dodewaard near the Waal, they wandered through Zetton, Valbourg, and around in front of Lienden and Elst, and finally circled back to the Waal upstream from Nijmegen. The whole area was so utterly flat and had so little cover that at times our pilots were unsure of their position, especially at night.

The Allies held Nijmegen and its bridge while the Germans held Arnhem, the two cities being only about ten miles apart. The river divided upstream and the branch that flowed by Arnhem was called the Neder Rijn, and the branch that flowed by Nijmegen was known as the Waal.

Rumour had it that a British Auster AOP (air observation post) had been shot down by German Fighters—Focke Wulf Fw 190s—before 'B' Flight arrived; but we were told, "You guys don't have to worry. All you have to do is head for the bridge. It's ringed with every type of anti-aircraft gun available." This was said, of course, to bolster 'B' Flight's courage in accordance with the usual army psychology, but when the pilots stopped to think about it, we realized that we couldn't stay close to the bridge all the time. How were our little Austers, flying at 80 mph, supposed to beat German fighters to the bridge, when they were doing 400?

While our training back in England stood us in good stead, we abandoned a few things as we went along. The parachutes on which we sat turned out to be so uncomfortable and put some of our heads so close to the cabin roof, that we stopped using them.

For the most part, we didn't concern ourselves unduly about flying over the line, "gun-to-target." We had to know where that line was on the ground at the moment that every shell came down. Above it was the best place from which to provide corrections and trying to do so from a flank was much more difficult. In any case, if we managed to time it right, the shell was already supposed to have passed! We positioned ourselves to make a run across the front of the gun, so to speak. "Fire," we would say, and the guns would reply, "Shot—thirty—over," meaning they had fired and the time gun-to-target was thirty seconds. This gave the pilot time to get into position, to steady the aeroplane, and to grip the joystick between his knees, freeing both hands to hold his binoculars. Then he had to find the target in the lenses and wait for the shell to come down.

On a bumpy day, just as the pilot was set, the plane might give a sudden lurch and he would lose sight of everything. By the time he had things on an even keel, the round was down with the smoke blowing away—and he hadn't seen a thing. He had to go around and redo the whole procedure. In bad weather, a "shoot" could take much longer than at other times.

RANGING

Today we hear a great deal about radar-guided missiles that seem to hit the target every time. During the Second World War, the army was still using field, medium, and heavy artillery, which was usually located well to the rear, relatively safe from infantry attack, but close enough to hit enemy positions. The order to fire would come from a forward observation post carefully located on a high point, such as a hill or a church steeple. The observer would move or adjust the shells on to a target in a procedure referred to as "ranging." During the First World War, tethered observation balloons helped the batteries on the ground—and became a favourite target for enemy fighter aircraft. Balloon observers were thus probably the first to use parachutes in war.

To those who might not be familiar with what an artillery observer was up against, it might be of some help to explain that shells fired at the same range and elevation would not all land in the same place. There would be a spread of shell craters in the shape of a double cone, sharp at both ends and of some width in the centre—which became larger as the gun was fired at greater distances.

The bottom line to ranging was that if an observer was able to fire a number of shells at the same distance and could see that the number landing behind (or plus) the target, was equal to those landing in front (or minus), it could safely be assumed that the centre of the spread (or double cone) of shell craters was close enough to the target to justify firing until a hit was obtained. Alternatively, all guns in the battery or regiment could be called upon immediately to saturate the general area. Again, if the observer was trying to hit enemy infantry, crossing a field for example, the procedure was somewhat shortened, and four guns could be ranged instead of one. As many guns as were available could be called down as soon as one shell was in the general vicinity. Carrying out this procedure from the air gave us one tremendous advantage over an observer on the ground. We were able to see a great deal more and see very well.

However, there were disadvantages. As observers in the air, we were always on the move—keeping out of the way of our own shells, staying extremely alert at all times, ready to dive down and fly as close as possible to the ground to evade enemy fighters. As well, we had to keep the aircraft straight and level in order to focus the field glasses on the target. We had to know the precise moment that the shell was expected and provide needed corrections (left or right, add or subtract). Also, as I've explained, we had to be in the best position we could manage when the shell landed, as close as possible to the line gun-to-target. The angles were always changing—if we were crossing the gun-to-target line when the shell landed we were ideally located and the angle was perfect. The further away we were from this position, the more difficult the job became.

While in the air, observation was much better than on the ground. On the other hand, our Auster was up there in plain sight of friend and foe alike. There was a chance of being attacked by enemy fighters and if we strayed too close to the forward areas or happened to fly over an enemy pocket of resistance, we were subject to ground fire.

Before takeoff, it was wise for pilots to know exactly where the gun positions were. Once we picked a target, we had a pretty good idea of the path the shells would take, and could try our best to avoid them whenever we gave the order to fire. The formula $4T^2$, where T was the time of flight, told us the height of the trajectory. For example, a time of thirty seconds put the shells 3,600 feet in the air and we seldom flew that high, but it had happened. In

Holland, the Flight heard about a pilot who had been killed when he was hit in the air by a 100-pound shell. More recently, a gunnery officer, who had served in Italy, told a group about how he had seen an Auster aircraft disintegrate right in front of his gun position—hit by a 25-pounder shell. It was only too easy for a pilot to become so involved in what he was doing that he simply lost track of the gun position when he gave the order to fire. There was quite a bit to do and think about when one was conducting a shoot from the air.

Of course a pilot could be sent up in a hurry, or when the division was just completing a move, or when some of the units had changed their gun positions. However, once the pilot got two rounds on the ground, fired in the same direction and at two different distances, the line gun-to-target was laid out quite clearly and the pilot could go on from there. Such a practice was not uncommon!

Strangely, one 25-pounder regiment in the 2nd Canadian Division wanted nothing to do with AOPs. Rumour suggested a plausible explanation. A certain AOP pilot, it seems, thought he had solved the problem of avoiding shells in the air by flying figure-eights just behind the gun positions. He could observe the fall of the shells fairly well and in reasonable safety, provided that the target was not too far away. Unfortunately, the Germans saw what he was up to. Calling in their own artillery, they saturated the area over which he seemed to be flying, and the regiment suffered casualties.

AOP pilots had also to be careful not to give away the location of their landing field, especially since it was usually located reasonably close to Divisional HQ. They were trained to carry out *concealed approaches,* descending to tree top height well away from the field and then working their way toward it, staying as low as possible.

THE BARGE

One evening, 'B' Flight was gathered in our farmhouse when we suddenly heard the sound of Bren guns and the more rapid firing of enemy Schmeissers. One of the group had served in Italy and recognized the sound. We were all surprised. It was uncomfortably close.

Not long after, on a miserably wet afternoon, a call came for somebody to take off immediately to "sink and destroy" a barge that was tied up on the German side of the river. The Germans held a partly demolished factory on the Canadian side, it was explained, and our patrols had reported recently that the enemy was there in some strength. That was from where the enemy night patrols were coming, hence the firing. They were bringing their supplies over at night on this barge.

The cloud was down to 800 feet and there was intermittent rain. After some discussion, I was sent off. Protests had done nothing to change the order from HQ. It had to be done—now! Whoever gave the order was obviously no flyer, since clouds and rain meant nothing to someone who stayed on the ground.

No sooner had I taken off than I was in the clouds and had to descend to 700–750 feet. Visibility was minimal and I found it necessary to edge a lot closer to the river than I had ever dared until the barge—of considerable size—came into view. It was tied up facing downstream at a wharf some distance from Arnhem. Directly behind the wharf was what looked like a huge, half-destroyed, steel factory with the roof missing. It must have been somewhere around Heveadorp, or further down the river toward the bend opposite Heteren.

I had been given the British 107th Medium Regiment. They were quite serious about wanting the barge out of the way and a 100-pound shell from their beautiful five and a half-inch gun did a great deal more damage than one from a 25-pounder field gun. Soon rounds began coming down short in the water and over into the steel factory. What a show of sparks that produced! Even when the rain blocked out the target, those big shells hitting the factory showed up bright and clear and that helped. Around and around I flew in the mist and rain with the joystick between my knees and both hands on my binoculars, each time a round was to come down.

Still the barge just sat there like a huge slab of rock, completely unaffected, even by shell fragments and splinters. Finally, it became obvious that hitting that thing was simply not going to happen. One round was in the water and the next in the factory with clockwork precision. I was right on line with each round directly opposite the centre of the barge. Every time I thought of tampering with the range, the next round convinced me that the mean point of impact (MPI) was right on target. The rain worsened and I was beginning to run out of gas with the big "E" for empty showing up on the gas gauge. I had fired fifty rounds! It was time to go home. Turning away, I decided to shoot just one more for the hell of it!

As that final round was about to come down, a rain squall partially blocked my view; but I thought I saw something that looked like a round, only this time it was off to the left, near the bow. There were no sparks, nor was there a water spout. Then everything was completely obscured and out of sight. Waiting for the rain to move off, I crept a bit closer. As the barge slowly came back into view, I thought I could see something red along the water line aft. Could the stern possibly be rising? My view cleared and I saw that the bow was down even with the water level. The shoot was over. With a great sigh of relief I was able to report, "Target sinking."

THE CHURCH SPIRE

The tall, white church spire, topped with a large, gold-painted wooden cross, helped to mark the general vicinity of the village from the air. Beyond that was the farm with its rather narrow field. The trees diminished somewhat, and beyond that was the large marshy area—with a derelict RAF Stirling bomber in the middle of it.

The counter-battery people asked for help in locating German 88-mm field guns that were firing mostly at dawn and at dusk. They requested 'B' Flight to set up patrols at these times to try and spot gun flashes and give them some map references or even to try to knock them out. Getting into my Auster in the dark with the luminous dials in front of me, I took off between the tall poplars with only the bright stars and no other lights. For me, this was a different experience, although, like all army pilots, I had done some night flying during my training back in England. (The most noticeable thing about night flying, other than the fact that one can't see much, is that it is generally smooth and there are no bumps. One often wished it were that way during the day. It would have made our shoots so much easier.)

I was flying back and forth between the two river branches when the sun came up. It was one of those beautiful sunny, cloudless days. I clutched my glasses and searched back and forth, from Arnhem on the right to the Waginengin area on the left. There were certainly plenty of houses on the far bank. On the right you could still see the many Churchill tanks on the main road close to the river and the city of Arnhem. One behind the other, they had been knocked out like clay pigeons as they had desperately tried to reach the Allied Airborne Troops trapped in the city. On the left, next to the main bridge, was a large, black railway bridge, torn and twisted. There were many towers of one sort or another along the far bank, like those that the fire station facilities used for drying fire hoses in this country. It seemed that the Germans also had lots of available observation posts (OPs). With so many, some had to be in use, but which ones?

Away to the left in the background was an open area with burnt out gliders or aircraft and a lot of earth works. Since HQ had asked the Flight to report anything at all that they noticed, I started to report these. Then I realized that this was probably the area where the airborne troops had landed in the attack on the city, the operation since dubbed *A Bridge Too Far*.

As carefully as I looked, I could see no movement whatsoever, nor was there any sign of a gun flash. Usually, when the Germans saw an observation aircraft flying around, they would not fire lest they be spotted and perhaps this was the case that day.

I kept checking the sky above and in front of me, remembering the day when I saw a German jet with swept wings going almost straight up at considerable speed. While I didn't think an Me 262 would bother a small plane like mine, I wasn't able to convince myself completely.

Another day, I spotted a large formation of Typhoon fighters with Allied white-stripe markings on them and I felt very secure. A few moments later two of them peeled off and dove straight for me. I rocked my wings back and forth so that they could not help but see my own *friendly* stripes. When they went roaring past I was very relieved. I almost felt their fingers itching to shoot at something. Perhaps they too had had a disappointing day!

Faster aircraft like the Typhoon and Mustang were not suitable for the work that I was doing, waiting for shells to come down, estimating corrections, and going through what was sometimes a long procedure. Slower machines were better for this purpose, but they were, of course, much more vulnerable from the air as well as from the ground. For this reason, there were standing orders that we were not to fly over enemy positions and were to keep at least one thousand yards back of the forward area.

Getting back to my story, I had not been able to spot anything in the bright morning sun. There was just nothing moving; so with the big "E" again beginning to show on the fuel gauge in front of the windscreen, I turned and headed for home. Looking ahead, I began to realize that I was in deep trouble. As far as the eye could see in front, as well as to the right and to the left, was a solid mass of moving cloud, the leading edge slowly passing beneath me. The very worst of it was that off to the left in the distance, sticking above the cloud, were the tops of tall buildings in the city of Nijmegen!

I cursed myself for not noticing this before. I remembered how it had been drilled into us repeatedly to keep a good lookout at all times—above, below, in front, left, right, and behind. Well, I had certainly been keeping a good lookout, but not behind and below. As I flew, I looked in vain for a break in the cloud layer. To do me any good, it would have to be an awfully big one since the cloud was very low—maybe even down to ground level! I got in touch with the field only to learn that the tops of the poplars were sticking into the bottom of the clouds. At least I did have some room—but how was I to get down there?

In a few minutes, my fuel would be gone and I was going to have to dead-stick-in. Unless I was very, very lucky, I could have a very serious argument with an obstacle such as a tree!

As I waited for the inevitable, I caught sight of something shining in the bright sun. It was the gold cross at the very top of the church spire, marking the general vicinity of the village. Then I knew what I could do. I would fly beyond it for some distance until I was past all of the trees and over the area of the bog, then I would let down.

Dropping through the cloud layer seemed to take forever, but suddenly I was flying in the grey light underneath, only a few feet above the marsh. Slowly and carefully I turned back the way I had come. In the distance in front of me, I could see the line of trees with the cloud-shrouded tops, but where was the field? As I approached the tree line—downwind, giving me more ground speed than I needed or wanted—I spotted an Aldis Lamp blinking brightly off to the left, but it was too late to help me. I was almost to the trees and unable to do anything but slam on more throttle and burst upward into the bright sun, to do the whole thing over again. This time, just as I got down—turning carefully, not wanting to stick a wing into the ground or get caught up in the clouds—I saw the blinking Aldis. I managed to turn toward it and flew between the poplars. I was able to touch down early and stop just before the dirt road at the end of the field.

I had learned a lesson that day. I didn't know exactly what it was, but from then on, I was very, very careful when looking around to always check both behind and below!

DREAM TARGET

It was my turn to take the evening sortie. I was flying back and forth from opposite Arnhem on the right to a point almost opposite Wageningen on the left. The light was beginning to fade and the gas getting low. I was about to turn for home, when I thought I saw something that looked like a gun flash, just an instantaneous pinpoint of light. Had I imagined it?

I wasted no time giving the 107th Medium Regiment a mike target. The first round came down minus and to the right. This was going to be my "dream shoot," I was going to clobber this gun position with every 100-pound shell that I could muster!

The pilots of 'B' Flight with one of their Auster aircraft. (L-R): Ray Morton, Bill Hagarty, "Suds" Sutherland, Mike Henderson, and Flight Commander George Nixon. *W. B. Hagarty*

Then all of a sudden my dream shoot was over, finished, done, ended. The radio had not gone dead, but it might just as well have. From the earphones came a guttural sound, like somebody barking in German. In vain I called my corrections. The guns couldn't hear a word I said and I couldn't hear them.

PRANG

I was returning to the field on one of those days when the cloud base was down to 800 feet and everything was sopping wet from intermittent rain and no wind. Coming in for a landing, I overshot—the brakes were useless on the wet grass. Back in England, we had been told not to *prang* an Auster head-on if we could possibly help it. "There is the hot engine, then the gas tank, the windshield, the instrument panel—and you." So with my last remaining airspeed, I slammed on rudder and shot sideways across the ditch at the end of the field. The right wing folded up like an accordion and so did the undercarriage.

About a day later, a British salvage vehicle arrived and the crew unbolted just about everything they could. They packed the Auster pieces away and drove off. A remark from one of the ground crew that, "She was overdue for an engine and flight check anyway," didn't really make me feel any better.

We managed to get by with only three aircraft, but it wasn't long until TJ226 was back with a new right wing and undercarriage and an engine that sounded a great deal better. And she flew like a dream. I was pleased to have my own machine back again.

THE WRONG MAP REFERENCE

When 'B' Flight first arrived, we were told to keep a good lookout—the Germans were rumoured to have captured an Auster. Nothing was heard or seen of it. Days passed and nobody brought up the subject again, but that was not the end of it.

As I was about to go up one sunny afternoon, one of the ground crew begged to be taken along. I hesitated because the Auster flew like a brick with two on board, but since this was not the first time the man had asked, and he was supposed to have one of the best pair of eyes in the Flight, I relented. We took off with everything looking quite peaceful in the bright sunlight. Suddenly the R/T came alive with a message, "*Peter Six, Peter Six*, you will engage and destroy the tower, map reference 123456. Over." Acknowledging, I thought that at last they had spotted one of those towers in use by the Germans on the far bank. When I studied my map, I saw that the reference was some considerable distance beyond the river. As far as I could see through my glasses, there was no tower anywhere in the vicinity. All I could see was one solitary white house located on the right side of a road, some distance beyond a village called Bennekom. The road itself stretched away into the distance at right angles from the river.

I replied, "*Peter Six, Peter Six.* Check map reference. Over." Every time I repeated this, I received the same answer—the map reference was correct. In vain I reported, "No tower visible at that reference." Finally a new voice came over the R/T, "*Peter Six, Peter Six*, *Sunray* here—you will engage and destroy the target given to you at map reference 123456. You are being given a direct order. Over."

Now if there was anything that could impress a young AOP pilot, it was the voice of *Sunray* coming over the R/T—especially from Divisional HQ! *Sunray* was of course code for "Commanding Officer." I realized at once exactly where I stood, even though they had told me back in England that senior army officers, as a rule, knew nothing about AOP or flying in general.

The first round from the 107th Medium Regiment came down about one hundred yards to the right of the village. I gave the order, "Less one degree

'B' Flight at their base in Holland during a visit from Squadron Commander, Major Dave Blyth. Capt Bill Hagarty is seated at left front. *W. B. Hagarty*

repeat. Over,"—which was to move left at the same range, as I wanted it to land on the road. The second round came down about three hundred yards to the left of the first. Suddenly I realized that the guns must be firing at almost their maximum range of eighteen thousand yards since one degree would have brought the shell over one hundred yards for each six thousand yards of range. Quickly, I gave the correction, "More forty minutes repeat. Over."

Studying the area carefully, I judged that the next one should be pretty close to the road, about where there was a cluster of houses, not far from the road junction just north of the village.

I gave the order to fire, looking at my watch that showed the seconds quite clearly. Then I steadied my glasses and got ready for the third round to come down. Just as I expected it to land, the cluster of houses suddenly disappeared in a very wide, deep red explosion, immediately followed by a huge tower of black smoke going straight up. There didn't seem to be any wind, but as the column rose to some considerable height, it slowly started to drift off to the right.

I flew away to the left and then off to the right, but there was no way I could see that wretched white house from either flank. As I flew back and forth wondering what I was going to do, the voice of *Sunray* came over the R/T once more, wanting to know why I wasn't continuing with the shoot as I had been ordered. I was not happy to find that *Sunray* had been listening.

As I looked up at the smoke column, I knew at once what I had to do: parachute or no, I would climb until I could see over the top. At over 7,000 feet, the white house finally came into view again. Flying back and forth I was able at last to observe five rounds, all at the same range—three plus and two minus—with each shell landing some considerable distance from the others.

It was going to take a lot more than fifty rounds to hit that thing. With fuel running low, I turned for home reporting, "MPI adjusted, record as target; over." As I looked ahead, I told my passenger to keep an eye out and I slumped down in my seat. I had no way of knowing that my afternoon sortie was still far from over.

AN UNFORTUNATE INCIDENT

As I headed back toward the Waal at about one third throttle, descending slowly, I tried not to think, but I couldn't help it—what a hell of a shoot that had been! I suddenly felt drained. I needed to get out and walk.

We had descended to around 1,500 feet when I felt a tap on my shoulder, "There's an Auster coming up behind us." I didn't even turn around. They've contacted the Flight and sent one of the guys up to check up on me, I thought, and this did nothing to improve the way I felt.

A short time later I was thumped on the shoulder and my passenger shouted in my ear, "This Auster is getting awfully close!" I turned to see an Auster coming up on my left. If I can see his number, I thought, I'll know who they sent up. Toward the rear of his fuselage, I saw dark green paint smeared over the place where the number should have been, and the pilot was wearing one of those tattered old helmets, like we wore back at Cambridge, flying open-cockpit Tiger Moths. This guy was certainly not one of us—so who was he?

My "visitor" moved even closer. We were now flying wingtip to wingtip. I watched the pilot lean over and slide back the window on the right side of the cabin. In his right hand I recognized what looked like a revolver! "What *is* the matter with this guy?" I asked myself. Then I remembered that the Germans had captured an Auster! From that moment I had only a single thought in my head—to keep from being shot!

If you want to make an Auster really move, you use the largest control surface, the rudder, so I began gyrating from one wingtip to the other. Each time I looked back, there he was, right behind me. When I attempted to straighten up, he edged closer. I tried everything I knew, but I just couldn't shake my shadow. He stuck like glue.

In desperation, I made a sudden steep turn to the right. Glancing behind, I saw my pursuer continuing around and away to the left. As we drew opposite, I fired my flare pistol. The flare fell away before it had travelled a fraction of the distance, but it had the desired effect. My pursuer stayed at a respectable distance. I got on the R/T and received a short, calm, yet dubious response.

By now we were over the Waal flying fairly low. As I turned for home my *visitor*, who was a bit higher, turned and came straight for me. The whole thing started all over again. I remember flying around a lighthouse on the edge of the river with his shadow right behind mine. I tried not to think what would happen when I ran out of gas; I knew that I couldn't keep this up and, of course, I had no time to try to reload my flare pistol. I thought of the heavy .45 revolver at my waist. With a recoil that took both hands to hold the muzzle down, it was next to useless. Frantically, I continued swinging this way and that.

The R/T finally came to life, "Fly over the field." All I could think of was, "I'm trying, I'm trying!" Gyrating over the trees, I saw the field in the distance, and so did my shadow who suddenly swung away. I was able to straighten up, climb a bit, and level off. As I looked back down to my left, I saw the him fly, at tree top height, right down the field from one end to the other. Then he turned and headed back in the direction of Arnhem.

The Flight commander's voice came over the R/T, "Follow him and see where he goes." I did so and saw my opponent reach a point about half way to the City of Arnhem, where he landed normally on a field with a few thin poplars on one side. Three other Austers were drawn up in a neat row, with some army vehicles under camouflage nets.

The next morning 'B' Flight received a signal, "'B' Flight Commander and the *pilot in question* will be at British Corps HQ at 14:00 hours sharp!" The flight commander and I arrived in front of an imposing building with sentries at the entrance. We were escorted up a wide flight of stairs into what appeared to be a ballroom where rows of empty chairs all faced towards one corner. Four or five army officers sat behind a large mahogany desk. On the wall was a huge map of the Nijmegen/Arnhem area. The flight commander and I sat down quietly in the front row.

A British Army major, with AOP wings on his chest, stood up and asked me to come forward. A very impressive-looking man and somehow vaguely familiar, I couldn't remember where I had seen him before. He wanted the answer to just one question, "Were you or were you not flying over enemy lines yesterday?" Stoutly I maintained that I was not. The major asked me to come forward and point out on the map, just where I thought the forward lines were. I took a pointer and traced the Neder Rijn, from Arnhem on the right to Wageningen on the left.

There was absolutely no truth to the notion that the Germans had captured an Auster, said the major. It was nothing more than rumour with no intelligence to support it. I don't remember much more, except that the major did say that it was absolutely impossible for one Auster to get away from another. He was dead right. There were no more questions, nor was there any discussion. The major was serious, firm, and polite. I felt that he had been quite decent about the whole thing. The other officers behind the desk said nothing and it was not long before the flight commander and I were dismissed.

On the way home, we wondered why nobody had told us that the other flight was arriving. It was also a surprise to see a landing strip so close to the forward area, and with so little cover. In deference to my pursuer, I thought I might have appeared—to somebody who was flying farther back and at a much lower altitude—to have been at a greater distance than I really was. I certainly knew that I had been flying close to the river. I remembered looking down on it on a number of my turns, but I was sure that I had not been flying on the other side.

The whole thing had been unfortunate and it was lucky that nobody had been hurt. I never heard another word about it for the rest of the war. I didn't hear from 5th Div HQ about the target either—but that was no surprise.

When the shock started to wear off, I realized that it had not been all bad. Through a series of mistakes and errors, including my own, we had destroyed some sort of ammunition dump, which must have been of considerable size and value to the enemy. I vowed that if I ever did get across the river, I would fly over Bennekom and have a really good look.

ARNHEM IS CAPTURED

British Corps had a plan to cross the river upstream and attack Arnhem from the right flank. Not long after the attack, 'B' Flight moved its field from Ewijk to a position across the river, somewhere between Duiven and Greffelkamp. One of the first pilots to go up came down with a bullet hole in his wing strut and didn't even know that he had been shot at!

I found myself over the edge of the city, watching a long line of Sherman tanks below and ahead, going up a main street toward a large intersection. As I drew nearer and could look down between the buildings, the street off to the right of the intersection came into full view. Before I knew what was happening, an 88-mm anti-tank gun on split trails, about four hundred to five hundred yards back, opened fire hitting the lead tank just as it started across. All the other tanks came to an abrupt halt—I could see infantry racing up towards the intersection on both sides of the column, hugging the buildings as they went. Realizing I could do nothing, I turned away.

Soon the Army was through the city and starting to move northwest. As I flew just past the city limits, I spotted a long column of enemy infantry with vehicles, horses, and carts, moving from right to left in the vicinity of Kompagnieberg, almost at the very limits of my vision. They were stretched out along a country road with the head of the columns disappearing into a forest. At supper that night, we read the daily report, that AOP had spotted infantry moving to the left at that location. The next day, Div HQ was all in a flap. Enemy infantry had overrun some of the artillery positions during the night and a battery commander had killed two German soldiers with his revolver, right outside his caravan! 'B' Flight at least had the satisfaction of knowing that they had warned HQ of the presence of the Germans.

Our Flight moved again, to an open space just northwest of the city, along the edge of a large evergreen forest.

I can't remember the exact location, but one day, without warning as I flew along in the sun, tracers began streaking past my right wing like meteors! I found myself staring at the instrument panel fully conscious of what

A contemporary wartime drawing by RCAF cartoonist Ricky depicting an Auster in an extremely dicey Air Observation Post predicament. While the original caption is unknown, the reader can easily invent one. *DND PL 30314*

was happening but I couldn't react. Unable to think, I froze. Suddenly they stopped—only to start up again. This time streaming past my left wing, seemingly even closer. At long last, I was able to get hold of myself. I put the stick hard over to the right and forward. As the ground came up to meet me, I saw farm houses, barns, haystacks, animals, fields, forest, country roads—and nothing else—no sign of tracers coming from anywhere. Cautiously I circled, not daring to take my eyes off the ground. Finally I crept away. Having been missed twice, I didn't want to risk not being missed a third time.

Much later, in August 1945, in a mess at Petawawa, Ontario, an officer described a certain time and place when he saw an Auster surrounded by tracers. He was sure it was going to be shot down. Remembering the same time and the place, I looked him square in the eye and said, "So was I!"

On another day, I saw a number of Sherman tanks almost directly beneath me, at the edge of an evergreen forest, in hull-down positions. They were firing with HE (heavy explosive) as fast as they could. I couldn't make out exactly at what they were firing being unable to see anything at all in the trees. As I was about to turn away, I spotted two enemy Tiger tanks moving along a forest trail. The Shermans must have been trying to neutralize them with HE. They just might like to know that the Tigers were moving off. I immediately got on the R/T only to find that my battery was dead. It occurred to me to go in low with a message drop, but only for a moment. Quickly I flew back to make my report on the ground.

Not long after, I was sent up to observe and report on a Typhoon "shoot." The Division was apparently held up in open space, somewhere east of Barneveld—Kootwijkerbroek or Gardererbroek. The 25-pounders were supposed to mark the target area with smoke. I arrived and the Typhoons came in at great speed and began circling, I heard "shot" over the R/T, with the time of flight and down came the smoke—one thousand yards short! Fortunately the Typhoons did not go in until I was able to shout over the R/T, "Target one thousand yards north of smoke!" The GPO (gun position officer), no doubt having registered with HE, simply forgot that smoke shells always fall short when fired at the same range.

It was certainly a beautiful sight to see those Typhoons going in one after the other, firing their rockets—which exploded with pink smoke—and then finishing off with their cannon. There did not seem to be any return fire from the ground. When it was all over and the Typhoons had left, one small German jeep-like vehicle came out of some bushes and went tearing along the road as if the whole 5th Canadian Armoured Division was behind him, tanks and all.

On the way back, I remembered Bennekom and turned toward the river. My fuel was low and I knew I wouldn't have much time. When I got there, I had no trouble finding what I was looking for. I found a wide circle on the ground with nothing on the inside and dirt all around the perimeter. All the trees radiated out flat on the ground. Nearby was what looked like the remains of a house. As I banked away, I thought to myself, it must have been quite a bang.

When I landed I heard the news—the Flight had been transferred to the 2nd Canadian Infantry Division, so the next day, we bid a hasty farewell to General Hoffmeister's valiant armoured warriors and headed off into Germany.

ON GERMAN SOIL
The 2nd Div was somewhere between Oldenburg and Bremen, and 'B' Flight was headed for an abandoned German fighter base to the south. The weather was closing in and there was no time to look for anything else. As it turned out, the fighter base was too far away to use on a day-to-day basis, but we were able to put most of our vehicles out of the rain, inside a large hangar that had been only partially destroyed. On the tarmac were the remains of some of the dreaded Fw 190s, Germany's best fighters.

Div HQ was calling for sorties and target registrations; but with the cloud base down to 800 feet and occasional drizzle, it was out of the question. We appeared to be way out on a flank, with nobody around. That night, the two men posted as sentries seemed more important than usual.

The next day the weather was worse and I decided to explore the base. In the pilots' quarters I found a lot of albums containing many pictures of aircraft, mostly in the air. In what appeared to be the CO's office, behind the desk was a framed picture of an Fw 190.

On the way back, I looked up to see a very tall British RSM (regimental sergeant major) on top of a rise, giving me a parade ground salute. "We are in desperate need of aid," was all he said. He had been in a truck with a dozen or so gunners, commanded by a young 2nd lieutenant. Somehow they had got lost and had hit a mine on one of the nearby country roads. We grabbed the Flight medical orderly and a few stretchers, put the windshield down flat on the jeep, and set off.

We came upon the truck. The 2nd Lieutenant had been blown through the opening in the roof where he had been standing; but other than being shaken up, he seemed to be all right. The rest of the men were in the same state, except for the driver. After administering morphine and carefully turning the jeep around, we put him on a stretcher and headed back. The men were given hot tea and biscuits. An ambulance arrived and finally a truck from their unit. Usually back at a reasonably safe distance from the forward areas, 'B' Flight found this sort of thing a new experience. There was more to come.

The next day, while the rain had stopped, the cloud base was still low and it was misty. Since HQ was again calling for sorties and registrations, the flight commander headed off in his jeep with his driver to find a suitable field so that we could be ready as soon as the weather cleared. About an hour later, things started to happen all at once. The squadron commander arrived in his jeep unexpectedly—2nd Div was calling again for sorties. Then an A/T (anti-tank) unit called to say an army pilot and his driver were at a nearby field dressing station—they had hit a mine!

The squadron commander, hearing the news, immediately disappeared. I took off to find a field from the air, as close as possible to the reference given by HQ. The flight vehicles, ordered to proceed by road, were to be given a map reference on the way. The other three aircraft would follow as soon as possible, although the weather had not improved.

As I flew along at about 700 feet, I came across the remains of a jeep. The letters "RB" on the crumpled canvas identified the flight commander's vehicle. Some soldiers were checking it for parts and I decided to give them a haircut. They ran like rabbits. Luckily I looked ahead to see the biggest and ugliest set of high-tension wires. It could easily have been a double tragedy for, by that time, the flight commander was dead.

Close to the map reference given for Div HQ was a farm house and a barn at the edge of a triangular field surrounded by tall evergreens where I was able to land and take off. Immediately I radioed the reference to the vehicles on the road, to the waiting aircraft, and to Div HQ. A short time later, a crew arrived to clear mines from the road into the farm. They left strict instructions to stay off all other side roads. As I circled, I noticed that the main road leading in the direction of Oldenburg was littered with fallen trees.

Our vehicles and planes arrived safely. After supper there was a bang and some smoke beyond the end of the field. We were unable to find very much, except the front part of a jeep. Some distance away in the field was a spare tire surrounded by knives, forks, and spoons sticking straight into the ground. 'B' Flight was coming to the realization that German soil, compared to that of Holland, was not a very safe place to be.

At the end of the war, the squadron commander was quoted as saying, "All my pilots took the same risks and they all had the same experiences." Although what is written here is an account of some of the things that happened to one AOP officer, it is more or less what happened to all of us.

POSTSCRIPT:
The following is excerpted from a letter received by the author from H. van Bentum of Woudenbourg, Holland in November of 1991, in response to a request for information.

"At the time, it (Bennekom) was an area that was barricaded by the Germans and anyone caught going in there was shot. A cousin of mine (Gerrik van Beek, Rynsteeg, Bennekom), who was a farmer living a mile north of there, told me that there was a mill in the centre of Bennekom without any arms and there was a German ammunition dump there; but he wasn't there at the time. If something like that happened (the explosion) no Dutch people would be allowed in the neighbourhood. The Germans never let us know how many people or how much equipment was lost."

Glossary

A/C
Air Commodore, rank immediately above G/C and below A/V/M.

A/M
Air Marshall, rank above Air Vice Marshall.

A/V/M
Air Vice Marshall, rank above Air Commodore and below A/M.

AA
Anti-aircraft fire (Ack-Ack).

AC1
Aircraftsman First Class, rank above AC2.

AC2
Aircraftsman second class, lowest rank in RCAF.

Ack-Ack
(AA) Anti-aircraft fire.

Actuals
Maps with current weather data for flight planning purposes.

Advance routing
Prior notification of operational units regarding ATA flights.

Advanced Flying Training School (AFTS)
Second phase of UK pilot training.

Advanced Flying Unit (AFU)
UK school for final pilot training before assignment to an operational training unit (OTU).

Ailerons
Moveable control surfaces on trailing edges of aircraft wings. Operated by control column or stick to control aircraft in rolling axis.

Air Observer School (AOS)
BCATP units formed with mostly civilian pilots to train Air Observers (responsible for navigation and bomb aiming) and later Navigators (responsible only for navigation).

Air OP
Air Observation Post or AOP, light aircraft flown by an Army officer to provide information for ranging field guns.

Air Transport Auxiliary (ATA)
Paramilitary organization formed with qualified, but over-age male pilots and women to ferry aircraft in the UK, usually from factory to squadron.

Aircrew Re-selection Board
Body responsible for approving requests for remustering (change of trade) by airmen.

Airfield Commandos
RAF/RCAF ground crew trained to defend their base against hostile ground troops.

Airframe
Structure of an aircraft.

Albemarle
RAF Armstrong-Whitworth twin-engined bomber and glider tug.

Aldis lamp
Light with shutter for signaling in Morse code.

Altimeter
Instrument giving an aircraft's altitude based on air pressure or ground-reflected radio signals.

Anson
Avro Anson, principal twin-engined training aircraft used in Canada along with much lesser numbers of Cessna Cranes and Airspeed Oxfords.

AOP
See Air OP.

AOS
See Air Observer School.

Arming wires
Safety devices to ensure that bombs did not detonate prematurely after release.

Army Co-op
Units assigned to help the army with photo-reconnaissance and ground attack.

ASL
Referring to height above sea level.

Astro (observation)
Navigation by means of stars and a sextant.

Astro hatch
Dome or opening in fuselage roof for navigator to take star shots.

Auster
British Taylorcraft Auster, single-engined, high-wing light aircraft used for artillery observation. See Air Observation Post and liaison flying.

Auto-lean/rich
Automatic fuel-mixture control.

Avenger
Grumman Avenger, American heavy single-engined torpedo bomber.

B55
British Airfield 55, temporary airfields built by Allies as they advanced across France were identified by numbers.

B&GS
Bombing and Gunnery School.

Balloon barrages
Groups of spaced out non-rigid balloons dangling cables, tethered around possible targets such as cities to obstruct enemy aircraft.

Barometric altimeter
Height gauge operating on air pressure.

Batman
On RAF squadrons, officer's servant.

Battle
Fairey Battle, RAF single-engined light bomber relegated to training duties with RCAF.

Battle dress
Combat, non-dress uniform with short jacket worn by RCAF, RAF, and Army.

Battle of Britain
Struggle for air supremacy over England won by RAF in September/October 1940, indefinitely delaying German invasion.

Battle of France
First meeting of RAF and Luftwaffe as British Expeditionary Force retreated across France to Dunkirk.

Beam Approach System
Means of making an IFT landing approach on an airfield using radio signals.

Beau
See Beaufighter.

Beaufighter
Bristol Beaufighter, much improved twin-engined heavy fighter development of Beaufort.

Beaufort
Bristol Beaufort, twin-engined torpedo bomber.

Bf 109
Messerschmitt Bf 109, widely used German single-engined, single-place fighter. Sometimes (erroneously) referred to as Me 109. (Bf: Bayerische Flugzeugwerke.)

Bleeding flaps
Gradual raising of landing flaps.

Blenheim
Bristol Blenheim, RAF twin-engined light bomber of early war years.

Blind flying
Operating an aircraft relying solely on instruments.

Blip

Image that an aircraft creates on a radar screen.

Blowing wheels down

Emergency method for lowering undercarriage with compressed air.

BOAC

British Overseas Airways Corporation, UK Government's former principal air carrier.

Bogey

Unidentified aircraft.

Bomber Command

Division of RAF/RCAF responsible for heavy strategic bombing aircraft and operations.

Boost

Intake manifold pressure for super-charged or *blown* (not necessarily supercharged) aircraft engines.

Boston

Douglas A-20 Boston, Americal light bomber used by RAF.

Bouncing bombs

Drum-shaped weapons designed by Sir Barnes Wallis to skip across the surface of the water in front of a dam. There they sank to a predetermined depth where the force of their explosion would be most effective.

Bren gun

British portable machine gun used by army.

British Commonwealth Air Training Plan (BCATP)

Massive scheme for training aircrew in Canada.

Buffalo

de Havilland DHC-5, twin-turboprop-powered Canadian short field trans-port.

Buzz Bomb

German V-1 "secret" weapon. Small jet-powered unmanned aircraft carry-ing 2,000-pound warhead. Precursor of cruise missile.

C-47

See Dakota.

Camera obscura

Room with lens in ceiling functioning as a large camera for simulated bomb-ing practice.

Cant

Cant Z-506, Italian tri-motored seaplane transport.

Captain

Officer in charge of an aircraft, usually the pilot (not a rank).

Carb heat

Means of preventing ice forming, restricting flow of air into carburetor.

Carburetor

Device for mixing fuel and air to be ignited in engine cylinders.

Caribou

de Havilland DHC-4, Canadian twin-piston-engined short takeoff and landing (STOL) transport.

Catalina

Consolidated PBY-5/5A Catalina/ Canso, widely used twin-engined American flying boat (or amphibian) long-range patrol bomber, also license-built in Russia.

Central Ferry Control

Body responsible for overall assignment of ATA pilots.

Chariots

Specially designed torpedoes with tandem seats for crewmen (charioteers) who would ride them to within range of a target.

Cheetah

Armstrong Siddeley Cheetah, British radial engine of 330 hp.

Chiefy

Senior NCO responsible for maintaining several aircraft.

Chocks
Triangular blocks fitted in front of wheels to prevent aircraft rolling inadvertently.

CI
Chief Instructor.

Circuit
Race track pattern followed by aircraft around an airfield prior to landing.

Clapped out
Worn out, the worse for wear.

CO
Commanding Officer.

Collector ring
Pipe circling radial engine to gather exhaust gases from cylinder exhaust stubs, safely discharging it into exhaust pipe(s).

Colonials
RAF airmen from Commonwealth countries.

Colour-of-the-day
Flare (of hue or combination of hues chosen daily) to identify friendly aircraft.

Come home
Retraction of wheels into their wells.

Commando
Curtiss C-46 Commando, American large twin-engined transport.

Commission
Traditionally a warrant conferring authority, with Pilot Officer as lowest commissioned RAF/RCAF rank.

Compass deviation
Variance in compass reading caused by metal in aircraft structure.

Controller
Ground-based officer responsible for directing fighters to enemy raiders.

Cookie
Very large bomb of 5,000–10,000 pounds or more.

Corsair
Vought-Sikorsky F-4U Corsair, heavy American single-seat, single-engine naval fighter.

Counter-battery people
Army section responsible for locating and silencing enemy artillery.

Coupe top
Transparent Plexiglas cockpit cover.

Crane
Cessna T-50 Crane, light American twin-engined aircraft used by RCAF as SFTS trainer.

Croix-de-Guere
French military decoration.

Cross-country (flight)
Point-to-point navigational flight (a requirement for pilot's wings).

Crossover feed
Provision for transferring fuel across the aircraft or from one wing tank to the other.

Crossover turn
A manoeuver in which one aircraft turns inside of another in order not to be left behind or to come abreast of leading a/c on final landing approach.

D-day
Code name for 6 June 1944 when Allied forces invaded continental Europe.

Dakota
Douglas DC-3 or C-47 Dakota, widely used American twin-engined transport/air liner.

Dam Busters
Name earned by 617 Squadron RAF after their successful raids on Sorpe, Mohne, and Eder dams.

Dash-7
de Havilland DHC-7, turbo-prop-powered Canadian four-engined feeder-liner.

Dash-8
de Havilland DHC-8, popular Turboprop-powered Canadian twin-engined feeder-liner.

Dauntless
Douglas Dauntless, American naval (carrier-borne) dive-bomber.

Dead reckoning
Navigating a plotted course with only a map, compass, timepiece and calculator.

Dead-stick landing
Approach and landing with no engine power.

Deck-level (on the deck)
Minimal height for flying.

Defiant
Bourlton-Paul Defiant, RAF single-engined two-place fighter fitted with gun turret.

DFC
Distinguished Flying Cross.

Differential throttle
Varying power to steer twin-engined aircraft while taxiing.

Dinghy
Inflatable life raft carried in aircraft.

Directional gyro
Navigational compass which can indicate a stable course.

Dispersal
Separate parking locations for aircraft to make them less vulnerable to air attack.

Div HQ
Division Headquarters.

Do (noun)
An offensive operation, 'Op' or mission.

Do 17
Dornier Do 17, twin-engined German light/medium bomber (first in series including Do 117, 217, and 215).

Dorsal fin
Fixed control surface above rear fuselage extending forward from fin.

Downwind leg
Part of circuit in which a pilot flies in the direction of the wind prior to turning into it for approach and landing.

Drift wires
Part of a bomb sight for measuring "crab" angle.

Drogue
See Target drogue.

Dropping zone
DZ, area where drogue-towing aircraft released their drogues for collection by airmen on ground.

Drum-feed
Means of supplying ammunition to machine gun or cannon from circular container.

DSO
Distinguished Service Order.

Dual
Flying with an instructor.

Elementary Flying Training School (EFTS)
First flying phase of BCATP using primary training aircraft such as the de Havilland Tiger Moth and Fleet Finch.

Elevators
Control surfaces on trailing edge of an aircraft's horizontal tailplane. Operated by moving the control column back or forward, changing pitch attitude of the aircraft.

Empennage
The tail of an aeroplane.

Engine fitter
Aero engine mechanic.

Engineer's panel
Engine instruments at flight engineer's position in aircraft.

Erks
Ground crew—fitters and riggers—who maintain aircraft.

ESN
Flare in enemy colour-of-the-day. Also *Sister*.

ETA
Estimated time of arrival.

Exactors

Hydraulic lines from throttle to engines in Westland Whirlwind.

Expired

See tour-expired.

F/C

Flight Commander, responsibility rather than a rank.

F/L

Flight Lieutenant, above Flying Officer and below Squadron Leader.

F/O

Flying Officer, rank above Pilot Officer and below Flight Lieutenant.

Fairchild 24

American single-engined light high-wing aircraft used for communications.

Faithful Annie

Avro Anson—to her crews.

Feathering (of props)

Rotating blades of an aircraft's propeller so that their width parallels general flow of air to minimize drag after engine failure.

Ferry pilot

Aircraft delivery pilot.

Ferry Pilots' Notes

Pocket book issued to ATA pilots with basic flying information on the aircraft they would be delivering (often never having flown the type).

Ferry pool

Group of aircraft delivery pilots.

Fighter affiliation

Simulated fighter attacks on bombers.

Fighter/bomber

Fighter fitted with bomb-racks for low-level attack or dive-bombing.

Finch

Fleet 16 Finch, RCAF two-place biplane elementary trainer.

Fire up

Start engine(s).

Fixed-pitch propeller

Props having blades that cannot be adjusted in flight.

Flak

Anti-aircraft fire. Also *AA*.

Flak ship

Small vessel equipped with batteries of anti-aircraft weapons to protect convoys from air attack.

Flaps (cooling)

Louvres controlling airflow through engine radiator or around an air-cooled engine.

Flaps (wing)

Surfaces that can be lowered into the air stream to slow an aircraft during landing or to bring the nose down. They also prevent stalling while allowing an aircraft to fly slowly.

Fleet Air Arm

Flying component of Royal Navy.

Flight

On fighter squadrons, unit of four aircraft (two sections) More with bomber squadrons.

Flight Engineer

Member of bomber crew responsible for engine operation.

Flight line

Aircraft parked in readiness.

Flying bomb

See Buzz Bomb.

Flying Wing

Post war RCAF unit at Winnipeg that actively operated aircraft.

Formate on

Take up station with (in formation).

Fuselage

The body of an aircraft.

Fw 190

Focke Wulf Fw 190, outstanding German single-place, single-radial-engined fighter.

G/C

Group Captain, rank above Wing Commander.

Gardening

Code for mine-laying by aircraft.

Gee

Navigation aid utilizing electronic pulses radiated from two stations.

General Duties

GD, RCAF trade for airmen assigned to miscellaneous ground work.

Geodetic construction

Sturdy and flexible basket-weave structure devised by Sir Barnes Wallis and used in Wellesley, Wellington, and Warwick bombers.

Glycol

Inline engine radiator coolant.

Go, No-go (situation)

When decision to fly or not is made by ATA pilot.

Go on the clocks

Fly on instruments.

Goose

Grumman G-18 Goose, American single-engined amphibious aircraft.

Grid ring and wires

Adjustable glass magnetic-compass top containing parallel sets of crossing wires.

Group

Unit comprising several wings.

Gun platform

Fighter aircraft as a weapons carrier.

Halifax

Handley Page Halifax, widely used RAF/RCAF four-engined heavy bomber.

Hampden

Handley Page Hampden, RAF twin-engined medium bomber.

Handling notes

Data on aircraft flying characteristics for ATA pilots and others.

Happy Valley

Industrial area in Germany heavily defended by flak batteries.

Hardened target

A military position such as a submarine pen protected by a depth of reinforced concrete.

Hardtack

Thin, very hard and dense biscuit used as emergency rations.

Hart

Hawker Hart, RAF single-engined prewar biplane light bomber.

Harvard

North American NA-66 Harvard, standard RCAF single-engined advanced trainer during the Second World War. American designed.

Havoc

Douglas Havoc, American night-fighter version of A-20 Boston light-bomber.

He 111

Heinkel He 111, German twin-engined medium bomber.

Heath Robinson (as adjective)

Comparing improvised aircraft modifications to whimsical inventions of a popular British cartoonist. Rube Goldberg would be American equivalent.

Hellcat

Grumman Hellcat, American naval fighter, successor to Wildcat, also used by Royal navy.

Hercules

Bristol Hercules, British radial aircraft engine alternative to R-R Merlin.

Hipper

German Pocket Battleship.

HMS *Hood*

British battlecruiser of 42,000 tons.

Hooter

RAF airfield klaxon horn for alerting airmen.

Hostile plot
Radar "blip" known to be an enemy aircraft.

Hudson
Lockheed Hudson, RAF/RCAF twin-engined medium bomber (US-built) development of Lockheed 14 airliner.

Hull down
When tanks have only their turrets visible.

Hunting
Unintended and barely perceptible oscillating movement of aircraft nose in level flight.

Hurricane
Hawker Hurricane, RAF single-seat, single-engine monoplane fighter; partner of the Spitfire in the Battle of Britain.

Hydraulicing
Obstruction of piston operation by oil build-up in bottom cylinders of a radial engine.

IFF
Identification, Friend or Foe, transponder device for recognizing friendly aircraft.

Initial Training School (ITS)
First pre-flight stage in BCATP.

Intelligence Section
RAF personnel devoted to collecting, interpreting, and utilizing latest information on enemy.

Intruder
Single aircraft, usually a Mosquito, raiding deep into occupied territory to harass enemy night-fighters returning to their bases or to attack targets of opportunity in daytime. In the latter role Bostons and Beaufighters and even Mitchells were occasionally used.

Irvin jacket
Upper part of fleece-lined two-piece RAF flying suit.

Jacobs
Jacobs L-4MB, American radial aircraft engine in 200–400 hp range.

J3 Cub
Piper J-3 Cub, very popular light two-seat, single-engined training aircraft.

Johnny Walker wandering mine
Explosive device capable of moving about underwater by repeatedly rising to the surface and sinking.

Joystick
Aircraft control column.

Ju 88
Junkers Ju 88, versatile German twin-engined medium bomber. Varients include Ju 188, 288, and 488.

Kestrel
Roll-Royce Kestrel, V-12 aero engine of 640-800 hp, predecessor of Peregrine and Merlin.

King George V Class
British 23,000-ton battleships.

Kite
Aircraft.

L 14
Document signed by pilot prior to flying, accepting an aircraft as serviceable.

LAC
Leading Aircraftsman, rank above AC1.

Lancaster
Avro Lancaster, very efficient four-engined RAF heavy bomber of the Second World War.

LG
Landing ground.

Liberator
Consolidated B-24 Liberator, long-range American four-engined heavy bomber.

Lightning
Lockheed P-38 Lightning, twin-engined American-built, long-range high-altitude fighter.

Link trainer
Single-place flight simulator to provide blind flying (instrument) experience for pilots.

Lodestar
Lockheed 18 Lodestar, American civil progenitor of Ventura.

Lorenz
System to aid night landing of aircraft.

Luftwaffe
German air force.

Lutzow
German 12,000-ton pocket battleship.

Lysander
Westland Lysander, RAF single-engined high-wing communications aircraft with exceptional short-field performance.

Mae West
RAF/RCAF inflatable life jacket.

Maggie
See Magister.

Magister
Miles Magister, RAF two-place, open cockpit, low-wing monoplane primary trainer.

Magnetic mines
Explosive devices which floated below the surface and rose beneath a ship, attracted by the metal of its hull.

Magnetic variation
Difference between true north and magnetic north.

Magneto
Device providing ignition spark for internal combustion engines.

Manchester
Avro Manchester, RAF twin-engined heavy bomber with unreliable R-R Vulture engines.

Manning Pool
Depot where RCAF recruits were kitted out and given basic drill training prior to streaming.

Maps and Signals Officer
ATA member in charge of Routeing Office.

Marauder
Martin Marauder, American twin-engined medium bomber also used by RAF.

Mark
Or Mk, designation for variant of an aircraft type, followed by Roman numeral.

Master
Miles Master, RAF two-place single-engined advanced trainer, equivalent to Harvard.

McKee Trans-Canada Trophy
Prestigious annual award to individual who has made important contribution to Canadian aviation.

Me 262
Messerschmitt Me 262, German twin-engined jet fighter.

Medium Regiment
Artillery unit equipped with guns in middle-range size.

Merlin
Rolls-Royce Merlin, widely used British V-12 aircraft engine ranging in power from 1,030 to 1,710 hp.

Meteorological office
ATA Ferry Pool location for weather information.

Meteorology basher
Officer responsible for briefing aircrew on weather.

Mike target
Object to be destroyed by artillery under direction of an AOP.

Mitchell
North American NA-62 Mitchell, American twin-engined medium bomber widely used by RAF and later by RCAF.

Mixture
Blend of fuel and air igniting in cylinders of internal combustion engine.

Mod
Modification.

Mosquito
de Havilland D.H. 98 twin-engined light bomber of wooden construction.

Mossie
See Mosquito.

Mustang
North American P-51 Mustang, very successful American fighter built to RAF order and specifications.

Nacelle
Streamlined housing for wing-mounted engine.

Nav light
Navigational lights on wing tips and tail, red for port and green for starboard with white on tail.

Nav
Navigator, part of a bomber's crew.

Navigational computer
Early device for calculating aircraft heading by triangulation, to compensate for wind and drift.

NCO
Non-commissioned officer.

NFT
Night flight test, to be sure that aircraft is serviceable.

Nomad
Northrop A-17A Nomad Two-place, single-engined monoplane, originally a USAAC attack bomber, used by the RCAF to tow target drogues.

Non-operational
Activities not directly involving the enemy such as test flights.

Number One
Lead pilot/aircraft in a section of fighter, or a formation of heavier aircraft.

Number Two
Second pilot/aircraft in a section of fighters, or a formation of heavier aircraft.

OC Flying
Officer-in-Command of flying operations.

Olives (in hydraulic system)
Means of preventing reverse flow of fluid in lines.

Op
See Operation.

Operation
(Op) Mission against the enemy.

Operational Training Unit (OTU)
School where aircrew were introduced to combat flying practices.

Operational type (aircraft)
An aircraft actively in service against the enemy.

Operational type (person)
An airman who has been in action.

Operations Officer
Unit member responsible for delivering flight assignments in Service or ATA.

Outlanders
Tongue-in-cheek reference to non-UK members of RAF.

Overload tanks
Large fuel tanks temporarily installed in aircraft fuselages for extra long range.

Oxford
Airspeed Oxford, British twin-engined training aircraft.

P/O
Pilot Officer, lowest commissioned rank in RCAF and RAF.

Pathfinders
Squadrons which located and marked targets for bomber streams.

Peregrine

Rolls-Royce Peregrine V-12 engine of 850 hp, used only in Westland Whirlwind.

Phony war

Early phase of the Second World War following British involvement but prior to active hostilities. Characterized by propaganda leaflet raids.

Pitot

Tube mounted outside of aircraft in air stream feeding air pressure to airspeed indicator.

Pongos

Research people responsible for innovative improvement in equipment. Also called *Boffins*.

Port

Left.

Prang

Crash (noun or verb) or damage (verb).

Prentice

Percival Prentice, British single-engined, low-wing basic trainer (postwar).

PT6A

Pratt & Whitney PT6, very widely used Canadian-designed turbo-prop engine.

Pull-through

The process of rotating an aircraft's propeller to prevent hydraulicing by flushing out any oil that may have accumulated in lower cylinders.

Pulps

Popular adventure story magazines from 1930s cheaply printed on newsprint.

Quadrant (power)

That part of the control pedestal which contains the throttle lever(s), propeller, and other engine controls.

R/T

Radio/telephone (for voice communication).

Rack and pinion

Method of rolling Whirlwind canopy back using cog wheel engaged in notched rail.

Radar altimeter

Instrument for ascertaining an aircraft's altitude using ground reflected radio or radar signals.

Ramrod

Daytime low-level operation in squadron strength against enemy airfield or comparable target.

Ranger

Night low-level, fighter attacks in flight or squadron strength with aircraft operating singly to cover greater area.

Ranging

Utilizing instructions from an AOP to adjusting the aiming of shells from a field gun.

RCAF Personnel Reception Centre

RCAF aircrew, upon arrival in the UK, were billeted at Bournemouth until further assignment. Also called *RCAF Holding Unit.*

Readiness

State of alert, pre 'Op' or prepared for scramble.

Ready room

Area set aside for aircrew to don flying suits and gear and to put in time prior to departure on an op.

Recce

Photographic-reconnaissance patrol.

Reflector sight

Electrically projected aiming device mounted inside fighter windscreen.

Reforming

Remanning and re-equipping a disbanded squadron.

Reid and Sigrist Slip and Turn Indicator

British turn and bank gauge showing slipping (or skidding) of aircraft.

Reliant
American Stinson Reliant, series of popular single-engined high-wing personal aircraft used for communications.

Remuster
To train for change of trade in the RCAF/RAF (e.g., observer to pilot).

Rhubarb
Daytime low-level operation by two aircraft against ground targets of opportunity.

Roadstead
Daytime low-level fighter attack on a marine target in squadron strength.

Ross rifle
Unsuccessful Canadian-designed First World War infantry weapon.

Round
Artillery shell.

Roundels
Concentric coloured-ring markings identifying RAF and British Commonwealth aircraft.

Routeing Office
Department at ATA Ferry Pool where safe flight routes were decided.

Rover
Torpedo bomber search and attack mission.

Royal Observer Corps
Organization of aircraft spotters to provide warning of approaching hostile aircraft.

Rudder
A control surface, the moveable after-portion of vertical tail, activated by pedals in cockpit to swing nose from side to side.

S.M. 82
Savoia-Marchetti S.M.82, Italian tri-motor low-wing transport comparable with DC-3.

S/L
Squadron Leader, rank above F/L and below W/C.

Salvo
Burst of fire from two or more guns at the same time.

Schmeisser
German light machine gun.

Schneider Trophy
Annual award for prestigious seaplane race, won outright by Britain in 1931.

Scramble
Rapid response (takeoff) by fighter pilots to warning of enemy approach.

Secret list
Roster of new weapons supposedly unknown to enemy.

Section
Two aircraft, half of a flight of fighters. With medium bombers, could be four aircraft.

Sergeant Pilot
Non-commissioned (NCO), rank below Pilot Officer.

Service Flying Training School (SFTS)
Third phase of BCATP in which pilots learned to fly higher-performance aircraft.

Servicing (noun)
Ground crew responsible for aircraft maintenance.

Sherman (tank)
American tank extensively used by Canadian Army.

Shoot
Series of shells fired from field gun directed by an AOP.

Short Service Commission
Agreement to serve specified period entered into by pilots in peace time.

Signal of delivery
Confirmation of ferried aircraft's arrival.

Sister

Flare in enemy colour-of-the-day. Also *ESN*.

Skidding

Turning aircraft solely with the rudder, keeping wings level.

Sleeve valve

Light and efficient alternative to standard poppet and exhaust valves of most reciprocating engines.

Slipstream

Airflow created by propellers around and behind behind flying aircraft.

Solenoid

Electrically operated relay.

Sortie

Raid or mission.

Spoiler

Device for disrupting airflow over wing and reducing lift.

Squadron hack

Aircraft available to squadron pilots for general transport.

Staff Officer

Airman of senior rank assigned to assist Air Attaché.

Stake truck

Transport vehicle with open deck and removable sides.

Stand by

Be ready for immediate action.

Stand down

To be relieved from service or stand by.

Starboard

Right.

Stirling

Short Stirling, RAF four-engined heavy bomber preceding Halifax and Lancaster.

Strafe/straffing

Attacking ground targets with cannon or machine gun fire from an aircraft.

Sweep

Low-level offensive action with aircraft flying abreast.

Swordfish

Fairey Swordfish, RAF large single-engined open-cockpit carrier-borne biplane torpedo bomber.

Tactical Exercise Unit

School for training crews in offensive practices.

Tallboy

Massive 12,000-pound deep-penetration bomb.

Target drogue

Tubular cloth gunnery target towed by an aircraft.

Target Drogue Operator

Aircrewman responsible for deploying drogue.

Tarmac

Tarmacadam, asphalt paved area in front of airport hangars.

Taurus

Bristol Taurus, British radial engine of 1,000 hp used in Beauforts.

Taxi aircraft/flight

Means of returning ATA pilots to their bases or ferry pools.

Telex

Teletype, early equivalent of fax machine.

Tempest

Hawker Tempest, RAF fighter, much improved development of Typhoon.

Three-pointer

Three-point landing, with tail wheel and both main wheels touching at same time.

Thunderbolt

Republic P-47 Thunderbolt, heavy American single-seat, single-engined fighter.

Tiffie

See Typhoon.

Tiger (tank)

Widely-used German heavy tank.

Tiger Moth
de Havilland D.H. 89 Tiger Moth, RAF and RCAF two-place biplane elementary trainer.

Tip-and-run
Daytime low-level nuisance raids by single or paired German fighters with a single bomb.

Tirpitz
German 43,000-ton battleship.

Tour expired
Relating to airmen who have completed a specified number of operational missions and are taken off Ops.

Tour
Specific number of operational missions flown by a fighter pilot or bomber aircrew before stepping down for leave and a new posting.

Tracer (ammunition)
Slug containing phosphorous which burns to illuminate its trajectory.

Tri-Pacer
Piper Tri-Pacer, American single-engined light aircraft.

Trim (tabs)
Smaller control surfaces set into trailing edges of elevators and rudder to control an aircraft's attitude or condition of flight.

Trimmed
Adjustment of trim tabs enabling aircraft to fly straight and level, hands off.

Turret Section
Department in bombing and gunnery School providing machine gun instruction.

Twin Otter
de Havilland DHC-6, turboprop-powered Canadian light twin-engined commuter liner.

Twin Wasp
Pratt & Whitney R-1830 Twin Wasp, radial engine in 1,200 hp range.

Twitchy
Noticeably nervous, unable to keep still.

Typhoon
Hawker Typhoon, RAF heavy single-seat, single-engined fighter, successor to the Hurricane.

U/C
Undercarriage.

Uncaging gyro
Freeing gyroscopic instruments (artificial horizon and directional gyro) from protective locking mechanism. Their readings remain steady to provide constant reference when aircraft manoeuvres.

Unfeathered
See Feathering.

USAAC
United States Army Air Corps.

USAAF
United States Army Air Force (succeeded USAAC).

V-2
German secret weapon, a large rocket carrying 2,000-pound warhead.

Vengeance
Vultee Vengeance, large American single-engined dive-bomber.

Ventura
Lockheed Ventura, RAF/RCAF twin-engined medium bomber (US-built) development of civil Lockheed 18 Lodestar airliner.

Venturi tube
Device attached to outside of aircraft in air stream, providing vacuum for gyro instruments.

Very pistol
Flare gun.

Visual purple

Goggles with lens darkly tinted to help aircrew adjust their eyes before flying at night.

Vulture

Rolls-Royce Vulture, unsuccessful aircraft engine comprised of two R-R Peregrine V-12s mated to form a twenty-four-cylinder engine of "X" configuration.

W/C

Wing Commander, rank above Squadron Leader usually held by leader of a squadron.

W/OP

Wireless Operator.

WAAF

Women's Auxilliary Air Force, distaff branch of RAF.

WAG

Wireless Air Gunner.

Warwick

Vickers Warwick, RAF heavy bomber, enlarged version of Wellington with same geodetic structure.

Wash out

Failure during flying training

Wastage rate

Pilot attrition through accidents and operational casualties.

Wellesley

Vickers Wellesley, RAF single-engined long-range light bomber of early war years.

Wellington

Vickers Wellington, widely used British twin-engined medium (originally heavy) bomber of unusual geodetic (basket-weave) construction conceived by Sir Barnes Wallis.

Whirly

See Westland Whirlwind.

Whitley

Armstrong Whitworth Whitley, RAF heavy-bomber, contemporary with but less successful than the Wellington, used mainly on Operational Training Units.

Wildcat

Grumman Wildcat, single-engined American naval fighter also flown by Royal Navy.

Wimpie

See Vickers Wellington.

Winco

Slang for Wing Commander.

Wing

A unit comprised of several squadrons.

Wings standard

Skill level required to earn pilot's wings.

Work-up

Training of a new squadron to combat readiness.

Yale

North American NA-64 Yale, American two-place advanced trainer, lower-powered predecessor of Harvard with fixed undercarriage.

Yoke

Control column in a large aircraft.

YP-J

Typical RAF aircraft fuselage markings with double letters designating squadron and single letter identifying aircraft.

YT-64

General Electric YT-64 turboprop engine of 3,000 plus hp. "Y" indicates prototype/pre-production status.

Index